American Crimes and
the Liberation of Paris

ALSO BY KENNETH D. ALFORD
AND FROM McFARLAND

*Hermann Göring and the Nazi Art Collection:
The Looting of Europe's Art Treasures
and Their Dispersal After World War II* (2012)

*Allied Looting in World War II: Thefts of Art,
Manuscripts, Stamps and Jewelry in Europe* (2011)

*Civil War Museum Treasures: Outstanding
Artifacts and the Stories Behind Them* (2008)

American Crimes and the Liberation of Paris

Robbery, Rape and Murder by Renegade GIs, 1944–1947

KENNETH D. ALFORD

McFarland & Company, Inc., Publishers
Jefferson, North Carolina

All photographs are courtesy U.S. National Archives unless noted otherwise.

LIBRARY OF CONGRESS CATALOGUING-IN-PUBLICATION DATA

Names: Alford, Kenneth D.
Title: American crimes and the liberation of Paris : robbery, rape and murder by renegade GIs, 1944–1947 / Kenneth D. Alford.
Description: Jefferson, North Carolina : McFarland & Company, Inc., Publishers, 2016. | Includes bibliographical references and index.
Identifiers: LCCN 2015043554 | ISBN 9780786496808 (softcover : acid free paper) | ISBN 9781476619439 (ebook)
Subjects: LCSH: World War, 1939–1945—Atrocities—France—Paris. | Military offenses—United States—History—20th century. | War crimes—France—Paris—History—20th century. | Organized crime—France—Paris—History—20th century. | Military atrocities—History—20th century. | Paris (France)—History—1940–1944.
Classification: LCC D804.U5 A44 2016 | DDC 940.54/0508913044361—dc23
LC record available at http://lccn.loc.gov/2015043554

BRITISH LIBRARY CATALOGUING DATA ARE AVAILABLE

© 2016 Kenneth D. Alford. All rights reserved

No part of this book may be reproduced or transmitted in any form or by any means, electronic or mechanical, including photocopying or recording, or by any information storage and retrieval system, without permission in writing from the publisher.

On the cover: The only known photograph of Manuel Martinez, a mug shot from the Police of Paris, France; American troops of the 28th Infantry Division pass the Arc de Triomphe and down the Champs Elysées (National Archives and Records Administration, USA)

Printed in the United States of America

McFarland & Company, Inc., Publishers
  Box 611, Jefferson, North Carolina 28640
    www.mcfarlandpub.com

Ackknowledgments

I am thankful to Holly Reed and Sharon Culley, archives specialists, National Archives, College Park; and Cathy Palombi and staff, the University of Virginia Law School. A special thanks to staff of the National Archives at St. Louis, Bryan K. McGraw, director; Eric Kilgore, Research Room supervisor; Eric Voelz, archivist; and Corey Stewart, Archive Specialist. My friend Lewis Levi was most helpful with the selection of photographs. My wife, Edda, is most supportive. Without her, my work would be unachievable.

All photographs are courtesy U.S. National Archives unless noted otherwise.

Table of Contents

Acknowledgments — v

Introduction — 1

1. The German Capture of Paris — 3
2. D-Day, June 6, 1944 — 10
3. The 29th Machine Records Unit — 26
4. The Hangings — 33
5. The Liberation of Paris — 39
6. Paris, City of Lights — 51
7. The Officer's Formal Mess — 63
8. The Mess and Billeting Office of the Hotel Astra — 69
9. The Black Market — 76
10. Paris Detention Barracks — 81
11. The Vincennes Gang — 88
12. The Channel Islands Crash — 103
13. The Voltaire Gang — 106
14. The Lola Murder — 116
15. The 2nd Battalion, 38th Infantry Regiment — 126
16. The Million-Dollar Battalion — 130
17. The Arrest of Men of the Million-Dollar Battalion — 144
18. The Cigarette Trials — 150
19. A Review of the Trials — 163

20. The Execution of Private Slovik	168
21. Postwar Paris	173
22. Martinez's Early Years	176
23. Martinez Returns to Germany	180
24. Springtime in Paris	189
25. Murder in La Place Pigalle	198
26. The Trials	208
27. Mannheim Prison: Maximum Security	213
28. The Inevitable End	218
Chapter Notes	223
Bibliography	227
Index	229

Introduction

The author served in post–World War II Germany, 1956–1958, and gained firsthand knowledge of the profitable black market as well as the caste hierarchy of officers, enlisted men and African American soldiers.

World War II has been described as the United States' finest hour in production and valor, and indeed it was. American GIs in Europe were, for the most part, normal people caught up in the dilemma of just surviving—the basic instinct of human beings. This book, however, shows how a tiny percentage of these soldiers moved from mere survival to a criminal existence in the Paris underworld, a place of profitable black marketeering often involving robbery, rape, prostitution, and even murder.

During the war many Americans—and people the world over, for that matter—were addicted to nicotine and would go to almost any length to satisfy this craving. It was an era when everyone from the family physician to the grammar school teacher smoked, even while at their professions. Most restaurants sported a haze of smoke hanging downward from the yellowed, tobacco-tar stained ceilings. In the Paris of World War II, the population's craving for nicotine led to the theft of millions of cartons of cigarettes, which were then unlawfully sold in the city and ultimately resulted in the largest court-martial in the history of the U.S. Army. The most profitable commodities of the black market were cigarettes and gasoline. *American Crimes and the Liberation of Paris* follows in detail the goings-on of the gangs of American soldiers involved in these illegal activities.

The world's most democratic nation fought World War II with a segregated army. Most of the black soldiers in the army were used in noncombat military roles—in Quartermaster and Transportation units, for example. This gave them greater access to gasoline and other civilian-needed commodities as well as entry into Parisian gangland activities. This book tells their stories, including how Jim Crow justice doled out by the U.S. Army Judiciary resulted in more executions and longer prison terms for African American soldiers. This military system of criminal justice, police, prisons, and executions is closely examined. This book addresses those issues as a part of history—it is not the intent of the author to be insensitive to this topic, but rather to present history as it really occurred during this tragic war.

Many U.S. soldiers in World War II were draftees, representing a cross-section of the American populace. Like most countries, the United States is composed primarily of people with integrity, but there is always the criminal element. A conscripted army would naturally reflect the latter in the same proportion. This book is not about the 4,182,266 servicemen who served honorably in the European Theater of Operations, but rather focuses on the minuscule proportion of army lawbreakers who were involved in serious criminal black market activities. Fortunately, their acts did not tarnish America's image; these wayward felons dishonored only themselves.

1

The German Capture of Paris

How Adolf Hitler, an obscure corporal in World War I, gradually organized his Nazi followers into the strongest party in Germany and became Chancellor of the Reich on January 30, 1933, is a complicated story of cunning and faithless promises. It has been told many times, so we will skip that part of history and

French children help their elders push a cart loaded with their personal belongings from Paris in an effort to flee from the invading Nazis.

Left: A little girl slumped in a sleep of exhaustion over the shoulder of her father, who is trying to find safety from the German Army's advance into Paris. **Right:** Looking after oneself in the streets of Paris.

German Luftwaffe soldiers near the Eiffel Tower.

pick up with the Führer's quest for domination over Western Europe.

The conquest of Poland began on September 1, 1939. The Poles were hopelessly inferior in both numbers and equipment to the Germans. Hitler's mighty military machine, however, struck so suddenly and powerfully that the three Polish armies never had a chance to complete their mobilization. This "Blitzkrieg," or war of lightning speed and destruction, was something new—and something for which the Poles and their allies were not prepared.

The Luftwaffe, Hermann Göring's overwhelming air force, swept over Poland, wrecking planes and air bases, bombing railroads and bridges, and cutting telephone and telegraph wires.

1. The German Capture of Paris

The entrance to the Paris gasoline supply dump. Gasoline and cigarettes were the most profitable commodities on the Parisian black market during the German occupation.

The interior of the gasoline supply dump filled with cans of gasoline.

The Poles quickly surrendered, but this military action promoted both England and France to declare war on Germany.

By April 1940, it was clear that France and Britain were sticking together and would not consent to peace. Instead of driving westward into France, as might have been expected, Hitler launched an assault against little Norway and Denmark. He wanted to seize their fish and dairy products and protect the coastal waters through which his ships brought invaluable Swedish ores from the Norwegian port of Narvik. He also wanted to secure their airfields and ports, from which it would be easier to attack British vessels in the North Sea.

The conquest of Poland in less than a month had seemed a strategic miracle. The Northern Blitzkrieg, which conquered Denmark and captured most of Norway's leading ports and cities in half a day, was an even more brilliant feat. Everything had been meticulously prepared. Troops secretly concealed in ore ships had been escorted by destroyers, safely and unobserved, a thousand miles up the Norwegian coast. Parachute troops and airborne infantry were ready to descend from the sky. Nazi spies and traitorous agents were waiting to cooperate.

On May 10, 1940, one month after his Northern Blitzkrieg success, Hitler

1. The German Capture of Paris

Each cigar box in the warehouse was individually checked.

was ready for his supreme effort to knock France out of the war and subjugate Britain, and thereby shape the destiny of the German people for a thousand years. Imitating the German strategy of 1914, he avoided the difficult task of making a direct frontal assault on the strong fortifications of France's eastern frontier. Instead, his armies swept through the flat country of the Netherlands and Belgium, where his tanks and motorized troops could make a more rapid advance. In doing so, the German troops used the same Blitzkrieg methods that had been so successful in Poland.

Great Britain and France instantly responded to the German invasion of Belgium and the Netherlands. They rushed a large Allied relief force under General Henri Giraud northeast almost to the coast between Belgium and Holland. Too often, the Allies had been too few and too late. But in this case, in one of the ironies of war, the very speed and large size of the relief force contributed to a gigantic military disaster. The relief force marched too far to the north. On May 15, it was compelled by the overwhelming German numbers to retreat and began to be cut apart by the dive-bombers and quick-moving tank units of the enemy. The Allied forces fell into confusion, and most were eventually cut off from France and driven back toward the coast at Dunkirk.

France still had an army of 2 million front-line troops, but it was shoddily

8   American Crimes and the Liberation of Paris

Distribution of cigarettes for the occupying soldiers in a commissary store in Paris.

organized. On June 5, 1940, along a 100-mile front from Laon, France, to the English Channel, Hitler launched his second great offensive. In this Battle of France, he basically won a complete victory within four days as his columns of soldiers began to stream toward Paris.

Other German armies crashed through the Maginot Line as the French people comforted themselves with the idea that this fortification was impregnable. When it was broken, their morale collapsed. The fabulous speed and spectacular course of the campaign against the Western Powers filled the Germans with pride, but the rest of the world reacted with astonishment and anxiety.

Now the unimaginable happened: What could not be accomplished in four years from 1914 to 1918 with 6 million German soldiers suffering 2 million deaths in World War I now happened. Paris was declared an open city, and the Germans entered it without opposition on June 14, 1940.[1] In the middle of that month, Adolf Hitler made his first and only excursion to the conquered city, going on a whirlwind tour of three hours. During his sojourn there, he visited the most popular tourist attractions. Gazing upon Napoleon's tomb, he was heard to comment that this was the finest moment in his life. Thus began a 50-month occupation of Paris, France, the City of Lights.

The Germans, always great lovers of music, swarmed to the opera and to concerts, taking most of the seats so that few French could attend the performances. The German women also bought articles of clothing, which were difficult for the French to get. Most Parisians stayed home during the evenings, as the Germans monopolized the night spots around town. For many, reading was their sole pleasure. One woman proclaimed that she had read *Gone with the Wind* six times during the occupation; the book cost 400 francs and was on the German list of banned books. Parisians also listened to the BBC broadcasts, but they kept the sound of the radio low because they never knew when the Gestapo would call, and listening to the Allied radio was a serious offense.

These four years of severe and heavy-handed German occupation, with all of its consequences of mass arrests and deportations, joined with the military destruction of railway marshalling yards, viaducts, and bridges, disrupted the economic life of France. During the occupation, 10 percent of the Parisians happily joined with the Germans in supporting Hitler; 10 percent bitterly opposed the occupying force; and 80 percent just survived.

2

D-DAY, JUNE 6, 1944

As early as April 1943, the British Army began to review plans for an Anglo-American invasion of France. These plans were approved by President Franklin D. Roosevelt and Prime Minister Winston Churchill at their meeting in Quebec, Canada, that summer. From then on, for more than a year, vast supplies of men and war materials poured across the Atlantic and were piled up in England, Scotland, and Northern Ireland. Their import had for one objective—the invasion of Western Europe.

For this greatest amphibious operation in history, assembled in England were 8,000 planes; 800 ships, ranging in size from motor torpedo boats and PT boots to battleships with 16-inch guns; and an invasion fleet of more than 3,200 transports and landing crafts. At dawn, 6:30 a.m., June 6, 1944, the flotilla of landing ships of all shapes and sizes began disgorging its men and materiel upon the landing beaches. Battleships and destroyers kept enemy submarines away, while thousands of planes afforded a protective umbrella in the sky. Medium landing craft pushed ashore. Marvelous American "ducks"—heavy trucks that could do 40 miles per hour on the road, yet swim safely even in a choppy sea—shuttled back and forth between the large ships and the shore. Large numbers of airborne troops were set down a few miles inland to harass the enemy's rear, cut telephone and telegraph wires, and give the landing troops time to advance a mile or two inland and dig in.

General Dwight D. Eisenhower had been Allied Supreme Commander in the Mediterranean; on January 16, 1944, he went to London to head SHEAF (Supreme Headquarters of the Expeditionary Allied Forces). Under Eisenhower, the British General Bernard Law Montgomery, who had previously distinguished himself in North Africa, was to have overall command of the ground forces. It was decided not to attempt to land at one of the French ports, because they were heavily mined and protected by German guns, and because no single port would be large enough to receive the gigantic invasion force. Instead, the

2. D-Day, June 6, 1944

place selected for landing was a 50-mile stretch of open beach on the Normandy coast west of the mouth of the Seine.

Here the two landing points were secretly designated by code words: "Omaha Beach" and "Utah Beach," to the west near the Cotentin Peninsula, where American troops under Lieutenant General Omar N. Bradley were to land; and "Mulberry Beach," to the east, where Lieutenant General Miles C. Dempsey's British and Canadian forces were set to invade. Although all of these preparations had been going on for months and were necessarily known to thousands, the secret as to the time and place of the invasion was so well kept that not a word of it leaked out to the enemy. As a consequence, the Germans were caught by surprise. In spite of their boasts, they had not fully completed the fortifications of the Atlantic Wall. The greater part of their elite troops were in the Pas de Calais, opposite England's Dover coast.

The speed with which the mighty expeditionary armies were built up is almost incredible. In the first 24 hours, a quarter of a million men were put ashore in spite of unfavorable weather and in the teeth of fortified and violent opposition. By the 20th day, 1 million men were ashore. This successful amphibious operation was all the more remarkable given that the English Channel is always hazardous, with its choppy waters, swift currents, sudden storms, and 18 foot rise and fall of tide.

An ingenious invention known as Force Mulberry helped solve the almost superhuman engineering task of keeping these armies reinforced and supplied with food, munitions, and gasoline. Three days after D-Day, two "synthetic harbors" were created. More than 20 old battleships and transports were sunk in shallow water to form breakwaters running parallel to the landing beaches. Their superstructures, which were equipped with antiaircraft guns, stood out above water at high tide, forming a protective barrier against enemy air and naval craft and, most important, against the stormy waves. Inside the breakwaters, pontoon wharves were anchored and connected with the beaches by solid roadways made of great steel and concrete caissons that were towed across the English Channel and then sunk into place. With this system, transports could unload their cargoes alongside the pontoons and send them quickly ashore in a continuous stream over the roadways. In the great storm that swept the Bay of the Seine on June 19–22, 1944, the American synthetic harbor was smashed and piled up in a mass of tangled steel and wreckage on the beach. Fortunately, the other harbor held firm.

Seaman Junius J. Stout arrived with the delivery of the Mulberry Force in the capacity of a combat photographer working under the famous Hollywood director John Ford. He would later state:

American Liberty ships were deliberately scuttled off the Normandy beaches to provide makeshift breakwaters during the early days of the invasion. This scene shows 13 Liberty ships formed into a protective screen for the vessels unloading on the beach.

My unit shot motion pictures of the whole Operation Mulberry, the construction of the man-made harbor facilities designed to handle 8,000 tons of supplies a day. In the end it handled more. A fleet of old ships was brought across the Channel and purposefully sunk, nose to tail, in a row offshore. This bit was named Operation Gooseberry. It began on the second day. Those ships caught quite a bit of German artillery fire. Each time we sank one the Germans reported to Goebbels that another enemy vessel had been sunk by glorious German fire. On D–Day plus three, by the time the Nazis figured out what was happening, most of those ships were in position and the first of the big concrete Phoenix breakwaters was being pushed into position and sunk. There was an outer line of floating steel breakwaters, too. Finally came the three piers running from the beach straight out to deep water. These were called Whales, and LSTs came right up to them and unloaded in less than an hour.[1]

Junius J. Stout graduated from Fresno High School in June 1927 and then did postgraduate work and studied mechanical engineering at various California

2. D-Day, June 6, 1944

The waters were filled with shipping vessels as reinforcements and supplies were funneled ashore for the conquest of the Cherbourg peninsula. Balloon barges floated overhead to protect the ships from low-flying enemy airplanes; one balloon here rests on the deck of an LST. Headed inland were parades of trucks loaded with troops and supplies.

colleges. Living in Hollywood and with his father, Archibald J. Stout, working in the motion picture industry, Junius entered this profession as a soundman with various studios and gradually worked himself into the Camera Department.

At the age of 30, he joined the Navy Reserves as a Photographer Second Class on September 27, 1940, and was listed as a non-enlisted passenger on the USS *Minneapolis* sailing from Pearl Harbor on December 5, 1941, as an Assistant Cameraman, 20th Century Fox Movie Corporation. The USS *Minneapolis* had sailed for gunnery practice and was 20 miles away from Pearl Harbor during the December 7, 1941, Japanese attack on that base. This disaster, together with other losses, crippled U.S. forces and seriously diminished the country's air and naval power in the Pacific Ocean area.

With several years of experience as a motion picture photographer, Stout proved to be valuable to the U.S. Navy. Just three days after the Japanese bombing of Pearl Harbor, he was ordered to report to the Office of the Coordinator of Information, Washington, D.C. Here he prepared photographic equipment for a Southwest Pacific assignment.

In May 1942, he was transferred to Perth, Australia, serving with Patrol Wing 10, which was equipped with 14 Consolidated PBY-4 Catalina Flying Boats—the most widely used seaplanes in World War II. Stout's duties included taking motion pictures, still photography, and aerial mapping. In November 1942, he made a motion picture record of a special Dutch camp several hundred miles behind the Japanese lines in New Guinea.

Ordered back to Washington, D.C., Stout reported to the Office of Strategic Services (OSS) on May 15, 1943. Within two months, he was ordered to report to OSS's London Branch of Field Photography. There, he was assigned to John Ford's unit. It may have helped that Junius's father Archibald was a well-known cinematographer in Hollywood and had worked with Ford on previous movies.

Stout (6 feet tall, 190 pounds) was given a week's training in aerial gunnery in a B-17 and assigned to a B-26 Squadron of the Ninth Air Force. He made several combat flights over France, Belgium, and Holland and was recommended for an air medal. The medal was subsequently awarded: "For Meritorious achievement while participating in aerial flight against the enemy. Photographer's Mate First Class Stout served with distinction as Photographer-Gunner on a B-26 aircraft during numerous combat missions against heavily defended military objectives." His flying duties ended on April 10, 1944.[2]

In June 6, 1944, Ford's unit was in charge of documenting Operation Overlord, the D–Day invasion. Since photographing any battle is always an exercise of improvisation, Ford's job was to make sure everyone had a camera. He assigned Carl F. Marquard, Jr. (Brick), and Junius Stout to be lead cameramen in the first wave. Ford also supervised the process of fitting out some of the landing craft with automatic cameras that would start filming as soon as their ramps lowered.

On D+1 (June 7), Second Lieutenant Charles D. Gurley of the 2nd Infantry Division landed on Utah Beach. This Division's objective was to move up between the 1st Infantry Division and the badly shot-up 29th Infantry Division. Gurley, as platoon leader of Company E, 38th Infantry Regiment, noticed a lot of American dead bodies with bloody helmets as he completed this task.

While the battle raged fiercely and stubbornly at the eastern hinge of the Allied line around Caen, Bradley's columns cut across the base of the Cotentin Peninsula. Some of his forces then pushed northward to its tip and captured the great fortified port of Cherbourg on June 27, along with some 30,000

2. D-Day, June 6, 1944

Fatigued American infantrymen and a dog asleep on the town sidewalk, while fighting their way to Brest.

German prisoners. The Germans, however, had so completely ruined the port by sinking ships and demolishing landing facilities that it was many weeks before Cherbourg could be used for bringing in Allied supplies.

George Patton's Third Army broke out of Normandy on August 1, 1944, as most divisions went east in the direction of Paris and southeast toward the Loire River. General Troy H. Middleton, however, turned his forces in the opposite direction, moving west to capture the port city of Brest and clear the Brittany Peninsula. Second Lieutenant Charles D. Gurley, along with his unit, the 2nd Infantry Division, was part of this task force.

Task Force A was commanded by General Herbert L. Earnest and had a strength of about 3,500 men. It consisted of the 1st Tank Destroyer Brigade, the 159th Engineer Battalion, and the 15th Calvary Group under the command of Colonel John B. Reybold.

Reybold was born in 1900 in Pennsylvania; he attended the U.S. Military Academy at West Point and graduated on June 15, 1920. The young Reybold was then dispatched to the Cavalry School at Fort Riley, Kansas. He had a flair for managing both horses and the Cavalry. In 1925, Reybold was assigned to the Philippines, where he spent three years. Upon returning to the United

A battered Victrola provided music for American soldiers during a lull in the street fighting in Brest.

States, he held various duties in a multitude of military posts across the Southwest and completed a class in Advanced Equitation Classes in 1934. Afterward, he was sent to Fort Myer, Virginia, just across the Potomac River from Washington, D.C.

Upon leaving Washington, D.C., Reybold was called to serve in West Point as the Post Recreation Officer. In this capacity he was called upon for his flair for entertainment and the dramatic and was instrumental in bringing important theater productions to West Point along with some of the most interesting theater people of that day.

One of the roles most cherished by Reybold during his stay in Washington was his service at the White House as an aide to President Franklin D. Roosevelt. As part of his duties, he rode horses with the First Lady, Eleanor Roosevelt, mostly on the bridal paths along the Virginia side of the Potomac River near Fort Myer. Mrs. Roosevelt's favorite mount was Dottie, a chestnut mare that she rode at the President's Birthday Horse Show. On occasion, the pair would ride at the Roosevelt homestead in Hyde Park, New York. "She is a tireless rider, Mrs. Roosevelt," said Reybold.³ Reybold related that on one occasion Mrs. Roosevelt asked, "John, what would you like to do in the Army?" Without hesitation and quite prophetically, Reybold replied, "Mrs. Roosevelt, my dearest wish is to lead a regiment of the United States Cavalry into combat."⁴

Leaving West Point in June 1942 and searching for enrichment in his life, Reybold was assigned as Commanding Officer to the 15th Calvary Group. The unit had been reactivated at Fort Riley, Kansas, in 1942 under the command of Colonel Frank J. Richmond. The 15th moved to Camp Maxey, Texas, in the spring of 1943, and later maneuvered in Louisiana and the California desert under the command of Colonel Reybold.

After staging at Camp Shanks, New York, the 15th Cavalry embarked from New York City on March 1, 1944, aboard HMS *Queen Mary*, landing in Scotland on March 7. From the seaport in Scotland, the unit traveled south to Trowbridge, England, where it was immediately reorganized and redesignated the 15th Cavalry Group and assigned to General George Patton's Third Army. The 15th was given the mission of guarding the secrecy of the D-Day staging area in the vicinity of the port of Southampton. Following D-Day, the 15th was reassembled in Trowbridge in preparation for movement to France.

Sailing from Portland, England, on July 4, 1944, the unit landed on Utah Beach the following day. Its members then assumed responsibility for police duties and security of the vital port city of Cherbourg. For this assignment, the 15th Cavalry command post, with Colonel Reybold in command, was housed in the Chateau de Sotteville near the town of Les Rieux, about 15 miles south of Cherbourg. The men well remembered one notable event during their stay in Cherbourg: On July 20, they provided the escort for Prime Minister Winston Churchill during his tour of the docks, arsenal, and flying bomb launch sites in that city.

Task Force A assembled near Coutances, France, on August 1. This unit, which included the 15th Cavalry Group, received the assignment of cutting across the northern part of the peninsula to secure the vital bridges along the railroad from nearby Avranches to Brest. On the second day, Reybold's 15th Cavalry Group completed its job of loading a supply of K-rations for seven days and obtaining gasoline for 250 operational miles, a large supply of ammunition, and other needed combat supplies. Their personal equipment was left behind with the kitchen unit and other nonessential equipment. Silk escape maps were issued, and each vehicle displayed identification panels that could easily been seen by Allied aircraft.

The 15th Cavalry Group consisted of the 15th Cavalry Reconnaissance Squadron and the 17th Cavalry Reconnaissance Squadron. Its function, as the name implies, was reconnaissance to avoid ambush by the enemy of the main elements of men, tanks, and artillery. At 1 a.m. on August 3, Task Force A moved out from Avranches, headed to Dol-de-Bretagne, a distance of 25 miles. In the lead was C Troop of the 17th Cavalry Squadron, followed by the remainder of the 15th Cavalry Group and the rest of Task Force A. In those early morning hours, the Task Force was bombed and strafed by German aircraft. At about 6 a.m., the lead platoon of C Troop ran into a strongly defended roadblock a few miles prior to reaching Dol-de-Bretagne. Colonel Reybold was riding with C Troop. Fired upon by German soldiers, the colonel's young jeep driver was killed; Reybold was shot through the wrist as he was thrown from the jeep. Sergeant James R. Hanson was blown out of the half-track he was in; the next thing he remembered was the tail of the horse rubbing on his face as he was taken in a horse-drawn cart to the German aid station. Another soldier on the cart died. The platoon leader, Lieutenant Harold S. Garrison, was killed and the platoon suffered heavy losses in both men and vehicles, with 15 enlisted

A Frenchwoman reclining next to her German fiancé refused to leave the soldier, even after he was captured by American forces near Brest.

men taken prisoners by the Germans, including Reybold. Within 30 hours and 10 miles after entering a combat zone for the first time, the colonel heard the words: *"Für sie ist der Krieg vorbei."* This signal was sounded on the battlefield of Europe too many times in too many languages: "For you the war is over."

Within a short time, it was evident that no further progress could be made toward Dol-de-Bretagne, so the decision was quickly made for Task Force A to bypass this resistance by continuing some eight miles south, in the direction of the group's ultimate target of Brest.[5]

Lieutenant George Haas was a field artillery observer for Combat Command B of the 6th Armored Division. His job was to observe the countryside from a two-seated Piper Cub, identify enemy targets, and by wireless notify the artillery battalions of the exact locations of these objects. These observations were accurate. After the war a U.S. Air Corps officer asked a German general which aircraft he feared the most. Expecting an answer of the B-17 bomber or P-51 fighter, the Air Corps officer was surprised by the general's answer—the small gunless Piper Cub. The general clarified the statement by saying that once troops spotted the Piper Cub, they knew the men, tanks, and artillery would be destroyed within minutes by accurate, deadly artillery shelling.

Flying over Dol-de-Bretagne, Haas's plane was shot down by German 40-mm Ack Ack guns. The pilot was shot through the seat of the plane, with the bullets existing out of his shoulder. Critically wounded, he managed to crash land in an apple orchard just before he died. Haas's leg was broken in the crash. As he attempted to get out of the plane, a German shot in that direction; the bullet ricocheted off the ground and pierced the broken leg, causing a second break in the same leg. The wounded Haas was taken prisoner with the men of the 15th Cavalry Group.

On the afternoon of August 2, Captain Edward R. Clark, 0465864, 25th Armored Engineer Battalion, 6th Armored Division, was busy trying to set up a water purification unit for the following day. His group was traveling 30 to 50 miles per day and had to dismantle and reestablish the purification unit on a daily basis. Clark was told to set up the unit about 15 miles away in the town of Dinan, as this town was then being cleared of Germans by the 6th Armored Division, which would need a supply of water by 8:00 the next morning. At that time Clark, along with the 6th Armored Division, which had bypassed St. Malo, was heading for the main objective of Brest. Clark was expected to establish the purification base and radio back the location to headquarters. Late that night he went to bed—and the next thing he knew it was morning. After breakfast, he hurriedly jumped into a jeep with his driver, Private Sidney Warren, 32596504, and traveling at about 40 miles per hour headed toward Dinan.

About a mile from Dinan, the pair saw two Germans go into a building. The driver immediately slammed on the brakes as the Germans started firing from the windows of the buildings along the street. The first shots blew out the tires, and the two men jumped out of the jeep and started running, trying to hide in some tall bushes. The Germans had no trouble spotting them from a church tower, and stated firing again and throwing hand grenades. The two men threw down their carbines and came out with their hands up. Searching the two prisoners, the Germans took their watches and cigarettes and in "kindness" returned two cigarettes each to Warren and Clark. They found the pictures of Clark's family but returned them. Their raincoats and steel helmets were taken, but Clark requested the return of the helmet, fearing Allied bombing, and was allowed to keep it. As they left the area of capture, they passed the jeep, where the Germans stopped to look for candy, more cigarettes, and C-rations. The Germans hit the jackpot: They found seven cartons of cigarettes that Warren had hidden. Responding in "kind," they offered the two prisoners a drink from a bottle of cognac. Warren drank most of it down, but Clark passed, as he was feeling disgusted at having been captured so easily.

The Germans took their two prisoners and walked them toward the center of Dinan. As they were crossing a bridge, Clark noticed it was charged with explosives, awaiting the order to be blown up. Clark surmised that U.S. Army Intelligence had been told by local Frenchmen about the bridge and the 6th Armored Division had bypassed this village by going through Evernas, five miles south, thus resulting in his capture. As they walked into the town, the French on every side of the street were watching them. Clark noticed that none of them smiled or said hello, but when he looked closely they would slide their hands down along the side of their trousers and make a V with their fingers. The group continued walking at a quick pace, trudging up hills in the warm August sun. When the guards became thirsty, they stopped at a small building. One of the Germans went inside and came out with several glasses of champagne. This time Clark consumed the complete glass and wished he had more. They continued to walking for what seemed hours to Clark, before finally arriving at a rambling farmhouse.

About 50 yards from the farmhouse, Clark noticed a dead American soldier slumped down in a wheelbarrow with a 6th Armored Division patch on his shoulder. Clark concluded the soldier was left there for the shock value, to rattle other prisoners who were to be interrogated. He escorted into the building, where he found an elderly German lieutenant who spoke excellent English, along with a large picture of Adolf Hitler on the wall. The lieutenant asked the prisoners where their homes were, and both Clark and Warren answered with only their name, rank, and serial number. The Germans then separated the two prisoners. A younger German officer entered the room and started talking about President Franklin D. Roosevelt and his association with American Jews. Clark and Warren were then ordered out; as they left, they were joined by two German officers, who told them they were being taken to German headquarters.

Getting thirsty, Clark requested some water, but was told they could drink later. On the way they passed a large wagon with a drum of water. After the officers drank, they motioned Clark over to fill his canteen. Clark remembered "wondering—since I was a water purification officer and knowing a little about it—if the water was purified."[6] Even with his doubts, he had a long drink of water and filled up his canteen. As they continued walking, one of the German officers said he had been in Brownsville, Texas, just before the war. The city was about 20 miles from Clark's hometown, but Clark, still smarting from being captured, refused to discuss anything with the Germans. After about three miles, they arrived at a nice-looking two-story house on the outskirts of Dinan. There, in the headquarters building, Warren and Clark were interrogated again. They did not reveal any information, sticking to name, rank, and serial number. Late in the afternoon, they went to a well and, using a bucket of water, washed up. Then were then taken back to the house and went upstairs. Clark was hungry, as he had not eaten all day, and the pair were served cold pork and a half loaf of black bread. Exhausted, Clark piled up some old dirty mattresses and was soon sound asleep. When he awoke in the morning, he found three more Americans soldiers in the room along with himself and Warren.

Around 9:00 a.m. they were told to be ready to leave, but of course Clark did not know the exact time, as his watch had been taken. The German soldier who spoke English told Clark that he would soon be joining his own troops again. Clark wondered if they were going to be set free. He quickly caught on to the German joke when he went outside: There sat an old German truck masked with camouflage paint, and in the truck bed were two more American soldiers, both with wounds in their shoulders. Also in the bed of the truck were six badly wounded German soldiers. Sitting on top of the cab was a German with a lightweight machine gun.

After leaving the encampment and traveling about an hour, the group arrived at a port town (Dinard?) and drove to the ferry dock. A Frenchman came running from a nearby hotel and tried to give the American prisoners cigarettes, but the Germans motioned him away. Clark indicated with his canteen that he needed water and asked if the Frenchman could fill it. The Germans agreed, and the man left with the canteen and entered the hotel. Shortly thereafter the Frenchman returned with some hardtack cookies and the canteen, which had been filled with champagne.

Late in the afternoon of August 3, the ferry moved into the dock and the truck carrying the prisoners drove onto it. Clark noticed that several German soldiers accompanied by French women also got on the ferryboat. It took about 30 minutes to reach their destination, St. Malo. The truck was offloaded and drove to a German hospital, which was located underground and covered with concrete and steel at least 6 feet thick. The two wounded American and German soldiers were taken inside, while Clark and the others were guarded outside by the truck crew. Here Clark got acquainted with the three Americans who were not wounded.

The prisoners were eventually taken to an old French prison. There a German corporal who spoke good English told Clark to clean the place, as 60 wounded American soldiers were expected to arrive soon. The prison was quite a large place, three stories high, with an air raid shelter where a family of Dutch people lived, as their ship had been seized by the Germans. Within the enclosure were a barracks and a large mess hall that was to be used as a hospital. Clark and the four enlisted American soldiers immediately began cleaning the filth with brooms, scrubbing down the floors and unearthing some mattresses. The Germans furnished sheets and blankets as the beds were made to accommodate the wounded. It was now August 4, and the German corporal told Clark that a French major and a wounded American colonel would be arriving at about 1800 hours. About 30 minutes past that hour, five more American soldiers arrived along with the French major, but not the wounded colonel. One of the Americans was 6'2" tall, had been born in Russia, and spoke Russian fluently. Another newly arrived prisoner was Corporal George Horkott, 32476888. At the time they were arriving, American planes were dropping bombs on St. Malo.

Clark began a conversation with the Frenchman, who was a Civil Affairs Officer. Like Clark, he had entered Dinan thinking it had been captured by the Americans. The French major had been captured and sent to St. Malo. The two men were in a room alone when the major opened a suitcase crammed with eggs, cigarettes and cognac, which they drank immediately. They then had supper, with the major cooking the eggs with a big slice of balogna and more cognac. They discussed escape, but at that time the air raid alarm sounded and Clark ran for the shelter. When he returned, a bar was missing from the window and the French major was gone. Within the hour Clark was notified to be ready to move out in 30 minutes.

From their intelligence gathering activities, the Germans knew the U.S. Army was going to bypass the fortress city of St. Malo. General Bradley, however, changed his mind and decided that with American troops dispersing to the far corners of Brittany, the St. Malo harbor would be valuable as an auxiliary

2. D-Day, June 6, 1944

supply port. Used by the Germans as a naval base for coastal operations and as a supply base for the Channel Islands, St. Malo could accommodate medium-sized vessels and had facilities to unload cargo at the rate of a thousand tons per day. Although naval planners had informed General Eisenhower "that we are likely to be disappointed in its possibilities as a port," Bradley ordered St. Malo taken.

A picturesque port, St. Malo was the birthplace of Jacques Cartier and the home of the privateers who had harassed English shipping for three centuries. Across the Rance River, more than a mile to the west, the beaches of Dinard had been a favorite with British tourists. The defenses protecting both towns made up the fortress complex of St. Malo. Frenchmen had warned U.S. forces that about 10,000 German troops garrisoned the fortress.

The absence of Allied naval patrols offshore had allowed troop reinforcements and supplies to be brought into the harbor from the German-occupied Channel island of Jersey. The combat patrols from Jersey were all volunteers. The returning naval transport boats evacuated American prisoners and hundreds of wounded German soldiers from St. Malo; they were given medical care in the German section of the General Hospital on Jersey.[7]

Clark and his party of prisoners were among those withdrawn from St. Malo. Just prior to leaving the prison, Clark and his men loaded up all the blankets they could carry, along with bread and corned beef. As Clark was being transferred to the docks, American planes continued bombing and Germans fired back with antiaircraft flak guns. As they arrived at the dock, two German ambulances pulled up alongside a converted trawler. American Colonel John Black Reybold, 012342, jumped out immediately. Although his arm was in a sling, he opened the door to the other ambulance and started unloading American wounded. There were only 10 men, though the German corporal had earlier said there would be 60 wounded. Some were badly injured; one was completely burned, with his body encased in bandages. The burned victim was Sergeant James R. Hanson. To confirm his identity, the German medics requested the assistance of 22-year-old Corporal George Horkott, as he was a friend of the burned man. Sergeant Hanson was not expected to survive his wounds. All the prisoners, with the exception of Clark and Warren, were from the 15th Cavalry Group.

The wounded were loaded first on the starboard side of the open deck. Then Clark and the soldiers from the prison were brought onboard with their blankets and food. As the trawler sailed out under a full moon, the prisoners were taken to the sailors' quarters, where Clark arranged for bunks for the two men with him who were suffering from shoulder wounds. There was a small mess where they found tea, bread, and butter, which they ate when the guards were not looking. Colonel Reybold came down the ladder to the sailors' quarters and told Clark that he was up on the deck with the wounded. He had been moving the blankets to help the delirious burned sergeant; Reybold mentioned he would appreciate it if Corporal Horkott (Hanson's friend) would relieve him in two or three hours. Clark followed the colonel back up the ladder to see if he could help. Stepping between the wounded, he heard Reybold tell Hanson that everything was going to be all right and to take it easy. Next to Hanson was the wounded Lieutenant George C. Haas, Jr., 0447437, who stated he was very cold. Again the colonel emphasized that Hanson needed Horkott's help because of their friendship.

On August 5, eight German ships, including three landing barges, entered the St. Helier harbor from France. Some German troops arrived, along with 600 wounded German soldiers who had apparently been evacuated, and about 20 American prisoners. Finally Clark went to sleep. Upon awakening, he found himself in the port of St. Helier, Jersey Island.

Jersey Island

After the battle of St. Malo, the war basically bypassed Jersey as the Allied advanced northeast across Belgium and France. The airfields fell into neglect, with the Luftwaffe moving to other fronts. The only reminder of battle was an occasional raid on the ports by Allied bombers. The island mostly reverted back to its pre-D–Day commonplace existence. The most critical change was the population's isolation from the mainland and its supplies of coal, food, and basic necessities.

On August 5, 1944, when Captain Edwin Clark and the other 19 prisoners arrived on Jersey and were still aboard, the prisoners were given packages of cigarettes with Japanese inscriptions on the cartons. The eight wounded American soldiers along with Colonel Reybold and 200 to 300 German soldiers were offloaded first and taken to the German section of General Hospital. Some of the noncritical cases were taken to the Convalescent Hospital of the Luftwaffe at the Merton Hotel, also in St. Helier. Around noon, Clark and the 10 remaining soldiers were marched up the gangway and loaded into station wagons with bars on the windows. They were driven to the South Hill Military Prison in St. Helier. On the way they saw English people in the streets staring. No one waved as the French had done—they just stared, not recognizing the soldiers as Americans, as they had witnessed thousands of foreign workers coming to the island.

At the prison, the 10 soldiers were interrogated again. During Clark's interrogation, as he entered the office he was prepared to salute, but the interrogator actually got up and saluted Clark first. He was a German master sergeant by the name of Wagner, who had lived in England for five years just before the war. Afterward Captain Clark was housed with enlisted men. For the first two days they lived off the corned beef and bread they had brought from St. Malo. There was running water in the kitchen and the purification officer was concerned, but he gladly drank his fill of it. Straw mattresses and blankets were furnished to the prisoners. The fatigued Clark wrote: "After about the third day, in which we did nothing but sleep and I'm darn good at that—I sleep 24 hours a day—the men couldn't sleep quite that long but they came close to it. The only time I got up was for meals."[8]

Clark met the Rittmeister, Ickler, a German captain in the Cavalry and commander of the prison compound. The captain as described by Clark was like the German officers whom one sees in the movies, with a shaved head, very straight posture, and immaculate dress.

During the middle of August, the Germans quickly built a small frame house for the three captured U.S. officers. Located inside the upper enclosure, the wooden three-room house, about 25 by 15 feet, had a small porch overlooking the harbor. As the other two officers, Haas and Reybold, were still hospitalized, Clark moved in and had the house completely to himself. The enlisted men, privates and noncommissioned officers, all lived in a separate barracks in one big room, which was well ventilated and heated by a large wood-burning stove. They had wooden bunks with mattresses and a sufficient number of blankets.

After about a month of solitude for Clark, Colonel Reybold arrived in the prison, accompanied by Sergeant Wagner. Reybold reintroduced himself by saying, "Clark, as I have already introduced myself again, I have some cognac here that my German agent brought to me while I was in the hospital. Let's have a drink and hope to hell we're out of this place soon."[9]

Clark later reported that Colonel John Reybold turned out to be the most interesting and polished man he ever met in his life. The men began exchanging information and within a few minutes Clark realized the colonel was full of the latest news. It turned out the colonel had been receiving an English newspaper from his English nurse while he was in the hospital. The 50-year-old nurse, Meg, had furnished him with the paper apparently from a German source, as she also cared for the wounded German soldiers. Meg told Reybold that she had two sons in the British Army.

The colonel, in a proper military manner, began an inspection of the men on a daily basis and making corrections that benefited the camp in many positive aspects. Reybold was always willing to confront and argue with the camp commander about the deplorable conditions in the camp or about the way his men were being treated.

3

THE 29TH MACHINE RECORDS UNIT

Diary, 29th MRU—12

The Ground Force Replacement System was designed to assure dependable and timely arrival of qualified officers and enlisted men to replace men wounded and killed during the combat phases of the war. The newly arrivals were assigned to a replacement depot or replacement battalion located in the Communication Zone or the Combat Zone.

Assigned to the Ground Force Replacement System, the Forward Echelon of the 29th Machine Records Unit (MRU) was originally scheduled to arrive in France on July 18, 1944. As events materialized, this date turned out to be the alert date for departure from England to the Continent. Actually, the Detachment, as it was later called, did not leave Cheltenham until a day later.

There was much excitement prior to leaving, and a farewell party was given in the Tea House at the Bishop's Cleeve with beer and rations donated by the men. It was a gala occasion. Guests of honor included an enlisted man and his pretty English bride of that morning, and another couple who took the fatal step several days later. The MRU had certainly done its part in cementing Anglo-American relations. Both men, however, were soon separated from their English brides.

As the zero hour approached, duffel bags were well packed with all necessities, including beer bottles for cider and wine. The latter liquid ultimately proved to be a pipe dream that seldom materialized.

Early in the morning of July 19, 1944, the men of the 29th MRU pulled out with one machine trailer, one administrative trailer, one supply trailer, two generators, two tractors and one loaded for the occasion, one command car, and one truck, borrowed to transport the men. Everyone was in excellent spirits.

3. The 29th Machine Records Unit

It was a cool sunny day as they drove in the convoy, led by a Military Police motorcyclist toward Oxford over the beautiful rolling English countryside. Cattle and sheep grazed in the fields; apples in the orchards were rapidly becoming ripe; and the wheat, browned by the sun, was ready to be cut. Overhead were huge gliders being towed low to the earth. At many airfields, big heavy bombers rested idle on the ground. In the middle of the day, the convoy took time out to eat a scant lunch consisting of sandwiches and fruit juice. Around five o'clock that evening, the unit arrived at the Marshalling Area about eight miles outside of Southampton.

After camouflaging the three trailers, the men went to the area where they were quartered in two tents, got rid of their equipment, and proceeded to chow. The two meals at the Marshalling Area bore one distinction—corned beef—for supper and breakfast. But the men were hungry, so they ate heartily.

Shortly after morning chow, Lieutenant David E. Walsh informed the men they were leaving for the ship immediately. The command car and trailers departed first, followed by a truck full of enlisted men. There was much traffic on the road, and many military vehicles were headed at a snail's pace for the docks of Southampton. Before long, the group had passed through the busy city, arriving at the dock in time for a noon-day meal.

That afternoon the stevedores loaded the vehicles and equipment onto the ship, using mighty cranes and wenches capable of lifting the heaviest and most powerful of machines. It was nerve-wracking, to say the least, to see the men hoist the trailers into mid-air, leaving them dangling in nothingness, and then lower them into the hold of the ship. Any mishap would result in the destruction of expensive equipment, which would be extremely difficult to replace. All that worrying proved needless, however: The men knew their job, and none of the trailers was damaged. By midnight, the ship was completely loaded, and the men boarded.

Around 7 a.m. on July 21, 1944, the *Roger Griswold*, one of the earlier Liberty vessels, steamed out of Southampton Harbor, well loaded with men and equipment, on a short sea voyage. The expedition turned out to be a long trip from the length of time they remained on the ship.

It was a dismal overcast day, but most of the men went on deck to watch the shoreline of the Isle of Wight disappear. Before long, they were well into the English Channel and had joined the rest of the convoy headed toward France. It was a marvelous sight to see all the ships together, bound for the same destination. One quickly realized the careful planning that must have preceded such a vast movement—the largest convoy from England since D-Day, according to reports.

Late in the afternoon of July 21, the coast of France was sighted. After supper, they had reached their destination (Omaha Beach, as it was called by the Americans), east of Cherbourg. This was a surprise to most who expected to dock at Cherbourg, as many thought that their equipment was too bulky and too difficult to land on a beach.

The *Roger Griswold* cast anchor among hundreds of other ships waiting to be relieved of valuable equipment and personnel to reinforce the Allied drive into France. Ducks—the useful little water jeeps—were racing through crowded waters, and big barges were harbored alongside ships near shore, with stevedores busily unloading their cargo. In shallow waters were the breakwaters made from old ships: some brought to the shores of France for the occasion; some damaged in battle, including one old-time German destroyer; and all sunk to form a breakwater to ease the task of unloading. In the distance were the famous beaches of Normandy, where crack American amphibious troops had landed and fought the Germans and driven them back. This attack had spearheaded the Allies' drive into the Continent some six weeks ago after much bitter fighting, destroying once and for all the myth of an impregnable Fortress Europe.

The men of the 29th MRU would not forget their first night off the coast of France. As soon as dusk fell and they were comfortably lying in their bunks, the ack-ack guns commenced spurting, and the sky lit up like a 4th of July fireworks show. German planes were in the area, and their boys were taking shots at them.

Suddenly, the realization dawned that they were in the real combat zone, where they played for keeps. The more curious arose to watch the spectacle; others glanced up at the brightened sky, then turned over and went back to sleep. Soon the ack-ack stopped, and they knew Jerry had either been knocked out of the sky or was on his way elsewhere.

On July 25, 1944, the unloading commenced. By afternoon, the command car had been taken ashore. The stevedores, working hard and late into the evening, were unable to take off the trailers on the first day. But early on the morning of July 26, the trailers were hoisted out of the storage hold and onto the barges—one trailer and one tractor on one barge; two trailers and one tractor on another. Again there were tense moments as the trailers were suspended in mid-air before being lowered to the barge. Many of the men had visions of the equipment going to an untimely grave in Davy Jones's Locker. But the men who swung the trailers around like acrobats in a circus act knew their job; they got them safely on the barges and to the shore. They had been there since D-Day. Nevertheless, the men said a prayer and breathed a sigh of relief when at last the trailers rolled onto the beaches of Normandy.

The men were in good spirits as they drove through the French countryside, thick with hedgerows. For the first time they saw at close hand the destruction wrought by the war, which had so recently swept over this once-peaceful land. Cattle grazed in pitted fields. Bomb holes and what once had been German pill boxes and gun emplacements scarred the earth. Farmhouses were ravaged. Roofs were off of many; others had walls knocked out; in some, you could still see the furniture intact. The French people they encountered along the road seemed friendly. They nodded and waved as the convoy drove from the coast to the interior. The troops passed through Isigny, where General Leslie McNair, killed by "friendly bombing," was later buried. The sad little town, which had been badly hit, bore the scars of all its tragedy.

Around five o'clock that afternoon, the troops reached their destination: Advance Headquarters, Ground Force Replacement System (GFRS), on the outskirts of the tiny village La Hatainnerie, three or four miles beyond Isigny. The site was about eight miles from St. Lo, where the Americans and Nazis were locked in bitter battle over that much beleaguered town.

The Advance Headquarters was located in an apple orchard in typical hedgerow country. That night the members of the 29th MRU camouflaged their trailers and pitched pup tents, glad to be were off the ship and on the solid ground of France. To all of them it meant one thing—one step nearer the end of the war and going home.

The following morning, July 27, 1944, they picked up stakes and moved to another nearby field, which had been designated for the MRU. The men immediately placed the trailers in good spots and commenced camouflaging them. Some put up an administration tent for the coders. When the important jobs were accomplished, the men chose spots for their pup tents and dug in. Some inherited foxholes that had been evacuated by men who had moved to another area. Others got out the old pick and shovel and started digging up the earth. Foxholes varied in plan and depth. Some were four feet deep; some had compartments for duffel bags; some came with shelves; some featured gun racks; some were lined with paper or burlap bags or cardboard. All were made as comfortable as possible, often with a picture or two on display to bring back thoughts of home and a gentler way of life. Over these holes were pitched the pup tents, two men to a hole.

Meals at camp were good and a welcome relief from the steady diet of C-rations the men had been getting. The purified water was hard to drink at first, but they soon got used to it. They set up their own Lister bag, and the water tits were longingly marked as brandy, corn, four roses, gin, and rum—a reminder of happy days in the past and happy days to come.

On the night when the Americans launched their big offensive and pushed toward St. Lo, the MRU members could hear the guns booming in the distance, and the sky was brilliant with flares. The climate in Normandy was better than that in England—excellent, in fact, dry and invigorating. It was generally cool at night and in the morning, with a certain amount of moisture, but there was usually plenty of sunshine sandwiched in during the middle of the day. During the noon hour break, the grass was thick with GIs sprawled out on the ground, basking in the sun.

By August 1, 1944, their equipment was ready for operations, and they commenced servicing some 49,000 replacements. Seven days a week the men worked, many of them overtime, as the work piled up rapidly. Using punched-card tabulating machines, they conducted personnel accounting procedures by maintaining locator files and preparing replacement reports. In what little spare time they had, men wrote letters or read, checking a book out of the MRU library. The library, consisting mainly of Special Services books and a few donated by the enlisted men, had in it such books as *King Row, The Late George Apley, Studs Lonigan, Assignment in Brittnay, Cimarron, Jamaica Inn, Windswept, The Blazed Trail, The Bar 20 Rides Again, Random Harvest, A Connecticut Yankee at King Arthur's Court, The Story of Mankind, The Sea Wolf,* and *Night Flight,* to name a few.

In the evenings, many of the men frequented the nearby village. There they purchased perfume to send home or bought cider to fill up the bottles they had brought from England. Wine, unfortunately, was extremely scarce.

One day was especially exciting because a Mustang crashed a short distance from camp late that afternoon. Those who saw the plane go down and kick up the dirt said that it had been flying low with several other planes, and that it looked as if it had been playing around before it crashed into a hedgerow, bursting into flames.

Intermingled with these moments of excitement were moments of relaxation. One night a GI band from the 19th Replacement Depot entertained the men with some good hot swing. During the course of the evening, it was discovered that there was plenty of talent among the soldiers at camp. One chap, who had spent a great deal of time working around Washington, D.C., night spots, proved a big hit with the drums, which he beat with real rhythm. He also sang several songs, including such old favorites as *Easter Parade.*

Several nights later, a USO troupe, which had just crossed the Channel from England, put on an informal entertainment entitled "Show Time," consisting of songs, dancing, and wisecracks. The master of ceremonies was funny, but the big hit of the show was a pretty blond girl, Ronnie Reed, who had personality and sang soothing songs well. After the show, several of the GIs had sandwiches with the gals and drove them back to the hospitals where they were staying. The blond girl remarked that during the bombing the night before,

3. The 29th Machine Records Unit

the Germans had strafed the area right up to the hospital, but stopped when they reached the hospital buildings and did not commence strafing again until they had flown over them.

On the afternoon of August 12, 1944, the men of the 29th were told to fill up their foxholes as they were headed farther inland. The next morning after chow, they took down the camouflage nets and packed their supplies and duffel bags into the trailers. At 10:00 a.m., Captain George M. Barnett and the first group of enlisted men departed. Since transportation facilities were sadly lacking, the others got to their destination as best they could—several on a lumber truck, two in a jeep, and three on a water wagon. The last group went for an extended tour around the adjacent countryside before finally getting the water cans filled, reaching Canisy at five o'clock that afternoon. They would not forget the ride to Canisy that sunny day, as the dusty roads were crowded with vehicles carrying supplies to the front. Everywhere they looked, the men saw signs of war—farmhouses that had been shelled, fields that had been struck by bombs, trees that had been split in two. The battle-scarred St. Lo stood out above everything else, like a lonely graveyard, a symbol of the horror of modern warfare.

The town itself resembled a ghost town. Hardly a building had escaped the onslaught of war. Practically every home had been flattened like a pancake, with only a wall or two standing, which threatened to crumble at a moment's notice. Everywhere was tragedy. The debris had not been cleared, and it was apparent that not only American and German soldiers had died in this fierce struggle, but also many civilians, whose bodies lay beneath the uncleared ruins. Occasionally the troops saw a tired little Frenchwoman, generally clad all in black, returning from some refuge, hopelessly lost in the demolished city. These were the little people, bewildered and pathetic, caught in the maelstrom of war.

Everywhere was dust, and Military Police were directing traffic into and out of town. The men caught their breath as they drove through the town, taken by American soldiers just three weeks ago. There were factories that had been shelled, with all the windows broken. There was a home with only a wall standing and a picture, completely unharmed, hanging in its usual place. In the center of town there was a store with cars, dented and wrecked, in what was once a display window. Not far off was a theater with the sides knocked off, but the seats intact. The group passed a long narrow building that must have been a jail, as there were bars behind the shattered window panes. High above the town was a stone wall, which must have stood there for generations, with roses climbing over it and behind it, and tall green trees standing proudly up against the clear blue sky, untouched by battle. Every once in a while, a stench poisoned the fresh, clean air—the stench of death and of a dead city.

Seeing St. Lo made one think. Its fate displayed the outcome of war at its grimiest. As one GI remarked, if this was liberation, he did not want to be liberated. The soldiers could not imagine how anyone had emerged from the battle alive.

Headquarters for the Ground Force Replacement System was at the Chateau de Canisy, recently evacuated by the First Army, and after which the town was named—a tiny village, badly hit by the war, about four miles from St. Lo. The chateau was a tremendous L-shaped building that dated back several centuries. One could imagine counts and princes of the French aristocracy of a bygone period living in such a place. According to reports, the chateau was owned by a French count, who was residing in Paris at the time of the GFRS's stay on the grounds. The only member of the family present was his daughter, an attractive blond girl who was living in the chateau with the French people who worked around the place.

The chateau faced a small lake, on either side of which were tall, majestic pines, the tallest trees the men had seen since leaving the states. Generally speaking, the chateau had escaped the damage caused to many homes in the vicinity, although the roof revealed several small shell holes. One wing of the chateau was occupied by the family. The officers were billeted on one side of the lake, and the enlisted men, and the Headquarters, on the other side.

The 29th MRU had to be located at a different site. They were separated from the rest of the camp and were quartered behind the stables, now used as a supply room, in another apple orchard. The stables were protected on one side by a stone wall enclosing a garden in full bloom. The trailers were parked across the road in a clearing underneath a cluster of tall trees, which acted as a natural camouflage. They were further hidden with nets.

The men's love for their chosen spot ended abruptly when a scaffold was discovered on the other side of the garden wall. They soon learned that there had been many hangings there and that another one was scheduled for the following day. The hanging took place at five in the afternoon.

A curious crowd of enlisted men gathered to witness the grim affair through the shell hole on the other side of the garden wall. At the appointed time, a young Negro soldier, a white bag over his head, was marched up to the scaffold. Never once did he hesitate. He went up the 13 steps calmly and quietly in a military manner. He adjusted his noose. Then the trap was opened, and it was all over. A Negro chaplain stood by weeping, and several high-ranking officers acted as witnesses. The hangman was a professional who came from England for the job. Rumor spread that he was to officiate at some 50-odd hangings. According to reports, the Negro had raped a nine-year-old girl.

Shortly thereafter, the scaffold was removed, but the men of the 29th Machine Records Unit were left with a funny feeling in their hearts.[1]

4

The Hangings

The hanged man had not raped a young girl, but the hangman was, indeed, a professional: Mr. Thomas William Pierrepoint, 2 Tuner Avenue, Lidget Green, England.

The executed man's troubles began on June 14, 1944, when Aniela Skrzyinarz and her sister Zofia Sondej, both of whom lived in Vierville Sur Mer, France, were pulling a wagon on a road toward a field where they were going to milk cows. They met four African American soldiers with rifles. Two of the soldiers pushed the wagon through a gate into the field for the women, and one of them said in French that they wanted some milk. Aniela started to milk a cow and Zofia then went into the adjoining field to round up more cows. As she entered the second field, one of the soldiers pointed a rifle at her head and knocked her down. Zofia and the soldier were on the ground about 10 minutes. He tried to take her by force but she strongly resisted. Aniela continued to milk the cow, but then looked up and noticed that the three soldiers had disappeared. She walked into the adjoining field and the soldier who was watching her milk remained behind.

In the second field, Aniela saw one of the soldiers lying on her sister Zofia. She yelled to her sister, "What are you doing?" and she replied, "They put a rifle to my head." One of the soldiers seized Aniela, who tried to get away from him. He then fired a shot and Aniela, who was frightened, dropped to her knees. The soldier then came over and pointed the gun at Aniela's head, took her by the shoulder, and tried to push Private Clarence Whitfield away. Whitfield pushed back and seized Aniela and dragged her toward a hedge. One soldier left as Zofia heard a shot and saw her sister thrown to the ground. Zofia jumped up, ran home, and told Aniela's husband about the incident. Zofia returned to the field about 15 minutes later.

Meanwhile, Whitfield had thrown Aniela to the ground and fell on top of her. He laid his rifle down close beside her, lifted her dress, and raped her.

After Whitfield completed the act, he held one hand on her chest, partially lifted himself, and indicated by motions that he wished her to perform an unnatural sexual act. She "wouldn't do anything like that" and pretended she did not understand what he desired. She then heard her husband's voice. Whitfield arose and seized his rifle. Believing that he was going to shoot her or her husband, she seized the rifle. Her husband and an officer then entered the field. About 10 minutes elapsed between the time Whitfield threw her on the ground and the arrival of her husband.

Captain Roland L. Tauscher, Lieutenant James P. Webster, and Lieutenant Walter S. Siciah, all of the 3704th Quartermaster Truck Company, were sitting in the orderly room when Aniela's husband and Zofia arrived. Zofia excited to the point of being hysterical and kept yelling, "They are killing my sister and took advantage of her." The husband said in Polish, "Come with me." Lieutenant Siciah, who spoke Polish, went with them in a jeep to the pasture, followed by Captain Tauscher and Lieutenant Webster.

They passed an African American soldier on the road about 200 yards from the field. Then they crossed the first field into the second pasture, which was about 300 yards from the Skrzyinarz home. The husband called Aniela's name several times. On entering the second field they saw Whitfield, with a rifle at port arms, and Aniela. Both were struggling over the rifle and no one else was in either field. Lieutenant Siciah pushed Whitfield away from the woman and took the rifle. Aniela, who appeared upset and frightened, said to Lieutenant Siciah that she had been taken advantage of. Her husband struck Whitfield, who seemed surprised and asked why he struck him. Siciah asked him what he was doing there and he replied, "I am not doing anything here. I was passing through." Siciah said, "Don't lie to me." When Lieutenant Webster arrived, he asked the same question. Upon receiving a like reply, he ordered Whitfield to the true story.

The accused then said that the other fellows were involved and had run away. He said he was "getting something" and made a back-and-forth motion with his hand in front of his penis.

This act of violence would cost 20-year-old Private Clarence Whitfield his life. On August 12, 1944, at 4:50 p.m., he approached the hangman's scaffold and ascended the steps to the top of the platform, where Mr. Pierrepoint had taken his place.

CAPTAIN WHITE: "Private Whitfield, do you have a last statement to make to me as your chaplain before your death?
WHITFIELD: "Yes, what will you tell my mother?'
CAPTAIN WHITE: "Your mother will be told that you died in France."
WHITFIELD: "But I mean, will she get my insurance?"

4. The Hangings

CAPTAIN WHITE: "I will let the colonel answer that."
COLONEL WILLIAM WRIGHT: "Yes, she will get your insurance."[1]

Colonel Wright then gave the silent signal to Mr. Pierrepoint, who performed his function as executioner.

Whitfield had been inducted into the army on April 23, 1943, at Fort Bragg, North Carolina; committed his crime on June 14, 1944; and was executed on August 14, 1944. His time as an enlisted man lasted just 16 months. He would be an example of the punishment in store for the perpetrators of the 300 rapes that occurred in France during the first month following the D-Day invasion.

Only about 10 percent of all troops in the European Theater of Operations were African Americans, but the numbers of rapes committed by these troops in the first month following D-Day were greatly disproportionate to their representation. In June 1944 alone, 214 rape cases involving African Americans were tried in the Military Criminal Justice system. After the "public" hanging of Whitfield, there were only 46 rapes by Afro-Americans for the remainder of the entire war in Europe.[2]

Unfortunately within two months and less than 10 miles away from the scene of the Whitfield rape, three U.S. Army soldiers would murder a man and then rape the victim's daughter. The incident began at about 8:00 p.m. on the night of October 11, 1944, when Madame Lefebvre, her son Eugene, and her 19-year-old daughter Marguerite were at their home in La Pernelle, Normandy. August Lefebvre, the husband/father, was 500 yards away having dinner with his employer. Three American soldiers walked up to the Lefebure house and asked Eugene for cognac; the boy responded that there was no cognac in the house.

As the soldiers walked away, they noticed the young girl in the house and decided to return with the hopes of getting some "pussy." They made a mask for two of the men from the sleeves of an undershirt and one the soldiers used his handkerchief to hide his face. Returning about 10 minutes later, they knocked on the door and said, "Police." The door was locked, so the three soldiers prowled around the outside of the house; they broke a window and entered the house wearing white masks.

The Lefebvres yelled for help and ran from the house. As the family was running down the road, one of the soldiers, wearing his mask and a raincoat, caught Madame Lefebvre and threw her to the ground. She got up and ran toward a neighbor's house. As she reached the gate, one of the soldiers struck her on the head. Hearing the cries for help, the neighbor and his wife came out of the house. The soldier, who was bareheaded, ran in the direction of the Lefebvres' home.

Meanwhile, Lefebvre and his employer, at the latter's house, heard cries for help coming from the direction of the Lefebvre home. August Lefebvre immediately left for his house.

A few minutes later, Madame Lefebvre and her neighbors returned to their home. On their arrival, they found her husband clasping his stomach with his hands. He had been cut with a knife and was bleeding profusely. There was a wound about five centimeters long on the right side of his abdomen. He did not say how he had received it except to remark, "Oh, those salauds [dirty beasts]." An attempt was made to apply bandages and to find a doctor. Monsieur Lefebvre's face changed color, his speech failed, and in 15 minutes he was dead. He was 52 years old and had always been in good health. Lefebvre's employer arrived. In the courtyard of the Lefebvre house, he found an American helmet, gray in color, with a white arc painted on it.

Marguerite Lefebvre, who had left the house at the same time as her mother, ran down the road toward the home of her father's employer for a distance of about 25 meters. A soldier caught her at this point, threw her to the ground, and slapped her face. Another soldier was present, and both struck her, wrapped her head in a raincoat, forced her to her feet, and took her into a field. 'When she cried for help, one of the soldiers hit her with his knife. On reaching the field, one of them threw her to the ground and, while his companion held her, tore off her clothes. All three in turn raped her. This took about two hours. The soldiers then carried her to another field about two kilometers away and again repeatedly raped her. Two of the soldiers left, while the third remained asleep on top of her.

Marguerite crawled out from under him and escaped. She went first to the nearby home of a friend and then to her own home, arriving at about 1:30 in the early morning. She was exhausted and showed signs of having been struck and bitten on the face. Her clothes, which her mother gave to the police, were torn to pieces. It was necessary to hospitalize her, and she remained at the hospital for several months. Marguerite was unable to see the faces of her assailants, except for their eyes and mouths, since they wore white masks.

Written inside the helmet found by Lefebvre's boss was the name John Williams and the last four numbers of his army serial number. The following day, a pair of fatigue pants with blood stains on the fly and an undershirt minus the sleeves were found in Williams' duffle bag. It took less than two hours to tie Milbert Bailey and James L. Jones into this debauched crime. They were found guilty of murder and rape during a court-martial in Cherbourg, France, and sentenced: "To be hanged by the neck until dead."[3]

On April 19, 1945, the three men were taken from jail and brought, under guard, in an open quarter-ton truck to the village of Le Pernelle, the hometown

4. The Hangings

of the murder and rape victims. The truck halted about 20 yards from the scaffold, which had been erected in the side yard of the Lefebvre family's home. According to the army report: "The site of the execution was a hedge rowed field approximately 100 yards by 35 yards and adjacent to the house of the victims. The ground was covered with a blanket of grass and trees spotted the area but did not obstruct any view of the proceedings at the site. The weather was warm and clear with the sun shining."

Heading the execution procession were Lieutenant Colonel Henry L. Peck and Chaplain Lieutenant William L. Bell at his left; they were followed by the prisoners with guards on either side and behind them another guard carrying a brace board. The recorder, writing the details on a pad, followed directly behind. The brace board or collapse board was provided in case the prisoner collapsed, fainted, or became uncontrollable; if necessary, he would be strapped to the board and hanged with it attached. The board would not be needed in this execution.

One prisoner at a time and the escorts marched in a straight line directly to the feet of the scaffold. The commanding officer and the chaplain then proceeded up the stairs to the platform of the scaffold while the guards bound the prisoner's hands. As the prisoner and guards ascended the stairs, the recorder gave the command: "Attention." The prisoner, having been led up the stairs, was placed on the trap door. The recorder followed to the top step. At a signal from the commanding officer, the executioner's assistant bound the feet of the prisoner.

The commanding officer took his position in front and to the right of the prisoner, while the chaplain took his place in front and to the left. The commanding officer asked the prisoner if he had a statement to make to him before the execution was carried out. The prisoner said, "No, sir," and responded the same way when questioned by the chaplain.

The commanding officer then signaled the executioner, who cut the rope that released the weight and sprung the trap door. "The trap mechanism operated perfectly and the prisoner was precipitated through the open trap door clearly and hung suspended in the lower recess of the scaffold. The command 'Parade Rest' was given by the recorder. The body hung suspended with no sound or muscular movement but with a slight swaying motion. There were no visible signs or audible signs of emotional reaction from any official or observer."

These three proceedings took more than an hour. In a hanging, the executed is actually asphyxiated, which usually takes about 15 minutes before death. Witnessing these events were the son, Eugene Lefebvre, and the mother/wife, Madame Lefebvre—the family members of the murdered/raped victims. The families of the three executed men were notified that they had died from "Judicial Strangulation" in a non-battle status due to their own misconduct.[4] Their bodies would never be returned to their families.

The best explanation for the executions in the Lefebvres' yard is that they were carried out in the village where the crime was committed to show the locals that Americans were not the Nazis and that justice was served when U.S. troops committed crimes against the civilian population—at least that was the intent. But regardless, the U.S. Army had exclusive jurisdiction over its troops stationed in France as the result of an agreement between the U.S. and British governments and the French Committee of National Liberation. That agreement provided that the Allied service authorities would have sole jurisdiction over their respective forces and civilian nationals employed by those forces. The French police were authorized to arrest Allied troops for offenses against French civil law and to detain them until they were taken into custody by the appropriate Allied service authority. The certification of an Allied officer of field rank (colonel and above) sufficed to establish the identity of a member of his forces. Allied military authorities were to notify the French of any action taken against members of the Allied forces who were charged with offenses against persons under French jurisdiction.[5]

5

The Liberation of Paris

Behind the successful breakthrough of the American armies from the Normandy beachheads and the successful thrust of Patton's Third Army into the heart of France was the supply and service organization known as the Communication Zone or Com Z. It existed for one mission: To support ground and air forces in the assault driving into Germany. With a strength of 616,129 troops, Com Z was responsible for the rehabilitation of ports, reconstruction of railroads, building of airfields, and laying of pipelines in addition to moving supplies, equipment, and soldiers to the advancing armies.

Com Z was composed of engineers, quartermasters, truck companies, graves registration, port battalions, medical evacuation, units, hospitals, and much more. During the month of September, Com Z furnished the Combat Zone with 3.5 million gallons of gas each day and also purchased from French sources nearly 6 million pounds of potatoes and 3 million pounds of onions just some of the many supplies sent to the front lines. The truck companies of Com Z operated under blackout conditions, bombing, and strafing on a 24-hour basis. They often found themselves intermingled with tanks, half-tracks, and other combat vehicles headed for the battle front. It was the truck driver performing echelon maintenance between hauls that kept the wheels rolling over an ever-expanding Communication Zone. Railroads and pipelines for getting gasoline, oils, and lubricants to the army vehicles were constantly pushed forward.

The railroads were not as badly damaged as anticipated, although some key bridges as well as tunnels and railyard facilities were destroyed. Reconstruction of the railroad bridges started on June 19, just two weeks after D-Day, and a single 30-mile track running east from Cherbourg to Carentan was completed by July 5, 1944. After the breakthrough from the Cotentin Peninsula, the Engineer Service regiments repaired the railroad bridges immediately after capture. By August 20, the Cherbourg line was in operation for 175 miles, all the way to Le Mans, with the first army train arriving there three days later.

The Allied plans were to circle Paris with General George Patton's Third Army skirting south and General Omar Bradley's Army Group going northeast, the most direct route to Berlin. The armies would converge about 35 miles beyond Paris, leaving it surrounded, cutting off German supplies, and waiting for the isolated Germans to surrender. This was not the plan of Charles de Gaulle or Dietrich von Choltitz, German Commander of Paris, however.

The German plans called for the defense to take place within the city itself, resulting in the complete destruction of Paris. The *Springer Kommandoes* had been dispatched from Berlin and placed explosives under the 82 bridges crossing the Seine River, the Eiffel Tower, the Arc de Triomphe, Napoleon's tomb, and all historical monuments and buildings plus the industrial factories. All that was required was the order from General Von Choltitz, and Paris would be a complete wasteland.

A week previously, the monocle-wearing Prussian Von Choltitz had been in charge of a Panzer Army fighting the Allies in France. He was summoned by train to Hitler's Wolf's Lair in Rastenburg, Prussia. Meeting Hitler for only the second time, Von Choltitz was struck by his appearance and, after listening to the Führer and his continuing plans for war, realized the man was mad. It was in this atmosphere that he was promoted and placed in charge of the defense of Paris.

A few days after Von Choltitz took command of Paris, the French Forces of the Interior (FFI) under the influence of de Gaulle began an insurrection within the city. Receiving commands from Hitler's headquarters for the destruction of Paris, Von Choltitz stalled, realizing he was committing insubordination. Knowing it was only a matter of time before he would be relieved of his command by being arrested and his successor would give the order to ignite the explosives, Von Choltitz came up with a plan.

With the help of the Swedish General Consul, Raoul Nordling, he would invite the Allies to Paris! Through continued fighting by the FFI, demands by de Gaulle, and delivered messages by the Swedish consul, General Dwight D. Eisenhower relinquished control over the French 2nd Armored Division and ordered it, along with the U.S. 4th Infantry Division, to liberate Paris. With the bulk of the German army destroyed at the Falisie Gap, it took the two divisions a couple of days to liberate Paris without undue opposition. The liberation of Paris resulted in the capture of General Dietrich von Choltitz.

On the night of August 23, word came over the radio that Paris had been liberated. Actually fighting was still going on within the city, and it was several days before German resistance ceased. As the men of the 29th MRU sat around the loudspeaker listening to the exciting news, the horizon in back of the chateau was brightened by a tremendous rainbow, brilliant and beautiful, as if

5. The Liberation of Paris

it was a sign heralding the liberation of the city and all of France. They were now in the town of Canisy, where there had been much fighting—as the men of the 29th soon discovered while walking throughout the countryside in the evenings. Just a stone's throw away from the chateau were the railroad tracks, and a destroyed train was still lying there. It had been badly bombed, and sheets of steel struck out of the engine like the tentacles of an octopus. It was a passenger train, undoubtedly used by the Germans for troop purposes.

Everywhere they saw signs of battle: abandoned ammunition; long, narrow foxholes, just big enough to hide one man, dug deeply and hastily; a GI's overseas medic cap, part of a uniform, still bearing signs of blood and the straw neatly matted where the man had lain; machine gun clips, bullets, and mortar shells left by the fleeing Germans; and finally, five German tanks, several in good condition, but others badly burnt. One had been blown all to hell, and there was still a stench of death about it. Not far away lay a dead horse, still unburied, rotting into the ground. Most of the German tanks were filled with personal things left by the enemy—papers, letters, books, and ammunition, plenty of live ammunition. Everywhere there was silence—a strange silence that permeated the fields, a restful silence that had come after a fierce battle and destruction and death.

On the morning of August 23, 1944, Captain Walsh and the men of the 29th departed from Canisy, for Le Mans, approximately 130 miles away, taking the command car and two trailers. It was a cool, chilly day as they drove through the French countryside toward Le Mans—beautiful, rich farming land, very little of which had been touched by the war. Only the towns seemed to have borne the brunt of war, and practically every village they passed through had been hit. The town of Mortain, which the Americans took, lost, and retook from the Germans, was shattered beyond recognition. Only the homes on the outskirts of the town remained intact. Once in a while, they came across American and German tanks, smashed, burnt, and abandoned by the wayside. The men did not see many people, but those whom they saw were friendly and waved to them. Occasionally, they passed bewildered refugees going home in carts, on bicycles—old and young, dragging cows and dogs and other animals, returning with all the possessions they took with them when they suddenly departed as the fury of war had struck their land four years previously.

The 29th MRU reached the outskirts of Le Mans in the latter part of the afternoon, and the convoy stopped there for about 15 minutes. The people in the little houses along the roadside greeted them with tomatoes and plums until it seemed that they had almost stripped their gardens. Le Mans itself, a city of around 100,000 inhabitants, gave the soldiers a wild welcome. War had been kind to this city, and there was little fighting there. Everywhere the residents seemed glad to see the Americans. People stopped on the crowded streets, smiled, and waved. In contrast, there was only silence as carloads of German prisoners were herded through the streets. The enlisted men in their trucks swore as they passed, for they all hated the mess Germany had gotten them into.

Around five o'clock that afternoon, the 29th convoy stopped at a school building on the edge of town, which headquarters, GFRS, had taken over for its offices. The men went into the courtyard, where a hot meal was waiting. The people in the neighborhood were standing in the doorways watching as they emerged from the little school courtyard to return to the trucks. The Americans chatted with the French as best as they could, and gave them cigarettes and some of their rations. The French responded with gifts of big, ripe, delicious tomatoes. The soldiers then went to their living quarters, on the grounds of the chateau Perqucy, a small building located a mile and a half away from Le Mans.

At first the men of the MRU pitched their tents in a heavily forested area, but later they moved to an open field, which was drier and where their tents could derive some benefit from the sun. They shared the field with two big work horses, which were often noisier than they liked and which discovered the pine branches they used as mattresses were much to their taste.

None of the men dug in, as there was a little danger of air raids. The war was moving too rapidly, with the American Third Army driving toward Belgium. The MRU trailers were placed to the rear of the chateau. The 29th MRU had recently acquired an additional machine trailer, as it was servicing more and more replacement units that had arrived in France.

Living arrangements at the chateau Perqucy, as it was called, were very good. Everything was conveniently located, including pup tents, trailers, mess, barber's shop, and so forth. It was not quite so handy for the men assigned to headquarters, GFRS, who were driven to the school building to work in GI trucks each day.

To reach Paris was the goal of every American soldier overseas. Little did the men of the 29th MRU think when they landed on the shores of France that this dream would be realized. But now they were ordered to proceed to the heart of Paris.

On the afternoon of September 5, 1944, Captain Walsh and 14 enlisted men left Le Mans and arrived in Paris, after a trip of approximately 127 miles. Two days later, the remaining enlisted men departed for Paris. They stopped alongside the highway and consumed a hasty breakfast. On the main road to Paris, they saw a continual stream of trucks going in that direction. Civilian

5. *The Liberation of Paris*   43

Hungary Parisians reach out for the cigarettes and other bits offered by this American in front of the Hotel Majestic, former German Headquarters, Paris.

trucks and cars were jammed with people from all walks of life, on their way back to their homes throughout France. Many rode bicycles; some walked. The group even passed two people pushing baby carriages. One of the women was barefooted, and both were bound for Paris.

    The canvas tops of the trucks were rolled back so that all might see the big show. All along the road were abandoned and wrecked German vehicles, ruined villages, and damaged farmhouses. If you did not look closely, the countryside did not appear to have been badly damaged by the war. The convoy overtook many French trucks on the hills, and thus began the first hand-waving, V-for-victory signs, and distribution of cigarettes and candy. They heaved these articles from their trucks. The more hardy members of the group stood up in their trucks continually; toward the end of the day and its journey, they found themselves with extremely painful and disagreeable-looking wind-burnt eyes. The nearer they came to Paris, the more populated and citified the landscape became, and the emptier their pockets got. Little did they realize the monetary value or scarcity of cigarettes and candy in Paris.

Happy French children and young women of liberated Paris greet American soldiers.

Everywhere the French people were wild with excitement. The Yanks were getting a warm reception. In contrast, there was only silence as truckload after truckload of sorry-looking German prisoners passed the Americans, headed for the interior.

In Paris, it was the same story, repeated a thousand-fold. Everywhere Parisians greeted the soldiers warmly. They smiled, waved, chatted, and

5. The Liberation of Paris

A free French woman extends a welcome to one of the many liberators who had just entered the city of Paris.

swarmed around the truck whenever it stopped. They were happy that the Boche was gone, and they wanted to show their gratitude to the Americans for liberating their city. From the outskirts, the MRU troops proceeded into the heart of the city, and then got lost. They saw much of downtown Paris before they finally reached their destination, Le Jardin des Tuileries, where they were to park their trailers.

Le Jardin des Tuileries, started by Catherine de Medici in 1564, was an excellent spot for the MRU trailers, as the park was not yet open to the public

A liberator holds an infant as happiness abounds for the Parisian mother and sister.

and the tall trees offered a natural camouflage. The garden had been the scene of a ferocious little battle between the Germans and the Free French Forces, and there were still a half-dozen destroyed German tanks and vehicles lying around as testimony to the struggle that had ensued. The Americans were warned not to touch any of the abandoned German equipment, as it was

5. The Liberation of Paris

Top: American troops of the 28th Infantry Division pass the Arc de Triomphe and march down the Champs-Elysées. *Bottom:* The Stars and Stripes waves along with the French Tri-Colors over these happy faces of liberated Paris.

A color guard lead the parade of U.S. Army units along the Champs-Elysées under the Arc de Triomphe to celebrate the liberation of Paris from Nazi occupation. Parisians line the street to cheer the Stars and Stripes.

rumored that there were many live mines buried around the garden. A week after their arrival, several of the men witnessed the unearthing of the bodies of four German soldiers, who had been hastily buried in a shallow grave a short distance from the trailers. One Nazi had been bayoneted, and his face was frozen in an agonizing expression.

From foxhole to hotel was quite a jump, and the men could hardly believe their good fortune. Needless to say, they had no trouble in accustoming themselves to soft mattresses once more. The 29th MRU was quartered in the Hotel Ceramic on the Avenue Wagram, one block below the Arc de Triomphe. It was one of several hotels taken over by the Ground Force Replacement System and had been occupied by the Germans before their evacuation from the city. Built in 1904, it was small but fairly modern. The MRU was quartered on the fourth, fifth, and sixth floors, with two men to a room.

5. *The Liberation of Paris*   49

Toasting the liberation of Paris with a bottle of champagne and accompanied by two French women are, from left, T/Sgt. Shelton H. Crum of San Pedro, California, and Bud Cane, a *Stars and Stripes* reporter, from Princeton, New Jersey.

Many of the rooms had baths, and all the beds were soft and comfortable, some low and modern, with reading lights at the head of the bed. There was little electricity those first two weeks in Paris, and it was not uncommon to get caught with the lights going out right at the crucial moment when trimming a mustache or writing a letter. Hot water was practically nonexistent, and taking a bath was like a dip in the North Pole. Maid and hotel laundry service seemed amazing. The latter proved to be very expensive, but no complaints were made. This was the best deal that most of the men had ever experienced in the army, and certainly the pleasantest one they could have overseas.

Several blocks from the hotel was the Monte Carlo Restaurant, which the army had taken over and where chow was served. Food at first was rather poor because most provisions those days were bound for the front. The fare ran to C-rations, dehydrated potatoes and luncheon meat. Gradually it became better. Chow lines were usually long, and one GI timed the length of time it took him to get his mess kit cleaned, pegging it at 25 minutes. The chow lines also attracted the Parisians, who were curious and stopped to watch and examine their meal kits and their method of washing them. But for some the appeal went deeper than curiosity: They were near starvation. Few soldiers could forget the little old lady in black who made her nightly appearance, standing near the garbage pail, ready to take a little coffee or a scrap of food from their mess kits. One day they noticed a thin old man who had picked up a discarded jam can and was scraping the bottom for its meager contents. There were many like them.

Good cigarettes, they soon found, were scarce in Paris; Parisians would stop you in the streets and ask you if you had any to sell. They were nicotine starved and were willing to pay fabulous prices for a package, anywhere from 50 to 500 francs, with 100 francs being the usual selling price in the black market. Soon an order was issued forbidding American troops to sell cigarettes. One thing they did not have to worry about was policing duty: It was pounced upon.[1]

6

Paris, City of Lights

Paris is one of the most fascinating cities in the world—beautiful, cosmopolitan and gay, even in wartime. Amazingly, it had endured relatively little trouble in German hands. The Germans imposed a curfew and the Parisians were not allowed on the streets after a certain hour. Many times they were punished for some trivial offense, however, and were not permitted in the streets at all in the evening.

To all outward appearances, the city did not seem to have suffered much from German occupation. Even during the liberation, few of the buildings were damaged. Only the people suffered, especially the Jews. Families were separated, father and mother from child, with little likelihood of their ever being reunited. Many Jews were shipped to various parts of the Continent. One man, who was in the army when France fell in 1940, disappeared on a farm, where he remained during the occupation of his country. His wife, a charming intellectual woman, told of the fear of living in the occupied country and the horror she experienced upon witnessing the massacre of 16 innocent civilians by the Germans. Another woman's brother was taken prisoner after the armistice with Germany and shipped to a Nazi concentration camp, where he was imprisoned and remained for the duration of the occupation.

The officers and enlisted men from the Special Services Section, United Kingdom, moved into Paris to strengthen morale and provide the best of entertainment facilities for the 25,000 Allied soldiers who were anticipated to be on leave at any given time. Paris was to be a large leave center, and it would be necessary for Special Services to coordinate with the American Red Cross for bedding, meal facilities, and other factors affecting the welfare of the soldiers visiting the city. Additionally, 59,600 American soldiers and 5,200 British soldiers would be stationed within a 15-mile radius of Paris for the duration of the war. Also within a week or two of liberation, a large number of wives, future wives, and people seeking amusement arrived from London.

It was deemed imperative to have a large entertainment center in operation as soon as possible. Suitable theaters, cinemas, athletic fields, and gymnasiums had to be selected for this purpose. After an inspection tour of many theaters, it was decided the Olympia, Marignan, and Empire would be requisitioned.

It became evident early that in the Seine area there would be a great many hospitals and that these units would have to be serviced with a constant flow of entertainment. The USO was the usual source of amusement for hospitals, but it was soon discovered that there were more hospitals than the USO could cover. In turn, French artists were hired for the entertainment of the wounded and sick American soldiers. These artists were also utilized in the production and entertainment in the U.S. Army Theater Units. It was noted that the artist assignments "must be regarded as SECRET in the military sense."[1] One can only wonder why.

In spite of the German occupation, Paris emerged from the Germans' yoke in good spirits. Gradually the city came to life again. Subways started to run until 10 o'clock at night. Electricity was turned on in the buildings. Restaurants and sidewalk cafés opened. Theaters scheduled one film for 9:30 in the evening—old French, American and English films, such as *David Copperfield* and *Desire*. And once again, night clubs were doing good business—little hole-in-the-wall venues and swanky places where you could dance to a good band and drink champagne for 500 francs per bottle.

Paris was in many ways a combination of Washington and New York. The wide streets with the tall trees and the circles that were so confusing to drivers reminded one of Washington, D.C. But Paris was also a big city like New York, with a wealth of opera, theater and colorful night spots on after. It was a city of great historic interest as well, with many places to visit. The Eiffel Tower, built for the Paris World's Exposition during the last century, was a strange-looking edifice resembling a huge Texas oil structure that faced the Seine River. The Church of the Sacred Heart, ornate and oriental looking, was located on one of the highest points of the city with a magnificent view below. The Opera was rich in musical history. La Place de la Concorde, le Plaise du Louvre and Napoleon's Tomb drew their own crowds. Montmartre, the vivid night club district of Paris, was tough and atmospheric, serving as a rendezvous for artists, writers, actors and actresses. Notre Dame Cathedral, tremendous and awe-inspiring, had been started in 1163 and completed in 1325, with priceless stained glass windows (removed during the war) and relics from the holy land.

During their first Sunday in Paris, a group attended services in the Cathedral, where several weeks before a sniper inside the building had taken a shot at General de Gaulle as he walked down the aisle to worship. It was a miracle

6. Paris, City of Lights

de Gaulle was not killed. The men were much impressed by the high mass services—the beauty of the organ music and the chanting—indeed, an appropriate spot to pay homage to God. And nearby the Hotel Ceramic, just one block away, was the Arc de Triomphe, erected by Napoleon and a symbol of Paris. Beneath the Arc lies the Tomb of the Unknown Soldier from World War I, with an eternal flame that burns in his memory.

Paris, the men of the 29th MRU had always heard, was a city of style and beautiful women. They were not disappointed, for the Parisians were the nearest thing to American women they had seen since leaving the states: well groomed, smartly dressed and generally attractive, using lipstick and rouge. Many dyed their hair and went in for extreme clothing, such as brightly colored, exotic turbans. One woman said that the reason they wore such big hats was that the Germans had decreed that they wear small ones of a certain measurement. Parisian women, being ingenious, dug out their old clothing and emerged on the streets wearing new big hats that they wore in defiance.

The Parisians were friendly, pleasant, and eager to talk to the Yanks. They seemed more like Americans than the English, more casual, informal and less reserved than their British cousins. Most of the men liked them better than the English, because the French and the Americans were very much alike in terms of temperature.

Parisian shops were very lovely but very expensive. When they left Paris, the Germans had bought up everything that they could lay their hands on, but the French were smart and secretly stored away much of their finer articles in anticipation of that happy day when they could take them out of hiding, the day of liberation. The little French shop might have been a small shop in New York, but for the exorbitant prices. A pair of plastic earrings cost 750 francs; the same costume jewelry could be purchased in the United States for one or two dollars. Silk scarves sold for a similar price, and a small Belgian lace table cloth was priced at 1,750 francs. This was $35, almost a month's take home pay for most American soldiers. By far the best buy in Paris for the American soldier was perfume. Many of the men bought some Chanel or Milyneux to send home to their families—excellent perfume, reasonable in Paris, but carrying a high price tag in the United States.

There was plenty for the American soldier to do in Paris, with occasional imbibing being a popular pastime. In the evenings many GIs strolled down the Avenue des Champs-Elysées and lingered at one of the many little sidewalk cafés for a beer or a shot of cognac. Beer cost three francs per glass and was the nearest thing to American beer that the soldiers had encountered since leaving their home country. Cognac set one back 35 francs a shot; vermouth, 30 francs a glass; red wine, 200 francs a bottle; and champagne, from 385 francs up.

ENTERTAINMENT

Theatre & Address	Metro	Type Show	Time Show	Ticket Information
EMPIRE, *Avenue de Wagram*	Etoile Ternes	Theatre or other stage show	1430 2000	Tickets are required up to 15 mins. before the performance. At this time, the house is opened for admittance without tickets. Tickets may be obtained from all leave clubs.
OLYMPIA, *Boulevard des Capucines*	Opera Madeleine			
ENSA - MARIGNY, *Avenue Marigny (Champs-Elysées)*	Marbeuf			
MADELEINE, *19, rue de Surene*	Concorde Madeleine			
MARIGNAN, *19, Champs-Elysées*	Marbeuf	Movie	Cont. from 1400 2300	No tickets necessary. Free. Military personnel only.
ENSA - PARIS-CINEMA, *23, Champs-Elysées*	Marbeuf			
MADELEINE, *19, rue de Surene*	Concorde Madeleine	Movie	1800 2300	
SPECIAL-EVENTS	There are numerous special shows, concerts etc., presented from time to time. Inquire at the Information Desks of all leave clubs about these.			
THEATER AND OPERA *Tickets*	Tickets for French theaters and operas may be purchased at the ticket agencies located at the Olympia and Marignan theatres.			
FRENCH CINEMAS	Allied Military Personnel admitted at half-price.			

Entertainment flyers for GIs on pass.

Drinking was expensive—too much so for a modest pocketbook. Through liquor the American soldier learned that the franc did not go far—not half as far as their money went in England, for the current exchange value was two cents to the franc.

Paris was expensive, but fortunately there was much free entertainment

6. Paris, City of Lights

for military personnel. As noted earlier, Special Services took over several theaters, and many of the men went to the Cinéma Marignan on the Champs-Elysées to see such films as *The Song of Bernadette* with the Academy Award winner Jennifer Holt; *Sensations of 1945* with tap-dancer Eleanor Powell; and *Step Lively* with swooner Frank Sinatra and the lovely Gloria de Haven. The first movies at the Marignan were presented in a small preview theater, a theater within a theater, but as the number of GIs increased in Paris, movies were soon shown in the big main theater, a beautiful, modern building with soft, comfortable seats. The Marignan was open from 2 p.m. to 11 p.m. daily, with a policy of showing two different movies each week. The first movies shown were *Roger Touhy, Gangster, Song of Bernadette* and *Gildersleeve's Ghost*. The average attendance for this movie house was 30,000 troops per week.

In due time, Special Services commenced showing films three times a week in the Hotel Splendide, and later on, the Chambord. These features included such excellent movies as *Back Home in Indiana*, a warm-hearted, home-spun picture about horse racing; *Kings Row*, old but good; and *Two Girls and a Sailor*, a better than average musical.

A highlight of the military-sponsored entertainment was the show presented by the French for the Armed Forces in the Olympic Theater. This excellent three-hour variety show consisted of dancing (from toe-dancing to the inevitable can-can); pantomime in the Charlie Chaplin vein; juggling, acrobatics and swing; and finally, Fred Astaire, dancing a couple of nimble numbers in GI uniform. The Olympic Theater had opened September 18, 1944, with the production *Paris Presents*, being the first theater to reopen after the problem with scenery and necessary lighting was resolved. It had a staff of 120 including a chorus line of 20 girls. The Anita Avila Ballet had a pit orchestra consisting of the 35 members of the Fred Mele Orchestra. The Olympic initially offered one show nightly, with a matinee on Sunday.

Paris Presents was organized around the Willie Shore USO unit, which included Fred Astaire, plus leading French performers. This show ran for a month. After that, Paris was declared off limits as far as the USO was concerned, and it became necessary to staff the shows with French talent only. The average attendance was 20,000 soldiers every week.

The Madeleine Theater was a traditional-style theater seating approximately 800 people. The original intent was to use the theater as a base for British and American players, who formed a unit organized to operate as a stock company in Paris. The theater opened with a repertory of *Ten Little Indians* and *Three Cornered Moon*. These productions were followed by a cast of British and American soldiers performing in the play *The Male Animal*. The Katherine Cornell Company opened for one week with *The Barretts of Wimpole*

Street. The average weekly performance for the shows at the Madeleine Theater was 3,000 before the theater was converted into a cinema.

The Empire Theater opened with the GI production *Com Zee, Com Za*. The theater was staffed by approximately 120 civilians, including a pit band of 35 pieces. After a successful run of one month, the production was replaced with a French civilian show similar to that running in the Olympic Theater. A chorus line was added to the performance. The theater operated seven days a week with six matinee performances, playing to an average attendance of 11,000 per week.

In the early days the only condition of admission to a theater or cinema was the wearing of a U.S. Army uniform. The more popular live shows quickly filled every night and many disappointed troops were turned away. A Ticket Department was set up with the policy of admission by ticket only for the live shows. Every Saturday the number of soldiers for each combat unit was submitted to the Ticket Department and a percentage of tickets from the total number available was assigned to that unit for the following week. The American Red Cross billeted all the combat troops visiting Paris on leave, so the tickets were sent to this organization for distribution. After many committee meetings and much debate, 50 percent of the tickets were allocated to combat troops on leave and the remaining were set aside for garrison troops stationed in the Seine area. Later an Allied Ticket Allocation Committee was formed and held weekly meetings each Monday.

A certain number of seats were, of course, reserved for general officers. All ticket holders had to be in their seats 15 minutes before the performance. At that point, all vacant seats, including those of the general officers, were filled by waiting standbys.

Dance bands were plentiful and furnished to the various garrison units and hospitals in the Seine area. Large bands played one weekly concert at the Olympic Theater and at many army ceremonies. The biggest catch for the Special Services Section was to obtain the assignment of the Glenn Miller Band to its unit. Arrangements had been made for the band to appear before approximately 25,000 troops per week and also maintain their normal radio broadcast commitments. The Olympic Theater carried all the necessary equipment for a live broadcast. Unfortunately, Miller was killed, going missing over the English Channel in an airplane. This event led to some wisecracking among the troops, that they wished his music had died and he had lived.[2]

The Stage Door Canteen was operated on 144 Champs-Elysées by a French civilian in connection with the American Theater Wing, the same arrangement as made with the other Stage Door Canteens in London and the United States. The initial funding was $10,000 from the United States and an equal amount

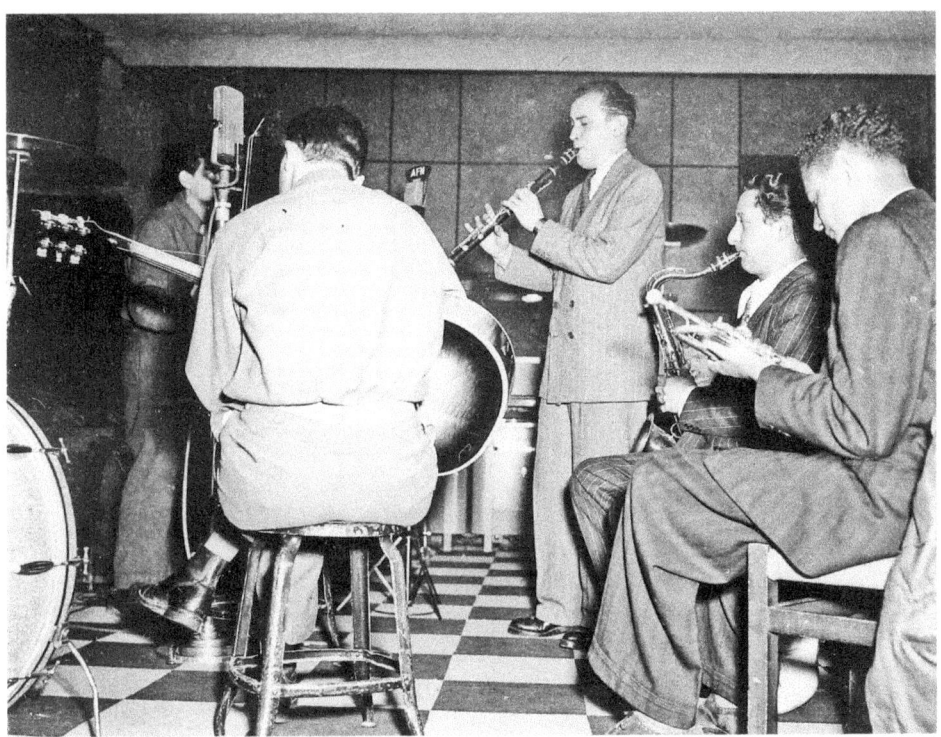

French musicians and members of Major Glenn Miller's American band of the American Expeditionary Forces join in a jam session broadcast over the Armed Forces Network from Paris studios.

from British sources. For its opening night, the Special Services Section furnished a band and arranged for an appearance by Marlene Dietrich. Soldiers were welcomed by French hostesses; they danced to good music and drank coffee, soft drinks and 1.5 percent alcohol-content beer and wine. About 3,000 soldiers were entertained each night.[3]

Regardless of the sanctioned entertainment, eight out of 10 soldiers headed for the notorious Pigalle section of town for amusement. Their Paris-wise buddies had tipped them off that they would get the best deal there. "Pig-Alley," as it came to be called, was the gaudiest, loosest honky-tonk section on the Continent or maybe the world. It was rather quiet during the day, but when darkness set in and the streets lit up and the streetwalkers start walking and hawking, it became what was known on Broadway as "out of this world." The prices charged by the ladies of the evening ranged from 250 francs (plus hotel room) upward to a corporal's pay, and they were not shy about asking for customers.

The opening night of the new Stage Door Canteen, Paris, sponsored by the American Theater Wing, found the Champs-Elysées jammed with soldiers and civilians waiting to get in.

The American Red Cross had entered Paris immediately after the city's liberation and requisitioned several hotels and staff to serve as Red Cross clubs. The staff personnel were given a security check and an army medical examination. Securing blankets and sheets was difficult; sporadic electricity and a lack of coal presented additional problems. The food for all American Red Cross activities was supplied by the U.S. Army Quartermaster Corps. Furniture was shipped from England and kitchen equipment was purchased through the U.S. Army.

The establishment of Paris as an important leave center brought with it the need for lodging, eating and recreational facilities for U.S. forces. The American Red Cross made available a number of clubs for all branches of the U.S. military. The first club to open in Paris, the Rainbow Corner, sponsored 10 hotels with sleeping accommodations for 826 soldiers. It was headquartered in the Hotel de Paris, a three-star hotel with 530 beds. The American Red Cross eventually opened 17 clubs: nine for enlisted men, five for officers, two for African American soldiers, and one, the Patio with 140 beds, for enlisted women. Thus it operated a total of 76 hotels containing 8,018 beds. The two American Red Cross clubs for African American enlisted men were the Potomac, Paris Lyon Palace with 256 beds, and Left Bank, Trianon Palace Hotel with 368 beds. Of the five officers clubs, the Independence, located within the Hotel Crillon, was rated four stars, with 330 beds; the Lafayette (Hotel Edouard) and Washington (Hotel du Louvre) were both three-star rated. The Officers Club for Women was the Normandy Hotel, with 291 beds and no star rating.

LEAVE CLUBS

1. AMERICAN RED CROSS

   a. Clubs for Enlisted Men :

CLUB	ADRESS	METRO
Boulevard Club	9, Boulevard des Italiens	Richelieu-Drouot
Columbia Club	2, Rue de l'Elysée	Marbeuf
Grand Central Club	108, Rue Saint-Lazare	Saint-Lazare
Left Bank Club*	1 bis, Rue de Vaugirard	Odéon
Patio Club (WAC)	239, Rue Saint-Honoré	Concorde
Pavillon Club	35, Rue de l'Echiquier	Strasbourg-St-Denis
Potomac Club*	11, Rue de Lyon	Gare de Lyon
Rainbow Corner	8, Boul. de la Madeleine	Madeleine
Transatlantic Club	8 bis, Place de la République	République
Union Terminal	5, Rue de Strasbourg	Gare de l'Est

   b. Clubs for officers :

CLUB	ADRESS	METRO
Independence Club	10, Place de la Concorde	Concorde
Lafayette Club	29, Avenue de l'Opéra	Opéra
Mayflower Club	53, Rue François-Ier	George-V
Washington Club	Place du Théâtre-Français	Palais-Royal
Officers' Club for Women	7, Rue de l'Echelle	Palais-Royal

   NOTE : *COLORED STAFF.

2. AEF CLUB, 2, Rue Scribe, métro Opera.
   Allied Expeditionary Forces Club. Leave and recreation center for all Allied troops established by Supreme Headquarters.

3. MISCELLANEOUS INFORMATION

   a. Most leave clubs include the following : information bureau, pressing service, coffee and doughnuts or snacks, photographers, shopping help, theater tickets, barber service, tours, dances.

   b. Bus tours operate morning and afternoon. Get your tickets in advance at your club.

   c. Eat your meals in the club where you are registered - by military order, clubs can serve only men who are registered. Coffee and doughnuts or snacks are available at all clubs to all US uniformed personnel.

   d. Men on day passes may take their rations to the ARC. Boulevard Club (EM) or to the ARC. Mayflower Club (Off) and receive a hot meal in exchange.

Club flyers handed out to GIs on pass in Paris.

All of the clubs served meals and had snack bars that offered coffee and doughnuts. Each club had extensive facilities that included information, the aforementioned theater tickets, check cashing services, a barber shop, manicures, shoe shines, clothes pressing, mending and sewing, a photo shop, laundry, money exchange, first aid, prophylactic station (army operated), a chiropodist, and cablegram services. Here a soldier could seek advice regarding a personal problem and get a sympathetic hearing or apply for a small loan, generally ranging from 200 to 1,000 francs ($4–$20).

The clubs likewise had extensive program activities, including dances, daily bus tours, shopping tours, a sketch artist, luncheon music, dinner music, walking tours, French classes, handball, fencing, wrestling, boxing, swimming, table tennis, dance classes, "date" bureaus, vaudeville shows and GI amateur nights. Of some importance, most of the clubs were staffed by attractive young American girls.[4]

In addition to these activities, a series of concerts were held at the Salle

Dancing at the "Couples Club," at 49 Rue de Pierre Charron: Soldiers and their French dates dance to the music of a U.S. Army band. This photo was taken in the balcony of the "Couples Club" on opening night. Notice the painting of President Franklin D. Roosevelt in the background. The club was under the auspices of the Army Exchange Service (PX) and offered fare such as hamburgers, soft drinks, and ice cream. There was a bar on the ground floor, a clubroom, and dancing on the balcony.

Pleyel, the Théâtre des Champs-Elysées and the Théâtre de l'Opéra. They featured the very best French civilian concert artists and visiting peforming stars such as Lily Pons, Andre Kostelanetz and Yehudi Menuhin.[5]

At any given time, 12,700 American soldiers were in Paris on a 48- or 72-hour pass, with 3,000 arriving daily. The passes were rationed by Captain Aileen M. Witting, WAC, in a fair and equitable manner, with combat troops receiving 75 percent of the passes. The army groups were notified of their availability daily, and this total was passed down the chain of command before finally arriving to the company commanders, who picked the allocated number of soldiers from their units. Quite often no advance notice was given; the men were simply pulled back from the front line, informed they had earned a pass to Paris and taken by jeep to a collection center. Here the ranking member was made group leader and the men set out for Paris by train or truck.

Six to 16 hours later, upon arriving in Paris, they reported to the Central Registration Bureau. The group leader collected 20 francs for each night for hotel rooms from each soldier and their passes. He presented these items to the Bureau representative, who stamped the reverse side. The group leader then went to the American Red Cross station and had rooms assigned for his unit when he turned over the money. When he returned and gave the men their passes, the soldiers were directed to their hotels either on foot or by metro.

Many of the men arriving were fresh from combat and covered with combat grime. Therefore a shower unit had been established in the barracks of the Headquarters Command, where the soldiers could go for a bath, a shave, and clean clothing in exchange for their dirty uniforms. Unfortunately the correct size of clothing could not always be made available, as the uniforms issued were the clothes cleaned from a previous group of visiting GIs.

Once in the hotel, the men were told to read the club bulletin boards, which gave the address of the 40 prophylactic stations in the vicinity of Paris. The soldier was issued or could purchase from the PX a prophylactic kit consisting of a wash cloth and a 5-gram tube of ointment. The soldier was told to insert 2.5 grams of the ointment into the urethra and apply the remainder around the penis. Alternatively, he could go to a prophylactic station where the treatment was applied by a medical corpsman. Here, after the soldier urinated and thoroughly washed the genitals, the corpsman, using a syringe, inserted a mercury compound into the penis opening. The patient squeezed the opening close and massaged the ointment up the urethra tube. A veteran said, "It gave a slight stinging sensation and do not use my name." As with the PX kit treatment, the ointment was also rubbed thoroughly on the penis and testicles. Next, wax paper was wrapped around the penis and scrotum as the soldier pulled up his pants; he kept this ointment on for several hours. This measure was intended to protect against sexually transmitted diseases (STDs) after one had engaged in copulation without a condom, but was recommended for additional protection when using one. The centrally located prophylactic stations treated an average of 1,627 American soldiers per day.

The 180 houses of prostitution in Paris were off limits, but it was estimated that about 68,000 women were streetwalkers. This number did not include the women available in bars, restaurants and other places frequented by the free-wheeling GIs. The Army Medical Corps estimated the 90 percent of all STDs in soldiers were contracted from streetwalkers.

Undoubtedly the least used facility by the combat soldiers was the golf course, located in nearby St. Cloud and accessible only by train. A French English-speaking civilian was in charge of the course and had available 36 dozen balls and 36 sets of clubs. Due to increased U.S. civilian use of the course on weekends, GIs were informed, "it will be necessary to limit use of the course at these times by prescribing the number of men to play at one time."[6] Apparently there was not a problem as no complaints were registered regarding usage of the golf course.

There were two heated swimming pools available in the city. Captain C.P. Eisemann made a request "to higher headquarters on the reservation of one of the pools for colored personnel. He made the statement, 'That's a hot question and I do not want to make the final decision.'"[7] The problem of supplying swimming suits was resolved by issuing the soldiers basketball trunks.

The soldiers returning from leave for the most part were happy. A typical remark was made by M.W. Eickenburg, 334 Infantry: "The Red Cross does about everything possible to help a man. I think they're doing a damned good job." There were some complaints, though. One man grumbled about the travel conditions on the train, and the excuse was "There is a war going on." Others, short of cash, grumbled about the cost of a room and meals, which amounted to 50 francs per day or $1; thus a 72-hour pass for lodging was almost one-fifth of a month's pay. All of the soldiers seemed to feel there was not enough time to see Paris, but overall the general morale of those returning to the Combat Zone was excellent.

This was Paris for the Combat Zone soldiers. But how did the permanent staff of Com Z fare?

7

The Officer's Formal Mess

The Seine Section Headquarters moved into the Ambassador Hotel and started operating a mess for American officers. The menu consisted of C-rations, K-rations, and 10-in-1s. It well suited the men until the British took over Maxim's, the most elegant bistro in Europe, for their officer's mess. Here, in the drab years after World War I, automobile tycoons and politicians of the Third Republic had elbowed out dukes and princes. In Maxim's, political careers were made and broken, and million-franc deals consummated with a U.S. sugar king or Bolivian tin baron.

Then came the Nazi occupation. German officers, many of them old habitués, took over Maxim's for their own. For a Frenchman to be seen entering its mahogany vestibule was equivalent to being tabbed a collaborator. After Paris's liberation, Maxim's was closed and turned over to the British for use as the staid Empire Club.

The conquering U.S. Army could not be one-upped by their British cousins, so they took over the Cercle Militaire, the French Army and Navy Club, for their officer's mess. It had been inaugurated by President Doumergue in 1928 and was used as a military club for French officers of the army and navy, offering restaurant facilities for approximately 300 people and a banquet capacity up to 600. It provided 100 officers' billets, of which approximately 40 rooms had private baths. Entertainment facilities provided included a library of 8,000 volumes, a large fencing room, a game room with billiard tables, a large lounge, and a theater with seating capacity of 500 on the ground floor and 150 in the balcony, as well as a bar where French officers could purchase drinks. The Cercle Militaire, due to its convenient central location close to the Gare St. Lazare, and its spaciousness, was especially suited for mess purposes.

The Cercle Militaire had been left by the Germans in a terrible state of dirt and deterioration, with furniture broken; leather arm chairs ripped open; doors wrenched off; locks, curtains, and metal works taken away; carpet

An American army truck delivering furnishings to the Paris officer's formal mess, located in the former Cercle Militaire.

shabby; china and glassware looted; oil stains in the lobby, which had been used as a garage; and refuse heaped everywhere. Of course, the Germans had also emptied the large wine cellar before leaving.

The French director supplied the army with the first members of the civilian staff by calling up some of his previous employees. Work was started immediately to put the building in proper condition, starting with the labor originally belonging to the club. This force was rapidly increased by personnel who were hired (400 were engaged on the second day) and set to work in shifts working from 7 a.m. to 11 p.m. In this way, the cleaning and painting of walls were carried out simultaneously, with new furniture and mess equipment selected from stocks in the U.S. depots and moved in. The work progressed rapidly despite the difficulty encountered in securing and repairing furniture and equipment.

When the Cercle Militaire first opened, its managers obtained a supply of German flour. This stock lasted for two weeks and was used to make French bread and French rolls, which were more popular than plain white bread. A contract with a civilian bakery was then negotiated to supply French bread and rolls.

7. The Officer's Formal Mess

The mess officers had the challenge of serving meals in rooms that were located one floor from the kitchen and had never before been used as dining rooms. Field ranges, augmented with electric hot-plates, were set up in two pantries on the first floor. The food was cooked in the main kitchen on the second floor, then carried to the first floor, where it was kept warm and dispensed to the waitresses serving this floor. Electric hot-plates were installed in the various dining rooms to keep the coffee hot. These hot-plates were purchased through the Service d'Aide aux Forces Alliés.

Another difficulty was dishwashing, because of the scarcity of china and a lack of space in the kitchen for setting up a second dishwashing machine. The breakage was rather high, due to the fact that china needed to be cleaned twice during each service.

It was decided that the Adjutant General's section would issue approximately 400 mess cards that would be a different color from those of the casual officer's mess. The casual officers' mess issued two different colored cards: a temporary mess card and a permanent membership card. Only officers on duty status were to be fed. Officers on leave and passes received their billets and meals from the Red Cross. Civilians in advisory or executive capacities who were U.S. citizens and on full-time duty with General of Special Staff Sections of the major military or naval headquarters located in Paris and who are performing duties commensurate with those of a commissioned officer are admitted by purchasing card A from the visiting officer's bureau at the Majestic Hotel. It was deemed necessary to have two officers check the cards at the doors; in addition, orders had to be checked for admittance. All of this activity took place under the control of General Pleas B. Rogers, the Commanding General of the Seine Section, who assigned two MP officers from the 382nd MP Battalion to assist at meal time.

The first bar to be put into operation was located on the second dining floor of the casual officer's mess. The bar had previously been used as such, so it was ready for use, with a seating capacity of approximately 150 persons. The first refreshment served was bottled beer, about a dozen bottles per day. The staff consisted of a cashier, a manager, and two waiters. Within the first week, one source of supply was located in Paris, which provided several cases of assorted spirits. The gross sales amounted to approximately 1,000 francs. The next improvement was the installation of draft beer. The sale of wine with meals in the dining rooms was also promulgated at this point.

About October 1, it was decided to take over the operation of the bar at the Hotel Lotti. Although the Germans had occupied these premises previously, which should have been sufficient cause to enable the U.S. Army to take possession without any obstacles, the building had to be taken virtually by force,

Brigadier General Pleas B. Rogers, commanding general, Seine Section, sits at his desk in his office, which overlooked the famous Place de l'Opéra in Paris. General Rogers was director of the leave program, which allowed thousands of American troops to visit the French capital for a brief rest.

as a small supply of champagne, cognac, liquors, and wine was stocked in the cellar.

From this point on, the chief problems were obtaining supplies of spirits and adopting a system of bookkeeping that was both flexible and foolproof. The sources of supplies increased rapidly in numbers and areas. The club began to deal with producers in Cognac, Bordeaux, Rheims, Epernay, Ay, and Marseilles. Shipments increased from several cases to several thousand cases. Items sold at the bar included all makes of champagne, cognacs, liquors, beer, aperitifs, red and white wines, and gin. The difficulties ordinarily encountered in obtaining them were enhanced by the unfamiliar business practices and laws governing French companies.

With the increase in volume of trade, improvements and expansions were made in the wine cellars, with wine racks being constructed. A tunnel with

7. The Officer's Formal Mess

branching rooms connecting the mess with the adjacent French police barracks was wired for lights and cleaned. This tunnel had been constructed by the Germans during their occupancy of these buildings. The staff was increased from three to nine. A sign painter was hired to maintain the ever-changing wine and spirits list.

In November, in addition to the regular monthly ration of scotch and gin, a special ration of other liquors was made possible through the purchase of a large quantity of assorted spirits that had been captured from the Germans. The warehousing was inadequate to handle this volume, which amounted to approximately 2,000 cases, so an agreement was reached with the well-known firm of Establishment Valette, St. Ouen, whereby it would furnish the storage space and staff necessary to manage the supply.

Numerous problems were encountered during the period of development. Sources of alcohol supply were most difficult to find. Quantities of spirits were practically nil in Paris itself, so the club was forced to look as far as 800 kilometers away. This brought out the problem of transporting the purchases to Paris. Government vehicles were denied for this purpose and rail wagons were impossible to obtain for spirits in that crucial period. Club managers were forced to use civilian wood- or coke-burning trucks, which further restricted the purchase fees set by the French government.

The Hotel Lotti, which had been opened September 25, 1944, had practically the same problems as the casual officer's mess. Although the American rations were not what the French chefs expected, they did an excellent job of preparing them attractively and tastefully. The French chefs were disappointed in opening canned vegetables, explaining that the vegetables were (over)cooked before they received them, so there was very little they could do other than warm them and serve them. Had they been fresh vegetables, these chefs could have used their culinary talents to advantage. The repetition in the menus of sausages and frankfurters was also very discouraging to the French cooks. When it came to serving C-rations, they just threw up their hands and said the Americans did not need cooks at all.

On October 1, a four-chair barber shop opened on the mezzanine floor of the Cercle Militaire, employing eight barbers. The prices for a haircut and a shave were 20 cents each. In the basement, a shoe shine booth with two boot blacks was established, shining shoes at 10 cents a shine. Adjoining the lounge on the first floor, a writing room, with 10 writing desks, was set up. In this room were pens, ink, and V-mails, with an Army Post Office collection box made available in the room.

An information booth, employing two young ladies, gave complete special services information. Special services supplied the officer's mess with tickets that were distributed to officers at the information booth. These tickets gave them free admittance at the theater in Paris: Empire & Olympia (variety shows), Marigny (English and American plays), and Madeleine (movies and plays). It was difficult for officers in Paris to book seats, for some places of entertainment were in great demand, such as the opera, the Folies Bergeres, and the Casino de Paris. These venues were sold out every night. The information girls directed the officers to the booking agencies and to the head porter of the mess, who managed to be supplied with a certain number of tickets every day.

Sunday night concerts in the Cercle Militaire lounge featured such well-known artists as Lola Bobesco, soloist of the great symphony orchestra of Paris, and Raphael Arroyo, a well-known Spanish pianist. In addition, a number of concerts were given by young artists who had just graduated from the Paris Conservatory of Music. These concerts were attended by approximately 150 to 200 officers and guests each Sunday night. On March 15, it was suggested by the mess council that dinner music be furnished in the messes in this section, to be funded by the bar profits of the operations. A trio—a violin, a cello, and a pianist—was hired to play dinner music from 7:30 to 10:30 six nights a week.

The Paris winter season, in spite of war circumstances, offered a wide range of amusements, from night clubs to concerts and lectures. Officers new in town were happy to receive detailed information from girls able to direct them through the jungle of this great city's night shows.

Needless to say, the generals of the Combat Zone were dissatisfied with the grand living conditions of the officers in the Communication Zone, and the officer's mess may have fueled this discontent. This mistrust stemmed from the feeling that rear area troops were better supplied than the combat soldiers, particularly with regard to such items as clothing and food. Also, they were living far better than the soldiers on the front lines. The staff of Com Z was referred to as demonstrating "lethargy and smugness." As pointed out by one U.S. general, "The Communication Zone exists for one purpose alone—serving the combat forces." General George Patton frankly stated that he trusted no one to the rear of his advanced section and usually planned his operations in partial defiance of those forces.[1]

Of course, the commanders of the forces at the front lines could not be too critical as much of SHAFE was headquartered in Paris, with the bulk of Eisenhower's staff located in Versailles—all within Com Z. They also entertained guests with an endless supply of whiskey and food that included sandwiches for the never-ending bridge games played by Chief of Staff W. Bedell Smith; his partner, a chief nurse; Eisenhower; and his chauffeur, Kay Summersby.

8

THE MESS AND BILLETING OFFICE OF THE HOTEL ASTRA

Rene C. Pollard, 0-267693, a civil employee of the Office of War Information (OWI), was hired on February 11, 1944, as Senior Administrative Officer, with a salary of $8,300 per year. He had been issued a uniform and War Department identification with the assimilated rank of a major but was classified as a Physiological Warfare Officer. At this time, a major in the U.S. Army was paid $3,300 per year and General Dwight D. Eisenhower, Supreme Commander, was making $8,800 per year. What qualification did Pollard possess to be awarded this salary? And would he improve his financial status while in Paris?

In May 1944, Pollard arrived in London, where he remained for two months. In August, he was sent to Brittany. Two months later, he was assigned to the Hotel Astra, 29 Rue de Caumartin, Paris, France, which had been taken over by the Office of War Information, as the mess and billeting officer.

Prior to the war, the OWI had created images that are among the most famous documentary photographs ever produced. Taken by a group of U.S. government photographers, the images show Americans in every part of the nation. In the early years, the project emphasized rural life and the negative impact of the Great Depression, farm mechanization, and the Dust Bowl. The noted photographer Ansel Adams was commissioned to create a photo mural for the Department of the Interior. The core of the OWI collection consists of about 164,000 black-and-white photographs.

The photographers in time turned their attention to the mobilization effort for World War II. In addition to patriotic works and photos playing up a wholesome image of America, OWI photographers covered less happy occasions. The OWI also documented social change, including the massive movement of women into the workforce and the advancement of African Americans in the military.[1]

Now in France, the OWI—all civilians—was a section that devoted itself to representing the U.S. Army's Communication Zone to the French people through its informational media. The OWI was responsible for conducting promotions on French radio programs in which it sought to ensure amicable relations between the army and the French people, whose country was traversed by the U.S. Army supply lines, in a campaign to keep the Red Ball Highway clear of civilian traffic and to turn in empty jerricans that they had found. These radio programs also sought to be "activity engaged in destroying the enemy psychologically." Depending on the problem, the OWI had a large working staff of international specialists who actually handled the day-to-day relationship between the U.S. Army and the French civilians. The American ambassador in France, while exercising a degree of control in certain fields of policy, had no administrative responsibility for the OWI.

The OWI drew it basic rations from the army; obtained transportation, oil, and gas from this source; and in general was attached to the army for maintenance, billeting, and transportation. The army exercised complete control over the OWI. Rene C. Pollard, in his position as mess and billeting officer, was of some concern owing to his large salary. In turn, the OWI's director was questioned regarding this position:

> **Q.** How would Mr. Pollard's duties as the manager, so to speak, of the Astra Hotel billet, mess, and bar—would be classified as psychological warfare?
> **A.** It is very difficult, sir, because all of our personnel [are] involved to a certain extent in psychological warfare activities. However, a great many of our individuals who are primarily assigned to either psychological warfare through Supreme Headquarters Allied Forces Europe, or the information activities in France have interchangeable duties and interchangeable activities, and it would be impossible to say that any one office had only connections with information or with psychological warfare on the other side.
> **Q.** Now, did Mr. Pollard have other duties outside of operating the billets and mess?
> **A.** He did not.[2]

The director's first answer is unfathomable. Let us examine Pollard's duties and actions.

Upon arriving in Paris, Pollard rented a large eight-room apartment at the fashionable 115 Avenue Henri Martin, which cost him a whopping $80 per month. He then hired Swiss-born Giuseppe Albertone, 58 years old and his 48-year-old French wife, Marie, for employment at the Hotel Astra. Pollard instructed the couple to report to his apartment as valet and chambermaid/cook. They visited the hotel just once each month to receive their pay and food ration tickets. Their services were needed for Pollard and his live-in girlfriend, Mrs. Mildred Blein, who was separated from her husband and whom Pollard

8. The Mess and Billeting Office of the Hotel Astra

intended to marry as soon as she obtained a divorce. Provisions consisting of salad oil, condensed milk, sauerkraut, pork, beets, lard, ham, hamburger, rolls, salt, sugar, flour, fish, and fowls were packed by the hotel cook or food steward in a large container and taken daily by Pollard from the Hotel Astra. They were enjoyed by the four occupants of the house. Additionally, Marie Albertone, the chambermaid, reported that a young employee of the hotel also brought by bags of coal.

During his free time, Pollard and Blein frequented the local horse racetracks, Le Tremblay and Autenil, and he won frequently. From the time he arrived in Paris until February 27, 1945, he used his winnings to purchased 43 postal money orders valued at $21,500 and sent them to his mother, Mrs. Helen Searle, of Woodside, Long Island, New York. Was he a lucky man or was he a crook?

As mess and billeting officer, Pollard was authorized to draw $5,000 from the U.S. Army Finance Division for funds to purchase foodstuffs and liquors for bar consumption. Assigned to the Hotel Astra and under Pollard's control was a Dodge station wagon and a GMC 2½-ton, 6 × 6 truck. They were to be used on trips in the purchase of supplies for the hotel.

Three weeks after taking the position in Paris, Pollard was approached by Roger Nazaret, a French civilian, who asked if he needed bread and eggs. Nazaret stated that should Pollard furnish the transportation, he would make it worthwhile for him. Pollard made arrangements for the French driver of the U.S. Army station wagon to travel with Nazaret on a 400-mile roundtrip. On their return, Nazaret delivered 40 kilos of butter and five dozen eggs to the mess of the Hotel Astra. Pollard paid for the merchandise and was given $800 for himself for the use of the army vehicle. Thus began a lucrative business in transportation, as the station wagon or the 2½-ton truck was on the road, driven by Frenchmen, almost every day under the safeguard of the U.S. Army.

Everything flowed smoothly with the "trucking business," with the exception of a minor bump on a trip for butter and eggs when two French drivers traveling to "parts unknown" were stopped by the French gendarmes. Pollard received a phone call late at night; the voice on the phone asked him if he had ordered 720 liters of Calvados. Pollard confirmed that he had ordered the apple brandy from the French region of Lower Normandy. He was then informed he needed to pay taxes on the brandy before the French authorities would release it.

The following morning, Pollard, dressed as a civilian technician "to bear more weight with the French," was picked up by the hotel chauffeur. They drove the short distance to Versailles and paid the tax, which amounted to $1,340. Pollard then requested the release of the butter, eggs, and cream, but was informed that the butter had been confiscated.

In need of champagne, cognac, and burgundy, the vehicles were sent scurrying to the French towns of Reims, Chablis, Champagne, and Cognac for these needed supplies. Nazaret, along with Frenchman Jean Pierre Baurche, Pollard's assistant, formed a partnership for purchasing liquor. They purchased 300 bottles of cognac needed for the Hotel Astra, as a cover, then bought as much as they could to load the GMC 2½-ton truck. Pollard received $7.60 for each bottle purchased above the 300 and Baurche received 25 percent of Pollard's profits. Baurche and the assigned civilian French driver of the U.S. Army truck left on this trip with an advance of $6,000 from Nazaret.

The truck returned to Paris and was met by Nazaret, who led the truck to a warehouse. It was unloaded there, with the exception of 300 bottles that were delivered to the hotel. The next day, Pollard received his commission of $5,200.

A few days later, the Hotel Astra supposedly needed more cognac. Pollard approached Nazaret, who stated he currently had more cognac than he could sell. Baurche, however, said he could dispose of the extra cognac. He had local connections, as he had been born in Paris in 1908. In 1932, he was in Algiers, where he married; family had one child. Before the war, Baurche had been a general agent dealing in wine in North Africa for the Society Albert Bichot, so he was well experienced in the sale of liquors. Conscripted into the French Army in Algiers in 1942, he remained there until he was sent to France in the fall of 1944 with the 34th Company of Q.G. Here Baurche's company was demobilized and he was detailed to Major Rene Pollard, Manager of the Mess, Hotel Astra.

Pollard obtained the needed funds from the U.S. Army Finance Division, requisitioned "his" truck, and sent Baurche to the town of Cognac, from whence he returned with 30 cases of liquor for the hotel bar. From this transaction Pollard pocketed $6,600. This became a regular routine for Pollard and Baurche, with Nazaret sometimes helping with the financing. Pollard rarely needed Nazaret's money: guarding against inflation or devaluation of the French franc, he had purchased fifteen 100,000-franc war bonds, having a total value of $30,000.

Alcohol was not the sole item in their illicit cargo. In Vire, Nazaret knew a man named Rene who took the men to farms and butcher shops where several hogs would be quartered and loaded onto the army truck. Upon return to Paris and on more than one occasion, the hogs would be delivered to a furrier located on Rue Diefhot across the street from the tobacconist; other hogs went to the Restaurant Nicols, Rue de Patiles Ecuries.

Due to the large amount of money he was forwarding through the U.S. Army postal system to the United States, Pollard came under suspicion by the

8. The Mess and Billeting Office of the Hotel Astra

Criminal Investigation Branch. On March 1, 1945, the Director of the Office of War Information was informed of this scheme. Pollard was immediately relieved of his duties and placed under house arrest at his fashionable apartment; six days later, he was restricted to quarters in the Hotel Astra.

On April 26, 1945, Pollard was court-martialed and found guilty of his crimes. He was fined $50,000 and confined to hard labor for six years, with an additional three years of imprisonment to be served if the fine was not paid. He was incarcerated in the federal prison in Atlanta, Georgia. If Rene Pollard had not sent the large money orders home, he would have returned from the war a rich man.

Unlike Arthur H. Lang, 0–825844, with the assimilated rank of captain, also ran afoul of the law in Paris. He served with the Army Exchange System (PX) in Paris. Lang wrote an endorsement stating that the bearer, Di Rosa Dominique, had been authorized to purchase all merchandise that might be used for the benefit and interest of the U.S. Army—writing that Lang was not authorized to make.

Like Pollard, Lang was living with a married woman, Maria Javelle, in Paris. He wrote the authorization at Javelle suggestion for a friend of hers. With this endorsement, Di Rosa Dominique purchased 20,000 bottles of cognac. It was when Javelle and Dominique attempted to purchase 600,000 additional bottles of cognac that a red flag went up, with the document being taken by the French police and turned over to an American military police officer.

The naive Arthur Lang had worked in a war plant and organized a Boy Scout pack in New York City. He left in his senior year at New York University to go overseas under contract to do his part in essential war work. He was impressed by the manner of handling accounts in the army and also learned "the French way of doing business." It does not appear the youthful Lang received any money for his wrongdoings, just the enjoyment of sleeping with Maria Javelle. For his crime, he received a sentence of total forfeitures and confinement at hard labor for five years in the U.S. penitentiary in Lewisburg, Pennsylvania.

Major Walter D. Snyder was assigned to Headquarters, 322nd Bombardment Group, Station A-89. This is his story about attending one of the Parisian USO dances:

> One evening he attended a dance given by the officers of the 322nd Bombardment Group. When it was over Snyder went with a Major Wray to another dance. They arrived there at approximately 1:00 a.m. It was extremely hot and crowded at this affair and he "had had quite a bit to drink," so the major left the building to get some air. He turned to the left and had walked about forty or fifty yards when

someone dumped a large container of water on him. Highly incensed by the incident, he had words with someone in a window on the left-hand side of the street. While he was arguing, a door four or five feet away and directly in front of him opened and two men appeared. They entered the argument, which soon progressed into a scuffle, and he was thrown to the ground. He arose and was thrown down again several times. His assailants left. He pursued them for about ten feet and another scuffle ensued, in which he was hit over the head with a chair and "pretty well beaten up."

Did this really happen? In the early morning hours, Monsieur Raymond Tanguy's doorbell rang. Inasmuch as his son was attending a dance, he opened the door. A very strongly built mustached American soldier stood at the door and asked for a girl. Tanguy answered, "There is no girl here," and tried to close the door. The American followed him into the passage beyond the door, jumped on him, and began to strike him with his fists. A struggle ensued, during which they fell in a gutter that runs through the passage. While he was on the ground, the American had his knees on Tanguy's body and caught him by the throat. He called for help and his wife, Madame Yvonne Tanguy, responded to his call. She pulled the American's hair and attempted to take his hands off her husband's throat. Holding Monsieur Tanguy with one hand, the soldier struck Madame Tanguy with the other hand, knocking her to the ground. At this point, an unnamed French soldier appeared. He stunned the American by kicking him in the head. Tanguy was able to free himself, after which he and his wife ran to their house. They found a watch near the gutter, midway in the passage that connects the street with the courtyard where the American had first struck him. The pair took the watch in the house and placed it on the kitchen table as they locked the door. Tanguy had been struck on the left upper part of his body and the left eye and was bitten on the right hand.

The American then yelled, "Help, help." The residents of the house next door were awakened by the noise. They turned on their lights and looked outside, where they observed the American standing in the street. In that house were Madame Reine-Marie Guilbert and her husband Monsieur Henri Nauche; they were staying with her mother, who was seriously ill. When the American knocked on their door, Madame Guilbert told him to go to bed. He then asked her, "How much money for you?" Her husband also told him to go to bed, to which the soldier replied, "Monsieur, come down. Me kill you." Nauche dressed himself and his wife remained at the window. The American rushed at the door of their house, breaking it down on the third attempt. Nauche hurried downstairs and found the American next to his ill mother-in-law's bed. He was assaulted, and both men fell on the ill woman's bed. They rolled off and the attacker started choking him. At this point, the wife arrived on the scene and

8. The Mess and Billeting Office of the Hotel Astra

struck the American on the head with a heavy broom. This stunned him and he released his grasp on Nauche. The couple managed to drag and push the American outside, but he succeeded in kicking Nauche several more times. As the pair reentered their home, the American soldier threw one of the shutters from the broken door at them. As the soldier staggered away, Nauche followed him; his wife left on a bicycle looking for the police.

A few minutes later, Major Walter D. Snyder walked into a public dance given by the USO and approached Lieutenant Frank E. Davis of the Military Police, telling him that some Frenchman had stolen his watch and then followed him to the dance. Aware that some harm had been inflicted on the major, a group of Military Police left the dance with him. It did not take long for Major Snyder to point the finger at the home of Nauche. With the help of the French police, who spoke English and had been summoned by Madame Guilbert, their next-door neighbor, Monsieur Raymond Tanguy, was identified as the person who had "stolen" the major's watch.

A key was produced and a door leading into a courtyard was opened. The group proceeded through the courtyard and went to the kitchen in the far left-hand corner, where a watch was picked up by an American MP from a table and delivered to Lieutenant Davis. This watch was the property of Major Snyder, who had remained outside the kitchen. Snyder expressed "that he wanted to kill these Frenchmen." The major was highly excited and used strong language because his watch had been stolen. Lieutenant Davis tried to remove the major from Tanguy's premises to prevent further fighting; he had to put a "hammer lock" on the major to get him out to the street. Snyder, along with the Military Police, returned to the dance. That would have been the end of the story, as Major Walter D. Snyder, as a U.S. officer, was above suspicion—with one grave exception.

Major Snyder and Lieutenant Davis soon left the dance hall. When they were outside, Snyder struck Davis four or five times about the face and head with his fist, knocking him down. While he was on the ground, the major hit him again and again. As a result of these blows, Davis sustained a broken tooth, a broken nose, and several bruises and cuts. Only then did the military authorities investigate the mayhem created by Major Snyder.[3]

The major's original story of being attacked by two assailants and his watch stolen would have definitely stuck, if only he had not viciously attacked Military Police Lieutenant Davis.

9

The Black Market

And now the seedy side of Paris. The economic situation, which was deranged by inflation and a black market, conceived by the Germans during their occupation of Paris to serve their own needs, dictated the bulk of the tasks for the U.S. Army, Criminal Investigation Branch (CID), in the winter of 1944–1945. With the high value of the franc and rigid control of the American dollar, many opportunities were afforded the American soldier in pilfering and misuse of critical supplies in an already flourishing black market. Smoothly operating unscrupulous French civilians, who made up the backbone of this underground activity, were capable of swallowing up untold quantities of goods.

In terms of theft, gasoline and the trucks containing this commodity were the biggest and most serious menace. Cigarettes were next in importance. But GI thieves had also made away with impressive amounts of food, mostly in 10-in-1 rations, and such PX items as razor blades, soap, chocolate, boots, and clothes. For all of these items, black market prices had remained stable for several months. A big Hershey bar sold for about $2; a khaki shirt, $20; cigarettes, $2.40 a pack; a 2½-ton, 6 × 6 cargo truck, $4,000. A case of cigarettes containing 50 cartons of 10 packs each would fetch $1,000; a 20-pound can of coffee was valued at $200. Gasoline was selling at $5.50 per gallon and an empty jerrican fetched $1.50. All proved irresistible bait for the eager American soldier.

The jerrican was a five-gallon tin of gasoline, so dubbed by the British, who picked them up from the Germans during the desert campaigns in North Africa. The term "Jerry" or "Jerries" was a name give to the German soldier by the Brits, and this label stuck for the Americans. The U.S. Army called the containers army cans, but the GIs stayed with the British name—jerrican. The superior merits of the can were copied by the British and later by the U.S. military. By D-Day, the Americans had stockpiled 12 million empty jerricans. Gasoline was shipped to the front by pipeline, railroad tank car, or tank truck, but it had to be delivered to the ultimate consumer in a jerrican.

9. The Black Market

At one of the Post Exchanges maintained for the thousands of enlisted men and women on duty at Headquarters Communication Zone in Paris are, from left, Corporal Gilbert E. Taylor, Ottawa, Illinois; Private James Martillotta, Albion, New York; Private Nellie Stratton, Santa Ana, California; and Private First Class Helen Bashara, Bismarck, North Dakota.

Into this black market situation stepped the American soldier. The librated Parisians greeted him with an emotional demonstration of overwhelming enthusiasm. Everyone in the capital showered kisses, hugs, and cognac on the Yank, who gave them back kisses, hugs, candy, coffee, and cigarettes from his rations. The soldiers stood at the Eiffel Tower or the Obelisk in the Place de la Concorde and just gave the stuff away.

The flush of liberation soon cooled, but the Parisian demand for army supplies remained as hot as ever. Some GIs still gave their rations away out of the goodness of their hearts, but others with sharper instincts decided to do business with the French people. The French people, in turn, were begging for a chance to pay for GI rations. The profits were so big and so easy to make that some soldiers decided to sell more than merely their own rations. In fact, some gave up soldiering for the marketing business, which offered more dough and a lot less chicken shit (a term used by GIs regarding army regulations that defied common sense).

They went AWOL from their units, which were mostly moving on beyond Paris, and stayed behind where the market and the money were. They moved into the upper brackets of the black market and became racketeers. Some of these men had criminal records in civilian life. When the opportunity for profitable crime came into their army life, they seized it. The biggest profits were to be made in gasoline and trucking rather than rations, so many American soldiers switched to these rackets. The underworld was quick to make friends with them. In bars, cafés, hotels, and houses of prostitution in the Montmartre and Montparnasse areas, the French gangsters made deals with the AWOL soldiers. The GIs agreed to sell gasoline and other commodities wholesale to the fences; they, in turn, would find retail outlets.

The first AWOL soldiers were gradually joined by others. Some of the new recruits came from the 97 truck companies assigned to the Red Ball Express—the trucking route over which 5,500 trucks delivered 12,000 tons of vital supplies from Cherbourg to the Combat Zone on a daily basis. The name Red Ball had been derived from prewar days, when it was used to denote a railway transportation service of a particularly high priority. The red ball as a symbol was

Loading trucks at Omaha Beach for the Red Ball Express.

9. The Black Market

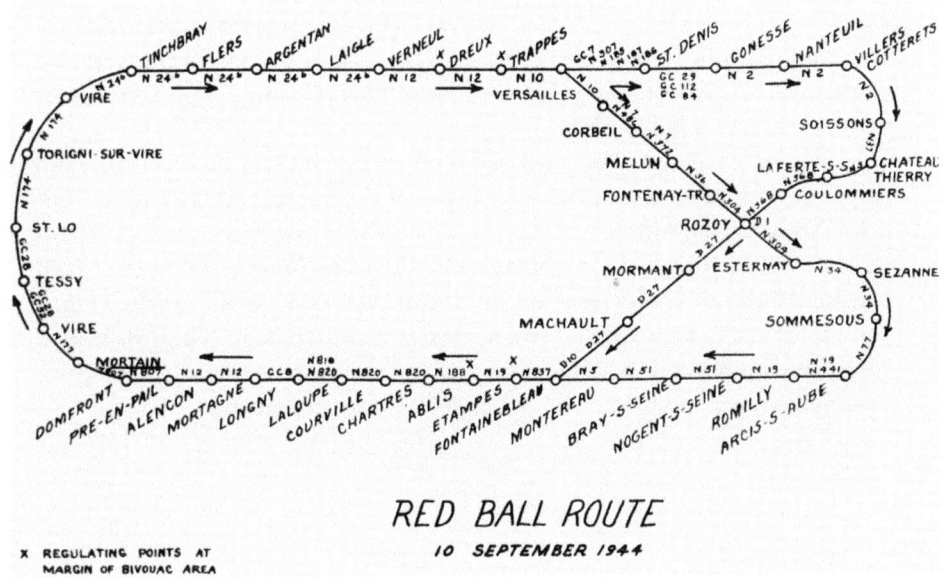

The Red Ball Route with a map drawn in the manner of the London Underground. Paris is located to the right of Versailles.

easy to follow on a truck route, with a direction arrow pointing the way. The trucks traveling on the one-way roads at 25 miles per hour brought with them truckloads of gas, which found a ready market. There was an almost endless supply of gasoline to be had, as the Red Ball Express was delivering about 250,000 gallons a day for the 50 infantry units and another 250,000 gallons for the 10 armored units in combat.

The other black marketeers were soldiers temporarily AWOL from the front. Some came back to Paris to look for a brief moment at the bright lights, liquor, and women and found things so pleasant that they forgot about going back to their outfits. Life in Paris was expensive, though. Champagne cost 500 or 600 francs a bottle, cognac cost 80 francs a drink, and women were expensive, too. At the fixed legal exchange rate of 50 francs to a dollar, it was easy to shoot in one evening all the money the soldier had brought with him. Through the cafés' grapevine, broke AWOLs soon heard about easy money to be made in the black market. Stealing trucks and gas took men, and there was plenty of money for everybody, so the older hands were more than ready to have new AWOL recruits join forces with them.

From such casual and haphazard beginnings, some of the gangs became highly organized outfits. Generally, one man served as the "brains." Occasionally he had previous experience in the United States. Men who had some speaking knowledge of French acted as gang contacts with the French operators. At least one member of the gang usually was AWOL from a trucking company, and sometimes he could induce other members of his old outfit to go AWOL with their trucks and join his gang.

During working hours, most of the men wore military uniforms to avoid suspicion while they were driving army trucks or handling army gasoline. "Off duty," however, they often wore civilian clothes borrowed from some girl's bedroom closet or bought in the French black market. One AWOL soldier paid $340 and $400 apiece for two suits. In almost every gang, there was the French equivalent of a U.S. gun moll, and sometimes several of them. The girls helped spend the money and came in handy for other uses, of course, but their principal value was to assist the contact men in lining up deals.[1]

10

Paris Detention Barracks

Many of these gang members, as well as some described in subsequent chapters, would eventually find themselves incarcerated in the Paris Detention Barracks. This facility was located in a former French military barracks named Caserne Mortier at 128 Boulevard Mortier, Paris. The function of the military jail was to confine all U.S. soldiers arrested in the Seine Section until they were tried or released. Soldiers who had not committed a crime other than being absent without official leave (AWOL) were jailed in a unit designated the Central Straggler Collection Point. The Paris Detention Barracks had a staff of 19 officers and 272 soldiers who served as guards, along with 26 German prisoners of war who were used as cooks and for cleaning and 2 POWs who were barbers. The Detention Barracks had room for 2,100 prisoners and was usually almost at its capacity. Its denizens included about 40 British soldiers.

The prison was built by the French in 1933. It consisted of three large buildings and several smaller structures, all made of bricks, concrete, and steel. They were enclosed with a quadrangle brick fence, 18 inches thick and 10 feet high, topped with barbed wire, with an 8-foot-wide apron of that wire also inside at the base of the wall. The quadrangle had three gated entrances, which were locked, barred and guarded by heavily armed soldiers. Each corner contained a watch tower with searchlights and guards on duty 24 hours a day. Inside the brick fence were 14 guard posts that patrolled constantly.

The three large buildings were referred to as Cages. On the ground floor of Cage A were the administrative offices and supply rooms. The second floor contained four large rooms for court-martial proceedings, along with the offices of the U.S. Legal Seine Section. The upper three floors were the Central Straggler Collection Point. The ground floor for Cage B contained supply rooms, a chapel, and miscellaneous offices; the remaining four floors housed men awaiting

WANTED   WANTED   WANTED

1. THE FOLLOWING DESCRIBED SOLDIERS ARE WANTED FOR DESERTION, ESCAPE FROM CONFINEMENT, FRAUD, FORGERY, AND OTHER MAJOR OFFENSES:

(a) PVT. RALPH HENSHAW KELLER, ASN. 11072354, AGE 22, HEIGHT 6'1½, WEIGHT 165, SLENDER BUILD, DARK EYES, DARK HAIR, MEDIUM DARK COMPLEXION, AIRPLANE AND PARACHUTE TATTOOED ON BOTH FOREARMS, SPEAKS FRENCH, AND IS A PERSUASIVE AND CONVINCING TALKER. SUBJECT MAY BE IMPERSONATING AN OFFICER AS HE WAS FORMERLY A LIEUTENANT.

(b) PVT. BERNARD W. TENNIS, ASN. 33227644, AGE 25, HEIGHT 5'9, WEIGHT 150, BLUE EYES, DARK HAIR, MAY BE DYED BLONDE, SALLOW COMPLEXION, SPEAKS WITH SOUTHERN ACCENT. AIRPLANE AND PARACHUTE TATTOOED ON BOTH FOREARMS.

2. REQUEST ALL FINANCE OFFICES, RTO OFFICES, AND AIRFIELDS BE NOTIFIED REGARDING THESE SOLDIERS AS THEY OBTAIN MONEY AND TRAVEL BY FALSE AND FRAUDULENT ORDERS. THEY MAY ALSO ATTEMPT TO ENTER SPAIN OR RETURN TO THE UNITED STATES.

3. REQUEST ANY INFORMATION OBTAINED PERTAINING TO SOLDIERS HEREIN DESCRIBED, BE TRANSMITTED TO THE THEATER PROVOST MARSHAL, APO 887, U. S. ARMY, OR TO THE NEAREST PROVOST MARSHAL'S OFFICE.

FOR THE THEATER PROVOST MARSHAL:

DISTRIBUTION:
TO ALL PM's AND CI DETACHMENTS.

H. M. SMICK
LT. COL., C.M.P.
ASST. EXECUTIVE

Wanted posters were provided to all MP battalions for AWOL soldiers.

trial. In the basement was a small room used for solitary confinement. Cage C's first floor was for supplies, while the remaining floors housed the soldiers who had been tried and convicted. Its basement also contained an area for solitary confinement. Surrounding Cages B and C was an additional barbed wire fence, 14 feet high, also with an 8-foot apron and one gate. No one, including the guards entering this gate, was allowed to take a weapon of any description inside the fence. The smaller buildings consisted of a mess hall, a dispensary, some small office buildings, and the death-house.

10. Paris Detention Barracks

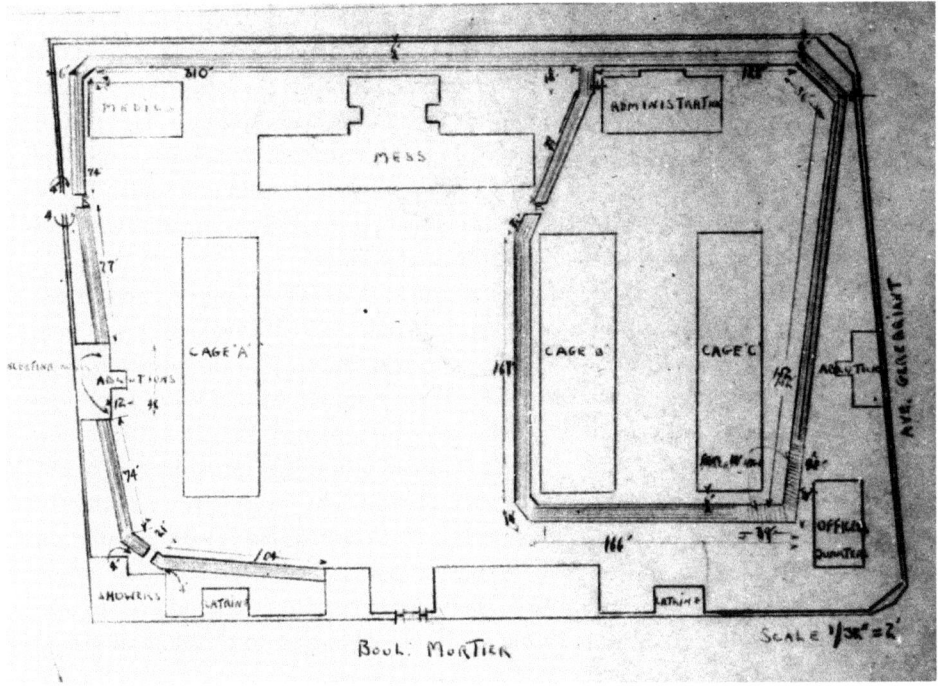

A sketch of the Paris Detention Barracks, with Cages A, B and C indicated. Cages B and C are surrounded by extra security fences.

The floors of the Cages housing prisoners had room capacities varying from 6 to 92 prisoners. The bunks were double decked, and each bunk had a straw-filled mattress and three blankets. The heat in the rooms was kept to the minimum needed for comfort because of the shortage of coal and fuel. Buckets were used for bathing and toilet facilities. Rigid records were kept to ensure each prisoner bathed once a week. Small mirrors were installed for shaving and grooming.

The mess hall for the prisoners was located on the ground floor of one of the smaller buildings. The second floor was contained a mess for the staff. All men were fed from the same kitchen. Due to the space constraints, only 350 prisoners could be fed at one time, so they were marched to their three daily meals in shifts. This took about two hours; the tables were cleared by the German POWs after each shift. Upon entering the mess hall, the prisoner was given a tin plate, an aluminum cup, and a spoon. He then went through the chow line and entered the mess hall, where there were tables but no seats. Standing silently, the prisoner ate his meal and left the utensils for the POW kitchen staff. The prisoners were then marched back to the Cages and searched before entering, to confirm that they had not squirreled away any food.

Tough prison rules? No, considering that less than 100 miles northeast, tens of thousands of American soldiers were living in an unheated hole in the ground with a frozen canteen of water and defecating in the same hole to avoid murderous artillery and machine gun fire. These were difficult days for all Americans, and these deserters would not be coddled. Prisoners were now rationed cigarettes, but were restricted to smoke in their individual cells. These rations were mostly distributed by the chaplain or Red Cross organization and gradually became two packs a week for each prisoner.

The solitary confinement areas in the basements of Cage B and C were about 15 × 40 feet, without heat or artificial light. No bathing facility was provided; a bucket was used for a latrine and was emptied by the prisoner. The prisoners in solitary confinement were first examined by a medical doctor to ensure they were physically fit. They were then placed on a starvation diet, consisting of a total of eight ounces of bread a day. The prisoners were not allowed to write letters, smoke, exercise, or read. They were given a change of clothing "when necessary." Considering that the regular prison population received a change of underwear only every two weeks, one wonders what "when necessary" describes. Once released, the solitary confines were required to take a hot shower, issued clean clothing and released back into the general prison population.

The death-house was a small brick and concrete building, just inside and to the right of the main entrance from Boulevard Mortier. In this building, on the left, was a guard office, two rooms for taking mug shots and fingerprints, and an office. To the right was a cell block (death row) with eight cells, an inadequate stand-up latrine and wash room used for shaving and brushing teeth, and a bucket to wash the prisoners' clothes. The cell doors were fastened with steel bolts locked in place with a heavy padlock. They were devoid of any furnishings except for a straw-filled mattress and five blankets. The seven British prisoners were issued four blankets as requested by the British authorities, as they slept on cement slabs and no heat was provided. The cells opened out to a rectangular court about 9 feet by 57 feet with no roof, but covered with a thick tangle of barbed wire, where the inmates could exercise individually for 15 minutes each day.

Meals in the death-house were brought to the cells by prisoners serving time in the Cages. The inmates were issued two packs of cigarettes a week and could smoke in their cells. A medical officer checked in each day to attend to the sick, and a chaplain visited two or three times a week and provided appropriate reading material. The cell block had a capacity for 36 men and currently 29 men were on death row. These prisoners were men awaiting execution, along with some others who were extremely dangerous. Presently on death

10. Paris Detention Barracks

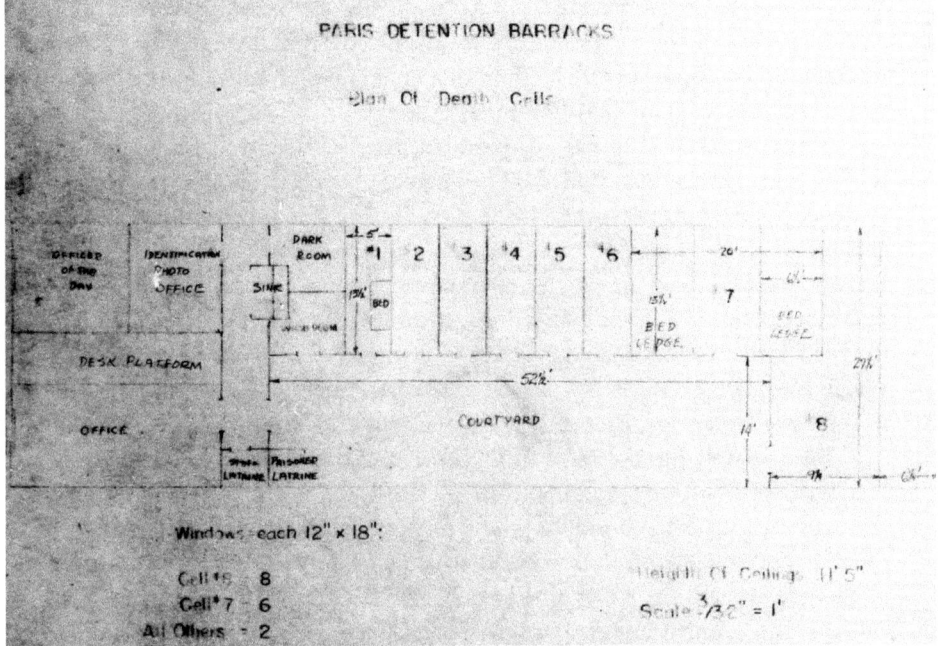

Death row in the Paris Detention Barracks.

row was Jerome Ciullo; two years later, Manuel Martinez would be sitting there. We will meet both of these men in later chapters.

The prisoners began their engagement at the Paris Detention Barracks by being arrested and entering through the front gate. They were then taken to a small room and searched for knives, pistols, razors, and any weapon considered dangerous. These articles were taken and an itemized receipt given in exchange. The weapons were stored in a room that was under constant guard. A determination was also made whether the prisoner would be classified as a straggler or held in confinement pending further investigation.

The AWOL soldier was then questioned to determine his unit and see if he had any articles in the Red Cross clubs or local hotels. If he answered in the affirmative, these items were collected and delivered to the prisoner later. He was placed in Cage A, Central Straggler Collection Point, with other soldiers in a close proximity of his unit. A copy of a delinquent report was sent to his company commander. The daily average number of releases was about 100 soldiers. Groups of 16 to 18 stragglers were sent by motor transport to their units. The remainder were given direct orders to return to their units and carefully informed of the consequences if they failed to obey. The six stragglers from

Italy were held indefinitely pending a decision on their fate from a higher authority. Overall, the total stragglers for any given day in the European Theater of Operations was about 500 soldiers—a small number considering this army consisted of more than 4 million men.

The suspected criminal was handled quite differently. His story is best told by considering a ruse pulled off by Sergeant Henry E. Franklin, who sought to write a report for the General Inspection Section on the processing prisoners at the Paris Detention Barracks. Franklin had himself arrested for converting British and American currencies to francs in a house of prostitution and was detained by the U.S. Criminal Investigation Division. They delivered him to the MPs with a confinement slip. He was then placed in a paddy wagon, a converted ambulance. One MP sat in the back with Franklin, while the other drove to the Paris Detention Barracks, a trip of about 15 minutes.

Immediately upon arrival, Franklin was escorted into a small house just inside the gate and frisked by a third MP for weapons. Then he went across the roadway to another building, where he was left alone for about ten minutes. An army guard called him into another room and told Franklin to empty his pockets of everything. All of his personal effects, money, pen knife, notebook, ribbons, and Combat Infantry Badge were taken except a handkerchief, a pencil, a religious medal, and a comb. The items taken were listed and placed in an envelope. On the walls were large clear signs warning the prisoners to give their true identity and not to attempt to conceal any items, including cigarettes, as smoking was forbidden for the prisoners. This no-smoking policy lasted for a surprisingly long seven months.

From this building Franklin was transferred to Cage C, where he was required to give his name and serial number and issued three blankets. He was led to a room with three latrine buckets and fifteen iron beds, eight of which were occupied; the room was not heated and had no lights. As it was noon when he was arrested, Franklin was marched over to the mess hall and fed some leftover rice and corned beef. The night was uneventful, except it was rather cold. Seeing some loose blankets, Franklin quickly took one. Prior to going to sleep he noticed all 15 beds were occupied by prisoners who had arrived that afternoon.

Awakened at 6 a.m., he was marched to the supply room, where each prisoner was given a cake of soap and a towel. Franklin thought they were going to wash, but instead the prisoners were taken directly to the mess hall for breakfast. After standing to eat, they were accompanied to the dispensary for a short-arm inspection which consisted of the medical technician telling the prisoners to "pull 'em out and milk 'em down." Each man exposed his penis and stroked it several times; if pus dripped out, it indicated the presence of gonorrhea or syphilis. From here the group moved to a shower room, where the guard told them there was something wrong with the plumbing and the water was cold; he informed them that they did not have to take a shower if they did not want to. No one showered. Instead, they washed in hand basins and were led back to their room. At this point, they were told to take all their belongings except the blankets. From here the men were taken to a supply room, where they stripped and placed all their clothing in an individual bag. The prisoners were issued a red fatigue uniform and three blankets, then marched to their assigned jail rooms in Cage C to await court-martial.

For exercise, the prisoners were required to perform 45 minutes of close order drill every day while wearing their red uniforms. The backs of the jackets and legs of the trousers were marked with the large letters PDB (Paris Detention Barracks). The men were not allowed to wear any decorations and could receive only visitors who were in the U.S. military, from 2 p.m. to 6 p.m. on Sundays. The inmates within the walls were used to do laundry, perform some kitchen work, and clean up the grounds.

The prisoners could send one letter a week. There were no PX facilities or Red Cross activities for them. A chaplain was assigned and held religious services. Prior to trial a prisoner was given a haircut, had the opportunity to shave and bathe, and was issued a clean Class A uniform without the hat.

Two medical officers were assigned to the Paris Detention Barracks, but not a dentist. Approximately 10 percent of the prisoners went on sick call every day. The most frequent cases treated were scabies, itch, lice, colds, respiratory diseases, and sexually transmitted diseases, with gonorrhea and syphilis appearing daily. Serious cases were sent by ambulance to the U.S. Army General Hospital.

After court-martial, prisoners serving less than six months were sent to the Seine Section Guardhouse. The others went to the Loire Disciplinary Training Center in Le Mans to serve their term. The most common types of cases brought to trial were drunk and disorderly conduct, desertion, black market activities, and simple assault without provocation—most of the offenders in the last case being paratroopers.[1]

11

THE VINCENNES GANG

This Vincennes gang of AWOL soldiers, which worked the Paris gasoline racket on a large scale, was one of the most successful and best organized GI racketeering rings in the European Theater of Operations. The take in the three months of the gang's operation was high, averaging around $20,000 per man.

To get gasoline for sale in the black market, the gang used two methods that were typical of GI gang operations. Gang members would drive around in their jeeps looking for parked vehicles with extra cans of gas in them; upon finding one, they would steal the gas. Occasionally they stole tires and tools if it did not involve too much trouble.

The other system of obtaining gasoline took more finesse, but paid bigger dividends. It involved going to an Army POL (petroleum oil lubrication) dump and getting a load of gasoline by fraud. There were several ways of doing this.

The easiest and simplest means was to drive the truck up to a dump and tell the GI attendant, "My commanding officer sent me down here to get gas." In the fall of 1944, so many outfits were moving forward, and the emphasis was so much on speed, that gas dumps serviced any and every military truck. There was no time to check whether a driver was telling the truth and no adequate system of requisitioning had been set up.

To get gas at other dumps, all the driver needed was a container. The fuel was regarded as expendable: As long as you turned in an empty jerrican, the dump would give you one full. For 250 empty jerricans, you could get that many full ones.

For the most part, however, the gangs succeeded not because of a perfect organization, but because it was easy to acquire and dispose of gasoline. As one convicted racketeer put it, "Any damn fool could make a fortune without even trying."

11. The Vincennes Gang

At a petroleum oil lubrication depot in France, jerricans are stacked into a pyramid shape, each containing 5,000 cans.

The leader of the Vincennes gang was Pfc. James Clyde Blackburn, 21 years of age, who had lived all his life with his parents in Vincennes, Indiana. He finished high school in 1941 and started college at Riverside California, attending for several months. Blackburn enlisted in the army at Fort Benjamin in Harrison, Indiana, on November 10, 1941, and took basic training at Kessler Field, Mississippi. Blackburn then went to Lowry Field, Colorado, where he attended

At a gasoline dump in France, soldiers load a 2½-ton truck from specially constructed wooden racks.

the Armaments School. He transferred into the prestigious Flying Cadets in October 1942, but was disqualified six months later for disciplinary reasons. He was sent to the hospital in Santa Barbara, California; while there, he dated a nurse, left the hospital without proper leave for thirteen hours, and, as a result, was disqualified for further air crew training.

Blackwell left the United States on December 28, 1943, and arrived in Glasgow, Scotland, about January 10, 1944. His unit, the 366th Fighter Bomber Group, went to England and was stationed at St. Pierre Dumount Airfield. From there, they proceeded to Laon, France. Here one of the 366th's functions was to provide air coverage for armored divisions. This was accomplished with the P-47s carrying 500-pound bombs and strafing enemy tanks, staff cars, and German soldiers.

Blackwell left the 366th for Paris on September 1, 1944. He went AWOL with two other soldiers, Booze Boyken and James E. Dugger, traveling in a 6 × 6 GMC army truck.

On arriving in Paris, Dugger and Boyken went to a night club, met some girls, and spent the night with them in their apartment, their names quickly forgotten. Blackburn made a quick connection with Madam Suzzane Fernande Durant, whose husband was absent; he moved in with her. The following day, the AWOLs went to 50 Rue Raynouard to the Blue Front Café and met Louise Bouvier, the owner. Dugger noticed she could speak some English and talked her into giving them a sightseeing tour of Paris. Dugger took an interest in Bouvier and, as her husband was also away, slept with her. This he continued to do anytime her husband was out of town. Bouvier told Dugger that some American soldiers were trying to sell her some cigarettes and gasoline, which she later purchased. It was here at this café that they learned about the black marketing of gasoline.

The three soldiers then drove their truck to the Eiffel Tower and stole 8 five gallon cans of gas from several 6 × 6 government cargo trucks. They took the gas back to the café at 50 Rue Raynoaurd and set up shop in an adjacent driveway. The following day they sold a few cans of gasoline for 8,000 francs each to some French civilians they had met in the Blue Front Café, who took the gas away on their bicycles.

The three soldiers stayed at various hotels in Paris and finally took an apartment at 2 Rue Marronners. Boyken and Dugger lived there only a couple of nights, then took rooms at the France Russe Hotel on Boulevard Grennelle. The name of the gang was apparently taken from the hometown of Blackburn, as Vincennes was on the other side of Paris.

During that time Walter B. Deason joined the gang. He was 20 years of age and had lived in Portola, California, before being inducted into the army on January 8, 1943. Deason received basic training in the United States and arrived in the United Kingdom in August 1943. He transferred to France during July 1944 and was stationed at Valognes with the Headquarters Communication Zone until about the middle of September 1944, at which time the unit moved to Paris.

On or about the September 25, 1944, Deason left his unit without obtaining permission and went to the Ideal Hotel, where he met Blackburn and six other soldiers who were also absent from their units. He did not know any of these soldiers when they first met. However, he did finally learn Blackburn's name and became very friendly with him. The other soldiers' true names were never revealed to him.

Drinking in the Blue Front Café, they began to meet other AWOL soldiers who had arrived in Paris. They included Eddie, Bill, Orville, John (John D. Carter), Dick, Paul, Woody (Woodrow W. Crockett), Bruce Deason (Walter B. Deason) and Duke, as well as two African Americans, Willie Smith and Jim. All of the AWOL gang members went by one name: Blackwell became Blackie,

Deason was Bruce, and Dugger was Jimmy. (For simplicity, only the last names will be used here, when known.)

Carter asked Deason if he wanted to make some easy money. He was told that the group had been stealing gasoline and selling it to the French. In a further conversation with Carter, Deason wanted to know what part he had to take; he was told he would have to deliver the gasoline after the gang had brought it into Paris. It was at this time that Deason learned they had a 6 × 6 GMC truck at their disposal, which was being kept in a garage near the Ideal Hotel.

Thus the Vincennes gang was formed. The area of Paris they frequented was Vincennes and Blackburn was from Vincennes—hence the double meaning of the gang's moniker. By now, Blackburn was wearing the civilian clothes of the husband of his girlfriend, Fernande Durant. He furnished her with money, food, and the better necessities of Paris.

One of the earlier members of the gang, Willie Smith, while drinking in the Blue Front Café with Dugger, asked him where he could sell some gasoline. Bouvier informed Dugger that she would purchase the gasoline for 800 francs per five-gallon jerrican. Smith stated that this was acceptable and that he would acquire the gasoline the next day. Smith returned the following day to the Blue Front Cafe with a full load of gasoline in 257 jerricans. A Frenchman met them and directed the truck to his garage. When Dugger, Willie Smith, Bouvier, and the Frenchman met in the garage, the Frenchman would purchase only 50 cans of the gas. Bouvier said she would take the remainder although she could not pay for the gasoline until the next day. Willie Smith was satisfied with that arrangement, so they unloaded the gasoline in the garage.

The next day Willie Smith went for his money. Bouvier told him she had sold the gasoline to a French captain who dealt in the black market. He had taken the gasoline but refused to pay for it. Dugger went to the Blue Front Café and Bouvier told him French Captain Sence had hijacked the gasoline and taken her husband's money and their wine. She further stated someone was looking for the captain for her. Later, while eating in the café, Bouvier phoned and asked Dugger to come to her apartment. He took Carter with him. When they arrived, Bouvier's husband, a gray-haired French officer, and the captain's chauffeur were in the apartment with Louise. Dugger was informed they knew the whereabouts of the rogue Captain Sence. Bouvier's husband and the two Frenchmen left to see the French captain who had stolen the gasoline. About 15 minutes later, they returned and said the captain refused to pay for the gas.

Dugger and Carter planned with the chauffeur to kidnap the captain; the plan was set for the following morning. The chauffeur would drive the captain to his favorite café and the two AWOL soldiers would take him hostage. The chauffeur would pick up Dugger and Carter at 6:30 a.m. and take them to the location of the café. If Captain Sence was alone in the car, the chauffeur would have the lights off; if the lights were on, he would have others in the car.

The following morning the car appeared with the lights off. Dugger and Carter, in uniform, stopped the car. They opened the back door, flashed their pistols in the direction of the French captain, got into the car, and instructed the "surprised" chauffeur to drive to Bouvier's address. Arriving at her house, Captain Sence was well aware that he was a hostage of the two armed men. Under duress, the captain wrote a note authorizing Bouvier to acquire 300,000 francs ($6,000) from his commander.

Bouvier left with the note as Dugger, Carter, and the hostage captain drank wine until the late evening. At that point, Dugger and Carter took off and left the drunken prisoner at Bouvier's apartment. A bit later, Willie Smith told Dugger that he had received his money from Bouvier for the gasoline.

It was now the Vincennes gang started to deal in large amounts of gasoline. Carter and Crockett, about the last part in September, brought a load of gasoline to the Blue Front Café. Dick, Paul, and Blackburn delivered the gas to two different garages on the west side of Paris. A Frenchman by the name of Felix showed them the way to the garages. At the first garage they delivered 35 five-gallon cans of gasoline and received 35,000 francs for them. At the next garage, 100 cans of gasoline were exchanged for 100,000 francs. Blackburn learned later that the MPs picked up the 100 cans of gas at the second garage, but it did not matter—the Vincennes gang had their money.

On September 28, 1944, Carter and Crockett took the truck and went out for a load of gasoline. They did not tell Deason where they were going, nor did he know where they would obtain this load. They returned around 4:30 p.m. and met at a prearranged restaurant with Blackburn and Deason. They then drove to the Blue Front Café at 50 Rue Raynourad.

Upon arriving at Bouvier's café, Blackburn and Deason met Dugger and Boyken. The four unloaded the truck, carrying 169 five-gallon cans of gasoline to the floor above the café. After they had finished, Blackburn gave Deason 19,000 francs, which represented one sixth of the amount Bouvier paid for the gasoline.

On October 6, 1944, Blackburn, Crockett, Carter, and Deason took the two trucks and drove to an Air Force base on route GC-19, where they picked up about 550 empty jerricans. They continued to Rambouillet, a gasoline dump, where they obtained 550 five-gallon cans of gasoline. One truck, operated by Blackburn and Crockett, loaded 250 cans; the other, operated by Carter and Deason, contained 300 gallons. The group returned to Paris to the Blue Front Café, where they met Willie Smith, Dick, and Paul. Willie Smith took the truck Deason was in. Carter, who was riding with him, took the other truckload of gasoline and drove it to the garage near the Ideal Hotel. Willie Smith took his truckload of gasoline and sold it to an unknown source.

The following day, Blackburn and Deason took the load of gasoline they had placed in the garage and sold it in five-gallon can lots to various people who called at the garage. Blackburn paid Carter, Dick, Paul, Crockett, and Willie Smith 25,000 francs each for their share of load. Deason and Blackburn evenly split the profit of about 150,000 francs on this deal.

After selling the two loads of gasoline, the gang did not operate for about a week. With their fast-earned cash, Blackburn and Deason each bought a large motorcycle to ride through the streets of Paris. Deason soon crashed his bike and badly hurt his left ankle and foot. Being AWOL, he had to seek the help of a French doctor for treatment and was bedridden. His girlfriend brought food and provided care for Deason, and Blackburn visited almost daily.

Apparently the Criminal Investigation Division had been tipped off by the French police, *Merceron*, that the Vincennes gang hangout was the Blue Front Café. On the afternoon of October 12, 1944, CID Agent James R. Thompson was in the café incognito. The phone rang and Bouvier (the owner and Dugger's girlfriend) answered. When the agent asked who was calling, she placed her hand over the phone receiver and said Dugger. She said Dugger would be in at 6:00 and was asking for money. Thompson made arrangements for additional Military Police to serve as reinforcements as he was expecting two to five gang members to show up.

Thompson then hid beneath the bar counter as two men in civilian clothes, Dugger and Carter, came into the bar. They had their backs to Thompson as they started a conversation with Bouvier in English. He watched through the mirror, got up with his gun drawn, and told the two men to put up their hands. Not knowing their temperaments, he ordered the men to get down on the floor with their hands out so they could not pull a gun. After reinforcements arrived, they were searched. Each man was carrying a gun: Dugger had a German P-38, 9-mm automatic.

Arrested that night was John Carter, James E. Dugger, and Booze Boyken. (Despite the author's extensive search, Booze Boyken was never identified but is believed to be Austin C. Dookie.) On the same night, Deason learned through the girlfriends of these fellows that they had been taken into custody. Deason, in turn, took the truck from the garage next to the Ideal Hotel and hid it in a garage at 87 Ave De la Bourdonnaise.

After the arrest of most of his gang, Blackburn half-heartedly decided to return to his unit, the 366th Fighter Bomber Group. On October 15, Deason and Blackburn drove the 6 x 6 government truck that Blackburn had originally

11. The Vincennes Gang

stolen from his unit to Brussels, Belgium. Blackburn "hoped" to find his unit close to the front lines of combat. The pair started one afternoon at one o'clock and arrived the next morning about eleven or twelve o'clock. Before leaving France they changed some French francs for Belgian money, about 4,000 francs. After arriving in Belgium, they found out the money that they had exchanged in the American Finance Office was no good; they then returned to Paris. On the way back they stayed one night in an English emergency camp at Amiens, France. The following day they returned to Paris and went to the Ideal Hotel, where Blackburn had a room in addition to his apartment. Deason and Willie Smith also stayed there. On this same day, Blackburn told Orville that the other boys of the Vincennes gang had been caught by the Military Police.

Not to be deterred from their criminal enterprise, Orville, Deason, and Blackburn began making arrangements to get more gas. About three days later, Orville and Blackburn took the latter's truck and went up Route 10 to a gasoline dump. There, they obtained 200 five-gallon cans of gasoline by showing a slip of paper which read:

> HQ. COM. Z. I certify that truck no. 4431272S is authorized to take 265 cans of gasoline necessary for the functioning of this unit.
> Signed, R.A. Dicks. Capt; Inf. Commanding.

A penciled notation was then made

> 200 cans issued because of gas shortage.
> Signed: Gerald Skipton, 2nd Lt. QMC.
> October 19, 1944

With that note (written by Blackburn), the truck was loaded with 1,000 gallons of gasoline. The pair brought it back to Paris and delivered it to a garage near Rue Mademoiselle. Orville and Blackburn received 700 francs per can for the gasoline—a total of 140,000 francs, which they split three ways (Orville, Deason, and Blackburn). During this trip Deason had stayed in Paris.

The following day, October 20, 1944, Orville and Blackburn returned to the same dump with another identical slip and obtained 250 five-gallon cans of gasoline. Again they returned to Paris. They took the gasoline to the garage on Avenue Bordannais, No. 87. Three or four French civilians took the gasoline away in a French truck and some was taken in French passenger cars. The men received 600 francs per can, for a total of 150,000 francs, again split three ways.

A day later, October 21, 1944, Deason took the 6 × 6 truck and drove it to the same gasoline dump. Using a slip of paper he had made out, he procured 200 five-gallon cans of gasoline. Deason returned to Paris on the same day, taking the gasoline by himself to the garage at No. 87 Avenue Bordannais. He sold it in small lots to various French citizens. Deason received 132,000 francs for this load, which he split with Blackburn. In just three days, Blackburn had collected $2,580 from the sale of black market gasoline. By comparison, in the army he was earning less than $600 per year.

A week later Blackburn purchased a large French passenger car, a Hotchkiss, for 90,000 francs, at a garage across the street from the Tobosco Café & Bar. The Frenchman who sold the car was the proprietor of the garage. Prior to the purchase of the car, Blackburn had bought a motorcycle for 24,000 francs from a motor dealer on Boulevard Grenelle. Now he traded this motorcycle plus 25,000 francs for a larger motorcycle, a Montebane. Blackburn, Deason and Orville were living the good life in Paris, and they hoped the war would never end.

On October 28, 1944, Orville and Blackburn returned to the original location of the gasoline dump on Route 10. Blackburn had made out a slip of paper worded from memory:

> 366 Fighter Group, 28-10-44. I certify that driver Pfc. Walter A. Butts [Orville] is authorized to take 250 cans of gasoline, necessary for the proper functioning of our unit vehicles.
> Signed: Major M. Urich ASAAF.

The major whose name was used was in the same outfit from which Blackburn was AWOL. This slip of paper was taken up by Private Armand J. Coreno at the gas dump; on Route 10 near Rambouillet. Coreno was drafted into the Army in 1942 he arrived in France on or about August 26, 1944, and was assigned to the 29th Infantry Division. He was now doing guard duty at the gasoline dump, where his main duty was to see that no one took gasoline or oil without proper authority. During this week there were only a few drums of gasoline on this field, with the rest being oil and grease, so he issued no gasoline, but did give out oil and grease when shown proper identification.

That Saturday, about noon, a truck drove up with two American soldiers in it whom Coreno had never seen before. They first asked where the dump was that had the can gasoline; Coreno told them the dump had moved about 30 miles from this locality. The soldier who was riding in the truck gave him a slip of paper was made out to Walter Butts, a private, authorizing him to receive 250 cans of gasoline. Coreno then asked the soldier for his dog tags. Butts replied that he had left them at camp and produced a pay book with the name Walter Butts in it. Coreno told Butts the site did not have the 250 cans of gasoline, but did have the quantity in drums. Coreno figured it made no difference if the gas was in drums, so Butts figured out that he was entitled to 22 drums of gasoline.

Before the gasoline was loaded onto the truck, the driver and the soldier who called himself Butts fired some shots from the two guns they had in their possession. The driver, Blackburn, shot a clip of bullets from a P-38 German Luger at a C-ration can. Then Butts fired a clip of bullets from a small automatic at a C-ration can. Coreno showed an interest in the automatic and asked Butts if he wanted to sell it. Butts first said "no," but then said he would let Coreno have the automatic if he would help them load the gasoline, which he agreed to.

The group could get only 18 drums on the truck. Butts told Coreno that he had four additional drums due to them and they would return for the additional gasoline. Coreno told Butts that he would not be on post when they returned but would tell his relief to give it to him. The truck then pulled away with Blackburn driving and Butts (Orville), the passenger, returning to Paris.

Louie Gahagnon, a Frenchman, who was the bartender at the Tobosco Bar, had made contact with Orville and Blackburn for the sale of this load of gasoline. A Mr. Jean had come into the bar and asked the bartender if he had any connections that would allow him to purchase some gasoline, as he was in the transportation business. The Frenchman, Mr. Jean, had been a patron of the café for a long time and Gahagnon responded that he could probably get the gasoline for him. A deal was made, with Mr. Jean paying Louie 5 francs per liter and a separate deal being reached with Blackburn, who would commission Louie to sell the stolen gasoline at 10 francs per liter. The bartender was "working both sides of the street."

That day at about 2 p.m. Blackburn arrived at the bar and told Gahagnon that he had obtained the gasoline. Louie telephoned Mr. Jean, who met with Blackburn and Louie at the bar at 4:30 p.m. Mr. Jean, his friend, Blackburn, and the bartender then left and Blackburn directed the driver to a garage where he had parked the loaded truck. Mr. Jean wanted the truck to deliver the gasoline to his garage on Rue Vanneau, so he drove his car to the garage, followed by Blackburn in the truck. When they arrived, Mr. Jean started to pay for the gasoline—at which point, members of the Criminal Investigation Division arrived and arrested Blackburn.

The Frenchman, Mr. Jean, had notified U.S. Army Major Edler of the Theater Provost Marshal's Office of this illegal transaction: he was an intelligence officer in the French Army. The CID was notified and agents arrived at the garage at 2 p.m., where they waited for the truck to arrive and made the arrests. Mr. Jean upbraided Gahagnon for participating in black market activity. The French police were not notified and the French civilians left the scene. Did Louie Gahagnon, the bartender, tip off Mr. Jean regarding the activity of the Vincennes gang?

Blackburn was arrested in the garage. On October 28, 1944, Deason was arrested by agents of the 27th Criminal Investigation Section while drinking in a café. Orville was nowhere to be found. Blackburn told the authorities he did not know his last name but believed it started with an "R"; he described Orville as about 5 feet 8 inches tall, 125 to 140 pounds, with dark wavy hair, a dark showy beard, and a French complexion. Also still on the loose were Paul, Jim, Dick, and Willie Smith.[1]

The now broken Vincennes gang was just one gang of many in Paris. These groups organized with the same sweet, ruthless efficiency that marked the Capone mob of Chicago in the 1920s. It was easy for the former members of the Vincennes gang to melt into this underworld culture.

Living across town in the area of Vincennes, four miles from the center of Paris in the eastern suburbs, was another gasoline gang loosely connected to Private Johnnie L. Porter. He had been a truck driver with the 388th Engineer General Services, stationed on Utah Beach and carrying supplies on the Red Ball Express. Porter drove through Paris on September 1, 1944, with a truckload of gasoline in jerricans headed to the front lines. Returning to Utah Beach, he stopped in the nearby southern suburb of Porte d'Orléans, Paris. Here he met another soldier, Eddie, a light-colored African American of medium height and weight, who quickly became Porter's close buddy. They hid Porter's truck in a garage, moved into a hotel in Vincennes, and stole small quantities of gasoline and PX rations from Army trucks for spending money

The pair eventually met three AWOL soldiers: Hoyle S. Taylor, Gilbert Moses, and George Williams. Moses was wearing a helmet with "MP" inscribed with white paint. Williams was AWOL from the 14th Replacement Depot, one of eight such units in France. He flagged down a ride to Paris with "some half-track unit" and ended up at the Hotel de Paris in Vincennes. Here he met Moses and Taylor and a redheaded girl named Claudie, whom he called "Blondie" and spent the nights with.

These three men knew how to negotiate the black market. On finding out that Porter had a truck, they suggested using it to obtain a load of gasoline. One night Eddie, Moses, and Taylor took the truck. When they returned a few hours later, Porter saw them split a large sum of money and Eddie gave him 2,000 francs.

A week later they needed money. The foursome of Eddie, Taylor, Moses, and Porter took the truck and drove the backroads to a gasoline dump in Vincennes. French civilians were working at the dump loading various trucks. The gang members got in line with the empty trucks and the Frenchmen loaded their truck to capacity with 260 jerricans. Following instructions from Taylor, Porter drove out of the dump through an underpass east of Vincennes, turned left across a long bridge, and stopped at a red gate. Eddie and Taylor got out of the truck and talked with a Frenchman for a few minutes. When they returned, the Frenchman opened the gate and they drove in. They unloaded the cargo into a shed, Taylor was paid, and they left. Again Moses, Eddie, and Taylor split the money, with Porter receiving 6,000 francs from Eddie. The 260 cans of gasoline surely netted Taylor a profit of 208,000 francs, but all the "owner" of the truck received was 6,000 francs. Eddie promised Porter more when he had the change, but that never happened.

Later, the group met two other AWOL soldiers. Forrest L. Jones told them he had been working at a POL dump west of Paris and could help them obtain a load of gasoline. Jewel L. Jamison also joined the gang. A native of Chicago, he had guarded prisoners of war with the 3174th Quartermaster Service Company. Jamison, like every soldier in Europe, wanted to see Paris. It was intended to be a quick look, but he started drinking in a bar in Vincennes where there were some girls and forgot to go back. Here he met Williams and Porter.

On October 25, 1944, Jamison, Williams, Jones, and Porter left Vincennes at about 6:30 p.m. and drove the truck west to the gas dump near a big racetrack about 30 miles from Paris. When they arrived at the gate, Jones told the guard, "Going to the company," and he let them through. The group drove to the loading point. Jones, who knew the soldiers, told them they wanted a load of gasoline. They agreed, provided they received a cut of the money. The six of them loaded the truck and Porter headed for Paris.

That same night, the commander of the Company D, 156th Infantry Regiment, called his soldiers together and told them that practically every vehicle in the Seine Section was running on American gasoline and it was up to them to get out there and put a stop to it. Company D had been assigned to guard the gasoline dump at Nogent sur Marne located in the Vincennes Woods, the largest park in metro Paris, from which Porter and members of his gang had previously stolen gasoline. The guards, including Sergeant Lee R. Stelly, were given a list of trucks authorized to haul gasoline. That night, only vehicles loaded with gasoline were supposed to go into the gasoline dump at Vincennes. All other trucks leaving the dump toward Paris on the Red Ball Route should be empty.

Stelly was working MP duty in Vincennes when in the darkness he heard a truck coming from Paris. It was dragging a chain, so he knew it was a gasoline truck. The dragging chain grounded the truck and kept static electricity sparks from accidentally setting off fumes and burning up the truck and cargo. Stelly was standing across from the large Vincennes Wood park as the driver turned off the lights and made a left turn into the park. The driver drove about 150 yards in and turned the motor off. Stelly waited about five minutes and walked over to the truck. It was loaded with jerricans, but Stelly could not tell if they were full or empty. As he approached, one of the men was urinating, another was sitting in the cab of the truck, and a third was offloading a jerrican.

Stelly asked the men if the truck was loaded and if they were Red Ball drivers. The soldier responded "no," which seemed correct to Stelly: The drivers from the dump to a local train station were not Red Ball drivers. Stelly went around to the front of the truck, where he saw a big Red Ball painted on the bumper. Realizing that he was being lied to, Stelly told the men he would have to hold them and investigate their story. After three or four minutes of talking with the three soldiers, Stelly noticed an American soldier and three civilians with their hats pulled down low and dressed in overcoats coming toward the truck. They did not see Stelly in the darkness. The civilians were carrying a small handbag and asked the soldier accompanying them if the other three men were his friends. The three men apprehended by Stelly were pointing at him and making sure the newcomers saw he was carrying a gun.

By now, another MP had joined Stelly. Stelly radioed in and requested the officer of the day to come out as the pair arrested Jewel Jamison, George Williams, Forrest Jones, and Johnnie Porter. The four men were court-martialed. Hoyle S. Taylor, Gilbert Moses and Eddie were not apprehended and in all probability joined another gang.

The background of these gangs is best illustrated by Corporal James R. Mills, who deserted his company, the 441st Quartermaster Company, on September 9, 1944, while it was operating in Paris:

> About the end of August, I left my company area near Mennecy in charge of a detail and one truck to proceed to Gomez to a POL dump to pick up a load of gasoline. On the return trip in Paris we encountered another truck from my company which was broken down. The sergeant placed me in charge of the truck until my company could send a wrecker for it. I left my truck and in my absence it was picked up by the MPs, as I was informed by a Frenchman. I then went to a neighborhood hotel on the Boulevard de la Chapelle, where I stayed for two days. I then moved to certain other hotels, where I stayed with various prostitutes. I had 1,500 francs with me at this time. I spent the money for lodgings, meals, drinks, and women.
>
> I found a group of white and colored soldiers, AWOLs who frequented a whorehouse in the neighborhood of Rue Fluery [sic]. I joined this group. My job was to find Frenchmen who wanted to buy gasoline. I received a share of the money the gang received for the sale of the gasoline from the work I did. I do not know the names of any of these AWOLs. In this job, the gang I was working with ran about two truckloads of gasoline per week, which we sold to French civilians. My share of the proceeds per sale was about 15,000–18,000 francs [$300–$360] per job. I worked for this gang for about six weeks, then I joined another gang of three

11. The Vincennes Gang   101

colored soldiers, all AWOL.... I knew [of them] as William and Robert. I did not know the other soldier's name. I stayed with them about two weeks, during which time we sold about three partial truckloads of gasoline to French civilians. One load was 100 cans and two loads were 50 cans each. My job was the same as before—to locate and arrange the sales with the French civilians. My partners and I shared equally and I received about 20,000 francs while working with this gang.

I next joined a gang of five colored soldiers, AWOLs whom I knew as Curtis, Saul, Raymond, Madison, and Snowball. While with this gang, we ran two truckloads of gasoline and sold them to French civilians. I made the arrangement for the sales in each case. I received 12,000 francs as my share from the first deal. On the night of November 14, 1944, all six of the gang decided to run some gasoline, and all of us went in two U.S. Army trucks and one jeep to a POL [Petroleum, Oil, and Lubricants] dump near Soissons, where we obtained two full truckloads of gasoline by presenting a forged order signed by one of our gang; I don't know what it was. We got back into Paris about 2:30 on the morning of November 16, 1944. A lady who runs the Sphinx Hotel, Rue de la Chapelle, gave me the address of a French lady whom she said would buy our gasoline. This lady's name and address are Madame Camille Royer, 43 or 53 Rue Marcadet, Paris, France. I went there and arranged with her to sell her both truckloads of gasoline at 500 francs a can. I and Madame took one truck to her garage but couldn't get through the small gate to unload.

An employee at this garage whom I now know to be Mouton Rene, 20 Quai de la L'Oire [sic], Paris, 19, guided me and Madison to another garage at 76 Rue Stevenson, where a Frenchman whom I now know to be M. Queulvee and his employees were unloading our truck when the MP came. A Frenchman took us through a door and hid us in a French truck, where the MPs found us. Madame Camille Royer was to pay us when the gasoline was delivered.

Queulvée would later assert that Madame Royer had purchased the gasoline from the African American soldiers and that he, in turn, intended to buy it from her.

On November 16, 1944, at about 1:30 p.m., Sergeants John D. Bell and James P. Lassetter both of the 382nd Military Police Battalion, observed that a 6 × 6, 2½-ton U.S. government truck, heavily laden with gasoline jerricans and covered with a tarpaulin, drove to the entrance of a garage owned and operated by Henri François Queulvée, located at 76 Rue Stephenson, Paris, France. A African American soldier drove the truck. Immediately preceding the approach of the truck to the garage entrance, another African American soldier dismounted and ran toward the garage. The door was closed, but upon the approach it opened to permit the truck to enter and then closed again. The circumstances excited the suspicion of the two sergeants. Lassetter, armed with a carbine, was posted as guard with orders from Bell to allow no one to leave the garage. Bell went to the 787th Military Police Battalion headquarters and reported the incident observed by him. Approximately ten minutes later, he returned with First Lieutenant Sidney Fain and Sergeant John J. Smith, both of the 787th Military Police Battalion.

Lieutenant Fain knocked on the garage door and demanded entrance. After some delay, the door was opened by Queulvée. Fain, Lassetter, and Smith entered. Bell remained on guard outside. When the truck had halted in the garage, James Mills, Haywood Madison, and six French civilians, including Queulvée, commenced to remove the jerricans. A 6 × 6 truck when completely loaded will carry 260 jerricans of five gallons' capacity, and this truck was loaded to its approximate capacity.

About one fourth of the cans had been removed and placed in a civilian truck when Lieutenant Fain's party interrupted the proceedings. Each jerrican was filled with gasoline. Two tanks, each of a capacity of 55 gallons, stood on the floor of the garage and had a pump attached; each tank was full. Before the door was opened, Mills and Madison hid themselves in a civilian truck that stood in another part of the garage. They were discovered and with the French civilians were taken into custody and transported to the Military Police headquarters in Rue Wagram. James Mills and Haywood Madison were tried and received prison terms.[2]

12

THE CHANNEL ISLANDS CRASH

Paris was a city of liberation, but the war would continue for another ten months and the armies had to be supplied. Lieutenant Robert B. Blackler had been assigned to the 31st Transportation Group, Ninth Air Corps, and his primary mission was flying cargo from England in support of Allied troops in France. On the night of October 30, 1944, Lieutenant Blackler, piloting his Douglas C-47 Dakota military transport aircraft, left Villa Coublay Airfield. This was the airfield serving the most popular rest and recreation city in Europe—Paris. In addition to the crew of five, the C-47 had seven passengers. Three sailors were returning to Cherbourg after being on leave from their ship the USS *Atr-2*, a Class Rescue Tug. The other three passengers, all Merchant Marines, were assigned to the U.S. Army Transport Small Tug 674 assigned to the Cherbourg port. Photographer's Mate First Class Junius J. Stout was also on this plane. Astonishingly he was not registered as a crewmember or passenger, but it appears his final destination was to return to England with this crew.

The flight to Cherbourg from Paris was in overcast weather with visibility of four miles. About 15 miles from their destination, Radio Operator Joseph Fiset transmitted that due to electrical failure the lights were not visible on the plane. Lieutenant Blackler reported, "The mission was a transport mission which due to bad weather and a radar beam failure ended up over the German-occupied Channel Islands."

On the night of October 30, 1944, a large plane flew over Jersey Island with all of its navigation lights on. It circled the island twice as if the pilot was looking for a place to land. The observers on the ground thought it was a German mail plane, but after it had been overhead for some time the German guns opened up. The plane was hit and crashed into the sea at Bouley Bay Harbor, just off the north coast of the island.

Colonel John B. Reybold, Captain Edward R Clark, and Lieutenant George Haas—all prisoners of war on the Isle of Jersey—ran out of their building and looked at an airplane about 300 feet off the ground, with its landing lights on. The crew were shooting flares as the plane circled north. The officers figured the Allies had finally decided to take the island; when they heard a loud explosion, they thought this was the first of many bombs to be dropped.

The following day the Germans surmised the pilot had mistaken his bearings for Cherbourg. They told the POW officers that an American plane had been shot down and one officer, an American, had been rescued. Clark was informed that the officer would be in the hospital a few days, suffering from shock, as he had been in the cold water for quite some time. Somehow, only the plane's pilot was saved, as five bodies washed ashore in the bay that day and another body three days later.

As reported in an official Jersey document:

> The skies wept yesterday when the bodies of six young members of the American forces were laid to rest in the Allied War Cemetery in Howard Davis Park. The bodies were those of young airmen and passengers of the plane which was shot down over the north coast of the island on October 30th and their names were as follows: Lieutenant Ermine E.G. Pallentine, SP 3/c Edward J. Pycz, SP 3/c Timothy J. Manning, SP 3c William H. Kearns, 2nd Officer Woodrow W. Anderson and Junius J. Stout. The bodies of the latter four had lain overnight in St. Luke's Church, and the coffins of the first two mentioned, who were Roman Catholics, had been placed in the hall of the lodge at the main entrance of the park.
>
> The Dean of Jersey, the Very Reverent M. Le Marinel, M.A., conducted the services as the bodies of Manning, Kearns, Stout and Anderson were lowered into the grave and the Roman Catholic services for Pallentine and Pycz were conducted by the Reverent R.T. Arscott, parish priest of St. Mary and St. Peter's Roman Catholic Church.
>
> The skies opened and a heavy shower fell as the graveside ceremony was drawing to a conclusion.
>
> The principal mourners were the senior officer of the American prisoners of war in Jersey and the captain of the crashed plane, who had been saved. Also present were A.M. Countanche, Esq. Bailiff of Jersey; C.W. Duret Aubin, Esq. Attorney General; Dr. J.R. Hanna (Representative, the Order of St. John of Jerusalem and the British Red Cross); ...
>
> The firing party and guard of honor were supplied by German forces and German officers were present to pay their last respects to the dead.
>
> Wreaths were placed on the graves from the deceased's American comrades in the islands, from the German Reich, the States of Jersey, the Order of St. John and British Red Cross and the British Legion.
>
> The funeral arrangements, as usual for theses ceremonies, were carried out efficiently by Messrs. J.B. Le Quesne and Sons.

12. The Channel Islands Crash

A day prior to the funeral of his crew and passengers, Lieutenant Robert B. Blackler had arrived in the old British Garrison Military Prison on South Hill. The three officers—Reybold, Clark and Haas—pumped him dry of news in less than an hour. Blackler told them when the Germans began firing, he believed that the guns were from friendly fire at Cherbourg and that the reason for firing the flares was for identification.

The altitude was insufficient to bail out, so they crash-landed and struck water about 200 yards northwest of the tip of Jersey Island. As the plane crashed on the surface of the sea, none of the personnel on board were hurt. However, in throwing the life raft overboard, in the excitement someone forgot to pull the cord to release the carbon dioxide that would inflate the raft and it sank immediately. The men pulled on their life vests and started to shore, which was about 200 yards away. One member clung to the plane and sank with it. The channel was rough due to the high winds as they swam for the shore. Here the cliffs were 100 feet high with the surf beating against them; it pounded the men against the rocks and killed them. "S/Sgt Carroll was last seen by me attempting to climb out of the water onto a steep precipice bordering water. Because of the severe waves that were breaking against the shore, I think he was probably knocked unconscious and drowned, as were the other members of my crew. His body was not recovered."[1]

Blackler told his listeners that he swam away from the cliffs and remained in the water until the Germans threw him a rope. He would have nightmares of this event for the remainder of his life.

Ten days later, the body of radio operator, Sergeant Joseph E. Fiset, washed ashore. He was interred with the rest of his crew from the crashed plane. Two months after the crash, crewmember Private William H. Westemeier's body was recovered in the Samarés; he, too, was buried with the crew.[2]

Junius Stout's father, Archibard Job Stout was notified by the U.S. Navy that his son was killed on January 22, 1945. The father wrote, "Our last communication from him (Oct.26.1944). Where was he in the interim?"[3] The mixup was due to Stout not being registered on the plane flown by Blackler.

Today Roccanti is buried in the Brittany Cemetery, St. James, France. Stout, Gillespie, Pycz and Kearns are all buried in Colleville-sur-Mer, France.

13

The Voltaire Gang

American soldiers are killed; the war continues and the black market in Paris becomes even more lucrative as the Voltaire gang enrich themselves in Montparnasse, an area of Paris, on the left bank of the Seine River.

Dramatis Personae

Voltaire	Walter Medley
Jackie	John Maciejczak
Christiane	Jackie's girlfriend
Johnny	Herman M. Francis
Lidya	Lucienne Juielette Hubert, a 19-year-old prostitute; Johnny is a regular customer
Alvin Davis	Himself
Suzanne	Pauli Marly, Davis's girlfriend
Nicky	Ervine Furmann
Camellia	Herminne Slagmudler, a refugee and Nicky's girlfriend
David	Unknown and remained free of charges
Mama	Marie Debesse, manager of the Familia Hotel
Louis	Louis Debesse, owner of the Familia Hotel

Private Walter Medley, also known as "Voltaire," 33778404, 960th Quartermaster Service Company, deserted his company in early September 1944. Just prior to their departure for France, the 960th had been stationed in Wiltshire, England, the scene of a murder by a member of that company. The crime happened on June 17, 1944, when the men were drinking at a day room that dispensed beer, and the bartender refused to serve them any more beer at closing time. A fierce argument arose among the soldiers. During this time, Pfc. James E. Alexander, who was not involved, left and went to his barracks; he stood in the doorway watching as the argument escalated. Pvt. Benjamin Pygate then told Alexander, "Get back into the hut before I kill you." Alexander looked at him and Pygate kicked him in the groin. As Alexander fell forward from the kick, Pygate drew a knife from his pocket and plunged it into Alexander's neck, severing his carotid artery. Alexander quickly bled to death. Pygate was sentenced to death by musketry.[1] His execution was carried out on November 28, 1944, at the 2912th Disciplinary Training Center in England.

During Pygate's trial and execution, Voltaire had deserted the 960th Quartermaster Service Company. What is known about Voltaire from the time he went AWOL until December 15 comes from statements in the French police archives taken from two Parisians prostitutes and a convicted Frenchman. One of the prostitutes was Herminne Slagmulder, 21 years old, who was born in Belgium and known to the American GIs as Camelia. Her permanent address was the home of her parents living in Paris but her working address was at the hotel at 15 Rue de l'Quest. In September 1944, in the bar of the Hotel Daguerre, she became acquainted with an American soldier named Voltaire, who was with another soldier named Nick. In November, Camellia became acquainted with Maciejczak and three other African American soldiers, Cisol, Jimmy, and George. All members of the Voltaire gang, they lived at the Hotel Daguerre on 79 Rue Daguerre.

The other prostitute, Lucienne Juielette Hubert, blond, 19 years old, and known as Lidya, connected Voltaire, during this time frame, with an underground figure known as Monsieur Jean. Lidya had met him in the Chez Grilli located in the Hotel Daguerre, where he was having a drink with his wife. She watched as he had several drinks with American soldiers and purchased several cans of gasoline from their jeep parked in the courtyard of the café.

Lidya saw them again in the evening at the Cabaret Venus, where she went to dance every night. She began to understand that Monsieur Jean was a black marketer who worked with American AWOLs. She often "saw him in the company of a black American soldier by the name of Voltaire, who seemed to be the chief of a gang of colored and white soldiers, who dealt with American gasoline."

Monsieur Jean was 37-year-old Stephane Oudart, who in 1933 had been imprisoned for ten years for voluntary homicide. Indeed, he was the main buyer of the gasoline stolen from the U.S. POL depots by the Voltaire gang. The other buyers included Andre Thunderoz, a street flower vender, and Pierre Jacquier, manager of the L'Oriental Café.

Voltaire appeared to be about age 40, stocky, well developed at 200 pounds, with black hair streaked with gray. Why he took the *nom de plume* of the early 18th-century French Enlightenment writer, historian, and philosopher Voltaire is unknown.

His second-in-command, John Maciejczak, was a lanky 145-pound individual around 24 years old with a large scar over his left eye. Tattooed on his right arm was an American flag encircled by a streamer with the letters "USA." Also on that arm was a female Native American. The other arm contained a heart pierced by a dagger, with a traversing streamer bearing the name "John."

Voltaire and his gang members always wore their military uniforms. Voltaire would wear second lieutenant bars when he walked out on the street; he had a helmet with a lieutenant bar that he put on with toothpaste so it would rub off easily. This was in case he was suspected by anyone in authority: He could quickly remove and discard the lieutenant bars by rubbing off the toothpaste and become a private, his authorized rank. Maciejczak posed as a military policeman wearing an MP brassard and carrying a billy-club.

Then something happened on December, 15, 1944. Voltaire and Maciejczak left their gang and hotel with only the clothes on their backs and relocated several miles away, across the Seine River at another hotel. In all probability, the gang members were arrested and their trucks impounded by the Military Police while Voltaire and Maciejczak escaped.

About November 15, 1945, Ervin Furman and Herman M Francis went AWOL from the 542 Port Company located near Cherbourg. They hitchhiked to Paris. At that time Francis had 3,000 or 4,000 francs, so they stayed around Porte d'Orléans. A few days later they met Alvin Davis and went with him to Familia Hotel at 13 Rue Roger. Davis had a white soldier friend who was known as David and both lived at the Familia Hotel, so Furman and Francis moved into that hotel. On December 15, Camellia showed up at the hotel with Voltaire and his friend John Maciejczak, who rented two rooms. The hotel now housed six AWOLs: Voltaire, Davis, David, Francis, Furman and Maciejczak. They occupied rooms 9, 11, 14 and 18.

The Familia Hotel was owned by Louis Debesse, who had purchased the hotel in 1923. The 54-year-old owner did not take an active part in the hotel. Instead, it was managed by his portly wife, Marie, known to the gang as Mama.

Two days later, on December 17, the reorganized Voltaire gang found a jeep near the Arc de Triomphe. It was not demobilized, meaning the distributor cap had not been removed to prevent it from starting. They stole the jeep, with the six soldiers cramming themselves in to the four-passenger vehicle as Voltaire drove away. The group traveled 166 miles northeast toward the front lines to Charleroi, Belgium. Here they found three trucks parked in the street, two in one place and one in another. They entered the trucks, flipped the on-off switches, and with the left foot pushed the starters. As the trucks' motors zoomed into action, they drove off with two men in each truck, leaving behind the jeep.

In one of the trucks, they found a trip ticket dated 12–18–44 for vehicle

#4241953 and Voltaire wrote his name on the ticket. Voltaire and Francis drove the truck to the Valkenburg gasoline dump in the Netherlands and presented the trip ticket. The truck was loaded with 260 jerricans of gasoline, and Voltaire signed the receipt using the name 3453 Quartermaster Truck Company. The group returned to Paris about December 21 or 22. Voltaire stopped the trucks across the street from a service station at 136 Avenue Aristide Briand, Montrouge. He went inside and came out with Rene Alberte Nicoud, an old stocky man with a beard who climbed into the truck. The other two vehicles followed Voltaire's truck, which went in the direction of Malakoff, a southern suburb of Paris. There, they unloaded the gasoline. As soon as they finished, the man paid them 800 francs per can. The group then drove back to 136 Avenue A. Briand and let Nicoud off as he directed them into a garage. Voltaire had done business with this man before, so they felt safe about leaving the trucks there until their next job. From this venture, the Voltaire gang members earned about 30,000 francs ($600) each.

That Christmas, the gang ate dinner at the Familia Hotel with Mama, her husband, Camellia and Suzanne. Maciejczak's girlfriend, Christiane, was in the hospital at that time. Voltaire was Mama's favorite—she called him "ma petite Voltaire." A bit later Davis moved out and went to live with Suzanne, who was also known as Pauli Marly.

Just after Christmas, Lidya and four of her "professional" friends stopped by the Hotel Familia, where they had drinks in the bar with Voltaire, Davis, David, and Maciejczak, who were all in uniform. The manager, Marie, seemed very familiar with these soldiers, apparently knowing them well. After that, they walked to the cinema, accompanied by the Louis Debesse and his little niece. Following the show, the group returned to the hotel bar and continued drinking. Lidya then went upstairs with Francis to have sex in his rooms. She didn't register her name and it was the first time that she ever conducted "business" in that hotel. As Lidya was coming down the next morning, she heard Marie say, "I must bring some food to my little Voltaire" and saw her go toward the stairs with a tray and some food.

The next evening Lidya had an appointment with Francis at the same hotel. Upon arriving, she saw Furman with a woman, whom she knew very little about at that time, who was named Camellia and was now Furman's girlfriend. Francis paid Lidya, but as a client, she had told him that she wanted a bicycle. "He wanted me to stay with him all the time; he gave me 10,000 francs. I kept them but I didn't stay with him. Besides, I saw Furman give large sums of money to Camellia so that she could buy some clothes." Lidya refused to see Francis again, but she may well have given him a sexually transmitted disease—the clap.

During the first week in January, the Voltaire gang made another 252-mile trip to Valkenburg, the Netherlands. This area had just been cleared of the enemy, as it had been involved in the last major German offensive, the Battle of the Bulge. The gang counted on the hectic confusion of the battlefront and loaded up two trucks with about 260 cans of gasoline each. David and Maciejczak had the empty truck; Voltaire was more or less the boss and furnished the trip tickets. Furman drove one truck and Francis rode with him; Voltaire and Davis were in the other truck. On the way back, they had two flat tires on the rear. Voltaire stopped to help but David kept on going. The gang got back to Paris but David and Maciejczak, with the empty truck, did not return until two days later; during this time they had stolen 15 brand-new 45-caliber U.S. Army pistols and ammunition.

Francis took two guns, Voltaire two, Davis one, Furman two, Maciejczak two, and David either one or two. One load of gas was sold to "some man" on highway N20—about 245 cans at 800 francs per can. They left two of the trucks at the garage, but sold the other load the next day to Voltaire's old contact Monsieur Jean. They met him at the Familia Hotel, and he paid them for 245 jerricans at 800 francs per can in the kitchen in front of Mama.

With Monsieur Jean leading them in his personal car, the group pulled into a courtyard and unloaded the gasoline into a storeroom at night somewhere in Paris. The next day they took David's truck to the garage and stored it with the other two. All six split up the proceeds of this sale— about 65,000 francs each. A day later David and Davis left and went to the apartment where Davis was living with Suzanne. Here David, who was drunk, got into a fight with Davis, whom he threatened with his revolver. Davis gave him several blows with his fist and threw him out the door. The neighbors phoned the police. While Davis was pounding on the door, he was arrested by the Military Police; that was the last time he was seen by any of the Voltaire gang.

On January 15, 1945, Voltaire, Maciejczak and Furman went on a third job to obtain gasoline. Francis remained in the hotel as he had the clap and was too sick to travel. During this time Francis received a letter on blue paper from Davis, given to him in the Familia Hotel by Suzanne. It asked him to come by because Camellia had been crying all day; it said to not tell Mama. Francis did not go because he was afraid it was a trap to pick him up.

Before Friday, January 19, 1945, would be over, the Voltaire gang would be out of business in a deadly way. The events began in the early afternoon during a snow flurry, when an American officer ordered to requisition the private garage at 44 Avenue de Chatillon, where the gang kept their three trucks, found the loaded vehicles inside. He noticed some of the identification markings had been rubbed off. He notified the MPs, and the trucks were removed and driven to the Seine Section Impounding Area. Arrangements were made for the gasoline to be returned to the closest petroleum depot.

Around dusk, Francis and Maciejczak stopped at the hotel next to the garage to see the owner, as they wanted to use one of the trucks or possibly sell some small quantities of the gasoline by the can. While they were there, around 6:30 p.m. MP Sergeant Vincent Kenny, Pfc. Cephas Taylor, and Charles Chilengrerian, who were on roving patrol, were informed by Adrian Hileash of 44 Avenue de Chatillon that gasoline was being sold at his address. He went with the MPs in their jeep to this address. Upon arriving, the Frenchman was very excited and frightened and insisted they follow him into the apartment.

When Frenchmen such as Hileash put the finger on the AWOLs, they had a variety of motives. Frenchmen who had been ditched by their women in favor of richer Americans figured that turning the GIs in was an easy way to eliminate competition. In some cases, women just grew tired of the soldiers and wanted to get rid of them. Some of the French people counted on a reward from the American authorities. Still others were motivated by patriotism; they felt the black market was bad for their country.

Regardless of Hileash's reason, the MPs went with him to the location. Kenny went through to the garden in the back of the apartment. Here he caught Francis and brought him back into a small office in the apartment, inquiring about the whereabouts of the other man who was supposed to be with him. Francis said, "He beat it." After searching the area they found two .45 automatics, which Francis admitted having thrown away in the garden. The MPs took Francis, the pistols, and the money (about 22,000 francs) he had in his possession to the CID office and turned him over to agents Benjamin J. Peterson and Randall W. Murphey. The pair talked to Francis for a short time, with Francis stating that he would cooperate with Peterson and lead him to a place where at least one member of his gang was located. When he first came in, Francis admitted, "I suppose you know that I have been doing a little business." Then he explained that his gang had been selling gas. The soldier stated that when he had been picked up, he had gone to a garage to get a truck, but discovered that all three of the gang's trucks were gone.

After Francis was questioned at the CID office, he directed the agents to an address where some of his colleagues were supposed to be. There, at 38 Rue se Perceval, after a search of several rooms, they found Pvt. Alvin Davis hiding under the bed in Room 25. They took him into custody. A further search of the room turned up a new .45 automatic under a cabinet and about 17,000 francs in a cupboard. Davis denied that either the pistol or the money belonged to him. Kenny took Davis to the jeep as the agents questioned Pauli Marly (Suzanne), who was in the room with Davis. She gave them the address of the

Hotel Familia and told them they could probably find some of Davis's friends there. Leaving Suzanne's apartment, the Military Police went to a nearby café and telephoned for another patrol to join them. This unit arrived with Francis in one jeep and Davis in another and proceeded to the Hotel Familia.

Camellia had arrived at the Hotel Familia at about 6:30 p.m., but none of the gang was there. A few minutes later, Furman, Voltaire, and Maciejczak came in and learned that Francis had been arrested by the MPs. Camellia wanted to leave, but Furman told her that he she was going to eat with them and then sat down at the kitchen table. The three gang members and Camellia were sitting and standing up, as were the owner Louis Debesse, his wife Marie (Mama), the owner's sister-in-law, and her daughter (all of whom were living at the hotel). Voltaire had taken his shoes off, complaining that his feet hurt. The three gang members were carrying their weapons.

Arriving in front of the hotel, the Military Police squad left two MPs with the prisoners and the jeeps. Peterson gave instructions. Murphey's part was to cover anyone coming down the stairs and to cover Peterson and Chilengrerian, the MP interpreter. The front door was locked. When they rang the bell, the light in the office went out and the door was opened by a buzzer. They went in according to the plan: Sergeant Berry went upstairs to cover the top floor, Pfc. Stanley J. Romanauskas went around back to cover the exit, and Peterson and Chilengrerian went into the office, which was on the right side of the narrow hallway. Murphey heard Peterson say, "All right, get your hands up quick and come out." This was immediately followed by many shots fired in rapid succession. Murphey saw Peterson and Chilengrerian fall, and he got alongside the office door, up against the wall. When Voltaire rushed out of the office door, he had a .45 U.S. Army pistol in each hand, crossed so that he could cover both directions as he came out. He started firing as soon as he saw the MPs. Voltaire ran into the hallway as Murphey fired one shot into him. Voltaire turned toward him still shooting; as he got alongside, Voltaire fired again and stepped to one side. As he went past, Murphey fired again and Voltaire fell to his knees. As he started to rise, Murphey fired a fourth shot. Murphey asked Peterson how bad and where he had been hit. While Murphey was shooting it out, he heard a submachine gun firing in the rear courtyard.

Romanauskas, in the backyard, heard the volley of shots. Looking through the glass door from the outside, he saw a person start for the door. When he shot through the door, the man dropped in his tracks. Then Romanauskas recognized Agent Murphey as he entered the hallway with his gun smoking. Right after that, he heard the kitchen window open and Furman and Maciejczak leaped into the snow. As one of the forms jumped, Romanauskas fired his weapon and Maciejczak lay still where he landed. When Romanauskas shined

13. The Voltaire Gang   113

the flashlight on him, he didn't move. As Furman had leapt first, Romanauskas felt that he must have hit the other man who had followed Furman down with the Tommy gun. Somehow Romanauskas missed Furman as he ran away into the snow flurries. Romanauskas then ran inside. There he saw Agent Peterson and Pfc. Charles Chilengrerian lying on the floor. He asked Agent Murphey how he was; Murphy replied that he was all right, that he did not get hit.

Peterson said, "I think I'm dying. Can you get me to a hospital?" Romanauskas ran to the front door; it was locked, being the type of door that opens when you press a button. He told Peterson to pull himself out of the hallway and proclaimed that he would shoot the door off. Just as Romanauskas aimed to shoot, Murphey and a fat woman—the concierge—came over, and she pressed the buzzer to open the door. He took Peterson's pistol from him, ran outside, and got his jeep. In one vehicle was the radio operator Pfc. Kisley; in the other jeep were Sgt. Kenny and the driver holding one of the prisoners.

Peterson was in Romanauskas's jeep and Chilengrerian was in the other vehicle. As they turned and left for the 217th General Hospital, Peterson said, "I think I'm dying, so please notify my wife." Romanauskas attempted to encourage him: "We are almost there, just hold on." He reached the 217th General Hospital by radio and informed them of the emergency. When the jeep arrived at the hospital, personnel directed him with Peterson to the main surgery room. The wounded man was put on a stretcher and nurses and doctors started to work on him. The other jeep arrived minutes later with Chilengrerian.

Meanwhile, all this time, Sergeant Berry was on the top floor of the hotel observing the dead man lying on his stomach, while talking to the maid in the building. After Murphey and the MPs left the 217th General Hospital, they went up to the CID headquarters. Here, at about 11:30 p.m., Vincent S. Reilly received a telephone call from Agent Murphey reporting that a gunfight had taken place at about 10:30 at Hotel Familia, 13 Rue Roger, between three unknown deserters who had been trafficking in gasoline and Murphey, Peterson, and two MPs. Murphey further reported that Peterson and Pfc. Charles Chilengrerian, Co D, 709 MP Bn., U.S. Army, had been severely wounded, and that two of the deserters had been killed and one escaped.

Accompanied by Murphey, Reilly left for the Hotel Familia. At the hotel, he found Private Walter Medley, "Voltaire," 33778404, 960 Quartermaster Service Company, dead in the hall and Pfc. John J. Maciejczak, 36650214, dead in the courtyard underneath the kitchen window. In room 11, he located six revolvers and miscellaneous clothes and personal items; in room 9, he found the same. All of the items were U.S. Army property. Underneath the body of Voltaire were two U.S. Army pistols, and in the kitchen on the floor was a .45 sub-machine gun.

During their interrogation, Louis Debesse, the hotel keeper, and Marie Debesse, his wife, lied. They stated that the three soldiers had come to the hotel at 5:30 p.m., that it was the first time they had been there, and that the men had left about 6 p.m. but came back shortly thereafter. They further stated that before the shooting the men had entered the kitchen and said that they were very tired, having just returned from Belgium. At the time of the shooting, they said, two African Americans and one white soldier were in the kitchen (the Debesses claimed not to know their names) as well as their niece and themselves. When the bell rang, Marie pressed the buzzer, Peterson and Chilengrerian entered the office and announced that they were military police, and the dead African American turned off the light and started shooting at the two officers.

About two hours later, Reilly again questioned the hotel keeper and his wife. This time, they stated that the soldiers had stayed at the hotel about one month ago but again claimed that they did not know their names. Neither of them revealed the presence of Hermine Slagmulder, alias Camellia, in the kitchen at the time of the shooting; subsequent investigation reveled that she was the girlfriend of Ervin E. Furman.

When the shooting had begun, Camellia hid under the table. She did not remember what happened after that point because she was so emotional. When the shooting stopped, she climbed out from under the table when someone switched on the light in the kitchen. The American policemen were in the corridor taking care of their wounded men. Louis Debesse went up to his wife, raised his fist, and said, "It is your fault if there is bloodshed." He started to hit her, but Camellia put herself in between the pair. At that moment, she noticed two revolvers lying on the kitchen floor, near the window. The window was open and she surmised that two of the gang had escaped. Camellia assumed the fleein men were Furman and Maciejczak.

She picked up the two revolvers and placed them in a little cupboard next to the kitchen stove. She then took a flashlight and went into the courtyard, where she saw Maciejczak's corpse. Camellia then left for room 10, which was occupied by the proprietor's sister-in-law and niece. The latter came up and joined her. She stayed in that room until morning and then came down at about 7:30 a.m., asking Mama if she knew where Furman was. Mama said that she didn't know. Camelia gave her 3,000 francs to give Furman in case he should come back, as she knew he was without money. She then left and did not return to that hotel.

That night the Military Police began looking for Furman. They went through some rooms at the Hotel Familia and found belongings of the gang. The CID agents searched other hotels in the area without any success. At about midnight, Furman arrived at Suzanne's hotel apartment and asked her to put him up. He made her understand that very serious things had happened at the Hotel Familia. She told him to leave at once because the MPs had just arrested Davis and would surely come back looking for him. Furman then immediately left. Sure enough, at 2 o'clock in the morning, the MPs came to fetch Suzanne and took her to their office for questioning.

The following day, Agent Murphey and his staff searched for Furman. They questioned Suzanne, Lidya, and Camellia and searched their apartments. They visited all military and civilian hospitals looking for a wounded man who fit his description as furnished by Camellia: "About 25 years old but looking like 18. Medium height (about 1 m. 68), thin, beardless, chocolate complexion, frizzled hair. No particular sign on the face or the body."

Furman remained missing in spite of wanted notices circulating throughout occupied Europe. He was apprehended in the evening of January 27, 1945, about 55 miles southwest of Paris, at Chartres in the home of Adrien Hebert. Hebert's connection was that he had worked in the garage at 44 Avenue de Chatillon where the Voltaire gang had kept their trucks. Why he hid Furman is unknown.

Of the last six members of the Voltaire gang, John Maciejczak and Voltaire (Walter Medley) were dead; David had been arrested and "fell through the cracks, as he could not be identified; and Ervine Furman, Alvin Davis and Norman M. Francis were court-martialed.

Furman, 24 years old and the father of two children, was a truck driver making $112 per month before his induction in the army at Fort Dix, New Jersey. He remained silent and refused to issue a statement. He pleaded innocent and was sentenced to prison.

Davis, 25 years old and unmarried, was a bellboy at $32 per month prior to induction into the army at Camp Shelby, Mississippi. Like Furman, he remained silent and pleaded innocent. He was found guilty.

Francis, 24 years old and unmarried, completed three years of high school and worked as a shipping clerk at $80 per month until his induction into the army at Fort Dix, New Jersey. He gave a sworn two-page statement of the gang's activities, thus making this chapter possible. Upon the advice of his lawyer, he pleaded innocent to his charges. He, too, was found guilty

All the men received long prison terms but were paroled from U.S. penitentiaries by 1948.[2]

14

The Lola Murder

Jerome M. Ciullo was born and raised in Wyandotte, Michigan, and attended Catholic school there until he was fourteen, when he was expelled for some minor infraction. His father died when he was seven years of age, and his mother went to work to support him and his two brothers. Both of the brothers enlisted in the navy and were given honorable discharges. After expulsion from school, Ciullo worked at six different places until he received his draft notice from the U.S. government. He then went to the local draft board and volunteered for the army. Not taking the usual seven days' leave, he reported for examination and was driven that day by bus to Detroit.

After basic training, he was transferred back to Detroit, to Rouge Park, and into a Military Police post, where he stayed until 1943. During that time Ciullo went AWOL for short periods of time because he was girl crazy. He transferred from there to Fort Sheridan in Illinois, then to Camp Reynolds in Pennsylvania on January 1, 1944. Three months later, he was sent to Camp Kilmer in New Jersey. From there, he sailed for England, arriving in Liverpool on April 1, 1944. That same day he was put aboard a convoy and driven to Manchester, England, where he was assigned to a motor truck company.

A couple of months later, Ciullo was in Sudbury, England, and assigned once again, to his disgust, to another Military Police outfit. The unit remained there for a couple of weeks before the whole outfit was shipped to Southampton in August 1944. Crossing the English Channel, the group arrived at the Omaha beachhead. They stayed for nearly a month, living peacefully in the mud—it rained almost all the time. After finally getting the orders to move forward, they were transferred by convoy to Rennes, France, where they took over an old German army camp to be used as a stockade for American soldiers.

Ciullo spent a couple of weeks in the same stockade for accidentally shooting a 38-mm English police pistol while on guard duty. In Rennes, he spent much of his time chasing the young French girls and being in uniform without

14. The Lola Murder

getting into much trouble, except for contracting gonorrhea. He did not exactly fit in this unit and subsequently was transferred to the 19th Replacement Depot for reassignment.

On December 6, Ciullo was picked up by the Military Police in Paris without a pass and put into the straggler Cage, then sent back to his unit. Five days later, he was AWOL for three days. Again arrested in Paris, he was returned to his unit. A week later, Ciullo caught a train to Paris and went to Place d'Italie, where he met a blond girl by the name of Odette. He returned to his unit, but the following night returned to Paris. Odette started talking to him about joining a gang. Ciullo responded that he wanted to think it over. That same night, he went back to the 19th Replacement Depot, thought it over, got his clothes, and went AWOL again on December 23, 1944.

Ciullo returned to Place d'Italie and told Odette that he wanted to join the gang. She then took him to an apartment at 63 Rue Baudricourt, where he met an American soldier nicknamed Hal (real first name Harold). He also was introduced to Hal's girlfriend Jacqueline, another American soldier named Joe, and a second French girl named Eileen. Hal asked Odette what Ciullo was doing there; she replied that Ciullo wanted to join this gang. When Hal asked Ciullo if he was AWOL, the latter responded that, as of that night, he was.

Hal was Harold Bell, 27 years old, an AWOL soldier from the 3rd Replacement Depot, Mortain, France. He had deserted his company five months previously on August 29, 1944. Traveling to Paris, he set up a business focused on obtaining and selling gasoline. A few days after arriving in the city, he began living with Jacqueline Cuegnez. Hal obtained trucks for hauling gasoline by pimping truck drivers such as James I. Suggs.

Suggs had the ideal job for the Parisian part-time black market. He drove a truck full of U.S. mail from the port city of Le Havre to Paris, a trip of 120 miles. He would normally finish the deliveries by 3 p.m. and was scheduled to stay overnight in nearby Saint Cloud. As long as he was back in Le Havre the next morning by 9 a.m., however, no questions were asked. In essence, he had 17 hours to use the truck in the ways that benefited him most. Several times, while working with Hal, Suggs had used the truck to travel to nearby fuel depots and obtain gasoline for the privilege of sleeping with a girl provided by Hal and Jacqueline.

When Ciullo arrived on December 23, Hal was in bed recuperating from an appendix operation. The group sat around until Christmas day, when they were invited to a French couple's house for dinner. That afternoon Jacqueline came back and said that she had located an American truck. Hal then asked her where. "Down at the Café Georgette, 67 Rue Baudricourt," she said. Hal was suspicious and put a revolver in his shirt and they went down to the café.

Hal started talking to an African American soldier who said his name was Suggs; Hal knew him by the name of Jackson, as he had previously used his truck. They discussed Suggs's identity and Hal suggested a place to hide his truck. Suggs was distrustful because of the questioning regarding his identity, so Hal suggested that he would stay with him at the café to ensure there would be no tricks, with Ciullo taking the truck to a French garage. Jacqueline had promised Suggs to get a girl for him in exchange for letting the gang use his truck.

The day after Christmas, Jacqueline brought a girl named Lola Alfreda Cartier to the apartment. Thus the group of Hal, Jacqueline, Suggs, Ciullo and Lola were present at 67 Rue Baudricourt. Suggs and Lola had intercourse as Ciullo shared the bed with them. The next day around one o'clock in the afternoon, Lola told Suggs that she didn't want to see him again.

Later Suggs, Hal and Ciullo took the truck out of the garage and drove 85 miles northwest to the port city of Rouen. They returned to Paris with 150 jerricans of gasoline and parked the truck in the French garage; they then returned to the apartment. The Frenchman who owned the garage sold the gasoline. After they got their money, Jacqueline went to see Madame Georgette, who owned the café they frequented, to see if any rooms were available. Jacqueline came back and told them she had the rooms.

In two days' time, Ciullo fell madly in love with Lola. He rented one room with Lola, and Hal and Jacqueline took another room. Joe, (another member of the gang) and Suggs shared a third room. By now Jack and another unidentified American soldier had joined the gang. Shortly thereafter, Joe, Suggs and Ciullo returned to Rouen and returned with 300 cans of gasoline. Through lots of double-talk with members of his unit, Suggs managed to keep his post as a truck driver and stayed out of trouble in regard to being AWOL.

On January 16, Mama Russky (Madam Vissokinsky) came into Ciullo and Lola's room. Ciullo he asked Mama Russky if she could buy a radio for him. She stated that she and Lola would purchase the radio the following morning. They had supper and, as Ciullo was taking shots from a French doctor for another case of gonorrhea, he had to wash himself with very hot water and use a purple disinfectant on and around his penis. Around 11:30 p.m., he got in bed, turned over, and went to sleep.

The next morning, January 17, 1945, around 9:30 a.m. when they woke up, Ciullo asked Lola if she was going with Mama Russky to buy the radio. She said she would, but didn't want to go right away. Ciullo reached up on the wall to turn the light switch on, but it did not work: The electricity was off from eight o'clock in the morning until noon. He then reached under the pillow and pulled out a German P.38 to play with it as he always did. The pistol contained a full clip but an empty chamber. Ciullo pointed it around the room, sighting

14. The Lola Murder

along the barrel at different objects and pretended to shoot the weapon. While he was doing this, an old man, Martin Vissokinsky, who cleaned up the apartment, walked in to start a fire in the fireplace. The old man had seen Ciullo dozens of times with the pistol playing this same mindless game, but this morning he told Ciullo harshly in French to put down the pistol—that something would happen.

Being a beginner at the language of French, a somewhat arrogant person of nineteen in the uniform of the United States, and a proud descendant of Italians, Ciullo replied that nothing would happen. The old man turned to make the fire. All the while, Ciullo was wondering what had started Vissokinsky's outburst. Abstractly and without conscious thought, he pulled back the extractor of the pistol, letting it fall down upon his left arm while he was lying on his back. As his hand hit his arm, Ciullo felt a slight jar and heard the loud report of a pistol going off. Lola, who was on Ciullo's left side and was lying on her right side with arms folded, received the bullet that shouldn't have been fired in her forehead. Ciullo leapt from the bed, frightened to the core of his being. He yanked open the door and ran out into the hall to the small courtyard, yelling, "I shot Lola; I killed Lola."

Ciullo ran into Hal's door and almost went through it. Hal said, "What's the matter? Calm down, take it easy." Ciullo told him, "I shot Lola." Hal asked him where. Ciullo said, "In the head." Hal then came back with Ciullo to the apartment. He looked at Lola and told Ciullo to get his clothes on.

Hal said, "We're getting the hell out of here."

Ciullo went back to the room, opened the door, and got a small cardboard box, which he put all of his possessions in. He went to the coat that was hanging on the wall with Lola's belongings, reached into the pocket, and pulled out two small wallets. He then went back to Hal's room and told him that he had everything. Hal looked through the two small wallets, finding one 5,000-franc note and two 200-franc notes. He searched everything else in this wallet but couldn't find anything except pictures of American soldiers. He threw Lola's identification card and the American pictures into the stove. Hal picked up the two suitcases that belonged to him. Ciullo picked up his box, and the pair went back downstairs to the front of the café. Ciullo put the box down, went into the café, gave the key to the owner, and told her they wouldn't be back all day.

The old man, Martin Vissokinsky, did not report the shooting? Not seeing Lola Alfred Cartier, café owner Georgette Cleyet went upstairs to her room, noticing that the light was on. It was about 5 p.m. After calling Lola and receiving no answer, she opened the door with a latch key and found the young woman dead on her bed. Cleyet immediately called her neighbor, Mr. Villars, and told him what she had seen; he phoned the French police.

Inspector Joseph Tavernier was dispatched to the scene of the crime at 67 Rue Baudricourt. There, he found Cartier dead on her bed, covered in her own blood. The wound to her head had most likely been created by a round object. He observed that Cartier seemed to be about 22 years old, had been living for a short time in a furnished room looking onto a yard, and had previously resided at 25 Rue Beranger at Fontainebleau. The hotel keeper told him that Cartier used to keep company with some American soldiers.

Tavernier questioned Georgette Cleyet, the 25-year-old acting housekeeper, who declared:

> This young woman is my tenant since the first of January. She came with a friend of hers named Jacqueline Cuegnez. Around the end of 1944, both of them asked for a room. Since this date they have each had one room on the third block looking on a yard: on the first floor Mademoiselle Cartier on the left corridor and Mademoiselle Cuegnez on the left. These two persons did not work; they lived from prostitution with the American soldiers.
>
> Mademoiselle Cuegnez never had any money, but her friend on the contrary had a lot, showing it to everyone and changing always big notes at the counter of my café. I must tell you that I have not seen Mademoiselle Cuegnez the whole day. As for Mademoiselle Cartier, I cannot say when I saw her for the last time.
>
> Signed after reading,
> S/S Cleyet

Inspector Joseph Tavernier then went into the victim's room. Here is his report:

> This room is situated in the third block on the yard, first floor on the left. We go in the room, 3 meters by 3. There is a lot of disorder and blood is on the floor. There is an iron bed, a table and two stools. The bed is on the left of the entrance. On the bed is the body of a young woman, aged 25 years, looking as if she was sleeping on her right side, the arm folded and the hand under the head. The left arm is along the body. She is normally covered with the sheet and blanket. The head is weltering in blood and has between the two eyes a wound of one centimeter just above the base of the nose, bleeding and surrounded with powder. The body is still warm and the rigidity is not complete. Everything seems to indicate that she has been killed during her sleep by shot at close range and that death was instantaneous. Under the bed we discovered a pair of shoes (American ones). On the table, the end of a meal, two plates, two glasses, three forks. Near the table, two stools, on one of them a book written in English. At the foot of this stool, the casing of the bullet that certainly killed the person, caliber 9 mm. The drawers of

Opposite, top: Jacqueline Cuegnez, a friend of Lola, lived across the courtyard in this messy room with her American lover. **Opposite, bottom:** The scene of the death of Alfreda Cartier, also known as Lola. The young, attractive Parisian prostitute was shot in the center of her forehead by a jealous, hot-headed, 19-year-old American soldier.

14. The Lola Murder

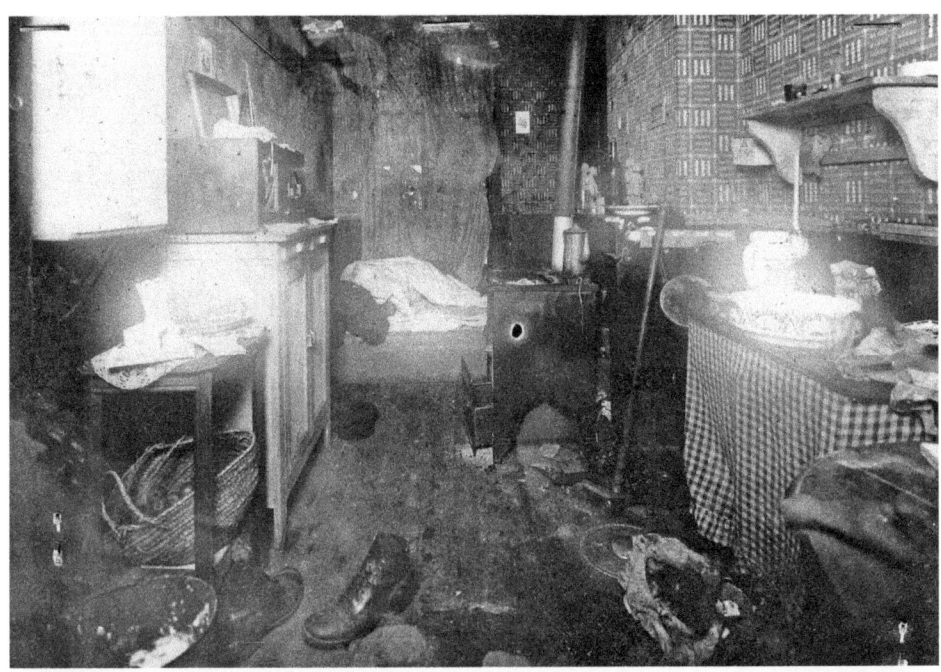

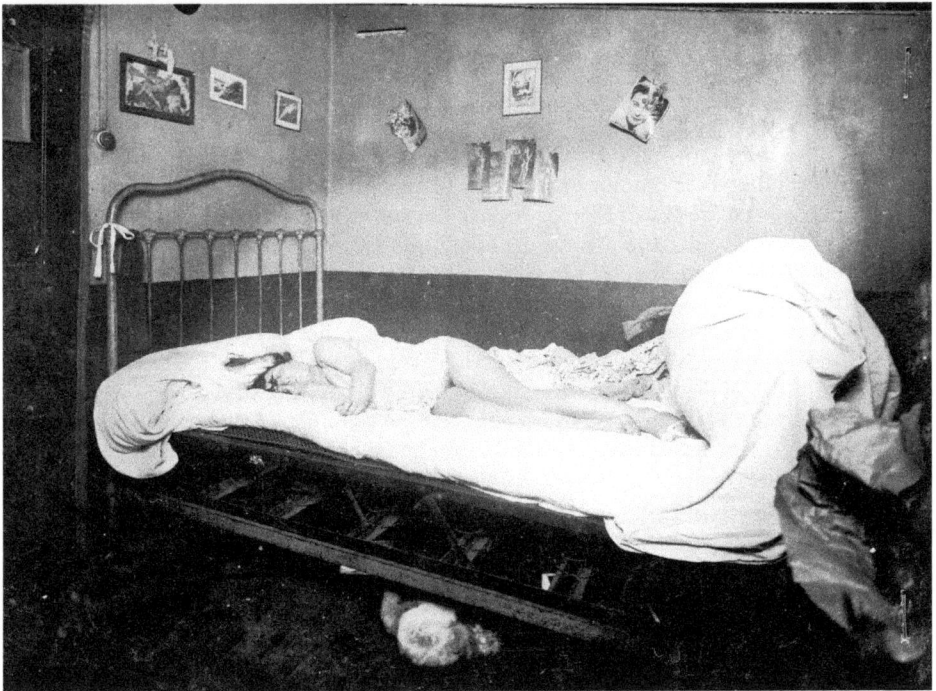

the sideboard have been searched; near the sideboard is a washbowl with colored red water (blood), where it seems the murderer washed his hands.

On the mantle we found a letter written by the victim, addressed to Mr. Jean Clavier, 21 Rue Ferrare, Fontainbleu, dated January 16, 1945, and in which she is asking for a revolver. It seems she fears something. We have been looking in vain for her identity, her bag, and money belonging to the victim, according to her landlord. It appears that theft is the motive of the crime.

Following our investigation, we ask to be taken in her friend's room. This room is situated in the same block, on the same floor, but on the right at the end of the corridor. Coming into the room we notice that the door is not closed and there is disorder inside, as if someone wanted to leave in a hurry.

The room is furnished with a bed, a table, two chairs, one sideboard and a stove for cooking. On the bed we discovered a little pink tablecloth with blood stains belonging to the victim's room. We also saw on the chimney the same cloth. In a corner of the room, we saw stained with blood a cap and two pairs of khaki pants in such as the Allied soldiers wear. The distinguishing mark and escutcheon of the cap have been torn off and burned in the stove with some other papers. We have been able to recover two buttons stamped with an American eagle and a piece of leather. On the mantle there are three glasses and a bottle with a little wine in it. The key of the room is found abandoned on a piece of furniture. On the table we found a little bit of oilcloth.

We went out leaving a policeman to keep the place intact until the judiciary authority arrived. We advised by telegram the attorney of the Republic, the police prefect, and the interested services of our administration.

Following this investigation, police obtained a statement from Michel Villars, born in 1900 in Paris, a rag dealer living at 67 Rue Baudricourt:

I live in a room on the first floor of the building at 67 Rue Baudricourt, on the same landing as the room of the victim, Mademoiselle Alfred Cartier. Our door is just opposite the one of this person. We did not know each other. This woman used to receive day and night some Allied soldiers, white and black, and was living from prostitution. She had a friend, a white soldier who used to take his meals with her and went away only when she had customers.

This pretend couple seemed to get on very well; they never quarreled and were always laughing. The day before the crime, Wednesday the 17th, we did not see her for the whole day at her friend's domicile. This day she stayed alone and went out only in the evening. We heard her come back around 23:00 hours. She was with many men; we were in bed and I cannot say how many there were or when they came. We heard all these persons play and laugh until midnight, but nothing after, not even someone going out.

We went to our work at a quarter past 7 in the morning and came back at 10. Everything seemed normal. We stayed in our room until 18:00 hours, but then came out at the call of Madame Cleyet, the proprietor, who had just discovered the body of Mademoiselle Alfred Cartier.

I approached and noticed my neighbor, whose head was weltering in her blood. I did nothing else.... I went home after the police assistance had been called.

14. The Lola Murder

Earlier that day, when Ciullo had left 67 Rue Baudricourt, while going out the door he looked for Hal, Jacqueline, and Jack. They were halfway down the street, so he picked up his box of clothes and ran after them. They got onto a metro car and went to the Montparnasse railroad station. Hal told Jacqueline to get some tickets for Cherbourg. She came back and said that there were no trains for Cherbourg. Hal told Jacqueline to get tickets for anyplace; he just wanted to get out of Paris. She finally got tickets for Le Mans, 130 miles west. Hal had told Ciullo to throw the gun away, but he responded "no" when asked whether he had done so. On the train, they met a Frenchman. Jacqueline got into a conversation with him and asked about places near Le Mans to stay for the night. The man suggested a small town called la Ferte-Bernard, 27 miles away from Le Mans.

The group arrived in that town about five o'clock and went to a hotel across from the railroad station. They stayed there for the night, got up at seven o'clock in the morning, caught the 7:30 train out of la Ferte-Bernard, and continued to Le Mans. Walking down the platform at the railroad station, they spotted two MPs. They about-faced and went the other way. Jacqueline was sent to find out when there was a train to Cherbourg, but there was no train bound for that city.

Hal told her to get tickets back to la Ferte-Bernard. The group got back on the train and returned to the town, but went to a different hotel. They stayed there almost a week.

Ciullo was visiting Hal's room on the first floor and talking with Jacqueline, Hal, and Raymond, a Frenchman who had joined them. Ciullo looked out the window and saw three MPs, two French policemen, and one French civilian who spoke English. Hal locked the door, then went over to the window and opened it. Hal looked out the window and, as nobody was in sight, jumped out first. Jacqueline went second, and Ciullo followed. Hal and Ciullo ran out of town to a farm. As they were standing by a creek, a woman yelled out of her window and asked what we were doing. Hal tried to tell her in French. She couldn't understand, so Ciullo told her in French that their truck was in the garage in town getting repaired and the Military Police were after them. The woman told them to come up to the house. Her husband met the pair and took them into the house; they stayed there from about 11:30 a.m. until 7:00 p.m.

Jacqueline found out where the two men were and came to the house with the farm woman and the Frenchman Raymond. They told Hal and Ciullo to get out of the house because the Military Police were coming. They ran over a little bridge across the creek, down a side street along the creek, and back into the middle of town. They kept going down the main street until they came to a bridge. While hiding under the bridge, Raymond looked back to see if they were being followed. Raymond now had Hal's gun. Ciullo asked Jacqueline where his gun was; Jacqueline replied that she had thrown it out the window. When Ciullo asked her why, Hal told him that it was a hot gun. Ciullo told Hal he didn't give a damn if it was a hot gun—he wanted that gun. Hal asked Ciullo why, but was rebuked that it was none of his business.

The group left the bridge and traveled about six miles to the town of St. Germaine-de-la-Coudre. Hal stayed there one night and returned to Paris. Ciullo stayed two nights and returned the next day as he was sick from his sexually transmitted disease. When Ciullo got back to Paris, the Military Police picked him up for going AWOL, unaware that he was wanted for murder, and sent him back to the 19th Replacement Depot. On January 31, 1945, the military authorities in Paris were notified that Ciullo was in the stockade at the 19th Depot; they ordered that he be transferred to the Paris Detention Barracks. Placed in a death row cell, from February 1 to March 15, Ciullo did not see anyone except two CID agents who wanted him to point out the other members of his gang.

On March 16, 1945, Lieutenant Reardon introduced himself as Ciullo's defense attorney. He had been appointed as Ciullo's counsel that morning and had come over to see if they could construct some sort of defense, as the trial would begin tomorrow.

The next day, Ciullo was taken to court and his trial began, with at least eighteen witnesses prepared to testify against him. Ciullo testified that he was in bed playing with his pistol and that Lola had told him to point the gun at her as she was not afraid of it. He did and accidentally shot her. The old man, Martin Vissokinsky, testified Lola was asleep when he came into the room. Most damaging was Suggs's testimony: "She told me Jerry [Ciullo] was mad at her and Jerry said he was going to shoot her."

In a 1953 appeal Ciullo wrote:

> There were two pictures taken of the body at a horizontal position that did not show depth in the picture to substantiate my truthful plea that I was in bed when the shooting happened.

Ciullo's last statement during the trial follows:

> PRESIDENT: Is there anything further you want to tell the court, Private Ciullo?
> WITNESS: Yes, sir, at the time that I shot this Lola, I wasn't positive if she was asleep or not, but she had her eyes closed. That's all.

The court ruled there was malice in the murder, as shown by the evidence that Ciullo argued and slapped Lola about two weeks before the murder, failed to summon medical aid after the shooting, and immediately fled the scene. Ciullo received a sentence of a dishonorable discharge, total forfeitures, and confinement to hard labor for life at the U.S. penitentiary in Lewisburg, Pennsylvania. In 1963, Ciullo was serving his time in the Fort Leavenworth prison in Kansas.

On April 18, 1945, Private Harold Bell, 32228342, was apprehended in Paris by members of the Military Police. He was dressed in civilian clothing, including black slippers. On June 12, 1945, he was found guilty of desertion and sentenced to dishonorable discharge, total forfeitures, and confinement to hard labor for life at the U.S. penitentiary in Lewisburg, Pennsylvania. Jacqueline Cuegnez was called to testify against Bell, but objected on the grounds she was his common-law wife.[1]

Arrested during one of these searches for the AWOL soldiers was Pfc. William Stribling. He had entered the service on June 7, 1943, at Fort Benning, Georgia, and later shipped overseas with the 656th Ordinance Ammunitions Company. After he "got hurt in a village that the Germans were counter-attacking" in France, he was hospitalized for two months and then assigned to a replacement depot. On May 4, 1945, Bill Stribling went AWOL from the 178th Reinforcement Company at Marburg, Germany. His destination was Paris, where he remained for 90 days prior to being apprehended by Corporal Leo Steinbrenner of the Military Police on August 6, 1945. Stribling was dressed in a combination of semi-military and civilian clothing, and Steinbrenner suspected him of being a long-term AWOL suspect when he approached him at 8:00 pm. Stribling had a fake pass and forged travel orders, but no dog tags or other identification. Within three months he was sent back in Marburg, Germany. He tried and court-martialed on November 7, 1945, for being AWOL, but not for any illegal activity in Paris. Would Stribling be so lucky again? We will meet him again in a later chapter.

15

The 2nd Battalion, 38th Infantry Regiment

During Clark and Reybold's confinement and the Machine Records Unit move into Paris, the port city of Brest was captured. The 2nd Infantry Division then took a complete reverse turn with the destination of St. Vith, Belgium. Second Lieutenant Charles D. Gurley, along with the 1,200 men of the 2nd Battalion, 38th Infantry Regiment, however, were relieved from the 2nd Battalion and assigned duty in Paris.

After a long 370-mile ride, Gurley and the officers of the 2nd Battalion were trucked to the Hotel Select on the corner of Rue de Charles and Rue de Cévennes. Here they had nice amenities with meals served in the hotel restaurant. The food was supplied by the U.S. Army Quartermaster Corps. The battalion headquarters was housed in a five-story mansion two blocks from the Eiffel Tower. The enlisted men were billeted in the Vincennes section, and all the men in the battalion had comfortable, soft beds with sheets. They did not know why they were pulled from combat and assigned to Paris until the 2nd Battalion officers met with an officer from Supreme Headquarters Allied Forces Europe (SHAFE), who told the assembled men that the trains were being raided as they approached and traveled through Paris. A large percentage of the cigarettes, food and PX supplies loaded at Cherbourg disappeared before they arrived at the army depot at Huy and Charleroi, Belgium. The officers were told that the soldiers of the 2nd Battalion were to ride the trains and shoot anyone who tried to take as much as a pack of cigarettes from the train.

After the breakthrough in Normandy, the army's concern with rolling supplies forward was so great that no one bothered much about policing the supply lines. Now they had to take action, because in September, October and November of 1944, GIs both at the front and in Paris were talking about the great cigarette mystery. Back in the United States, people were told that they had to go

15. The 2nd Battalion, 38th Infantry Regiment

without cigarettes because the men at the front were getting them. At the front and in the rear echelons in France, however, the shortage was so acute that the official cigarette rations were curtailed or suspended altogether.

The situation was so grave on the homefront that the U.S. Senate held a hearing on the matter and summoned the executives of the tobacco industry to Room 315 of the Senate Office Building. The senators and their important guest all smoked, and it did not take long for a layer of gray haze to fog the wall mirrors, obscure the windows, and dim the light of the 100-bulb candelabra. One concern: The people who wanted to start smoking could not, "because cigarettes are hard to get."[1] The tobacco executives responded they were producing 2.8 times more cigarettes now than nine years previously in 1935. When the hearing ended, a pretty secretary put down her cigarette and opened a window.

Of the 4.2 billion packs of cigarettes ordered by the U.S. Army and Navy in 1944, 77 million packs per month were slated for European distribution. According U.S. Army authorities, only 11 million packs, or 14 percent, reached their destination during any 30-day period.[2] One does not have to be a genius to figure out that 9.46 million packs of cigarettes were stolen and sold on the black market in France in one month alone. With a retail value of $2 per pack, the soldiers who stole the cigarettes surely received a $1 per pack, for a profit of $9.46 million—a fortune, considering that the average soldier was then making less than $800 per year.

At the same time, in French bars, cafés, hotels and other public places, plenty of civilians were smoking popular brands of American cigarettes. In Paris, you could buy for $2 a pack of U.S. cigarettes that had been intended for PX sale at $0.05 per pack. The whole cigarette situation became the subject of gags on the French stage and a general topic of conversation in all levels of society.

Gurley and his men of Company E were assigned the responsibility for guarding the trains from Argenteuil Rail Yard at Versailles to Vaugirard Rail Yard, near Montparnasse, on the left bank of the Seine in Paris, a distances of 14 miles. The 716th Railway Operating Battalion was accountable for the railroad traffic from Cherbourg to the army depots in Belgium, a route of 400 miles. Gurley reported to the lieutenant colonel in charge of this unit. He was seeking accommodations for three of his men at the Vaugirard Rail Yard, for that was the assigned number of men to ride a train for guard duty. In a loud and commanding voice, the lieutenant colonel demanded to know what he was doing there and raised hell that Gurley's men would interfere with his operation. He also told Gurley he did not have any rooms or buildings they could use.

When the slow-moving trains entered Paris, civilians would hop on and start throwing off cases of food—mostly 10-in-1 rations, or one field ration prepared for 10 soldiers for a day. The soldiers of Company E just out of combat had no problem shooting the French civilians, which soon put a stop to that type of pillaging. Yet the hottest items, cigarettes, continued to disappear. Gurley had a particular interest in the cigarette supply because his company had gone without cigarettes for two weeks while in Brittany.

The soldiers of the 2nd Battalion rode the trains three at a time, while working three days on and two days off. On one of his days off, Gurley and two of his officer friends from the Deep South were walking up the Champs-Elysées. As they approached the Arch de Triomphe, they passed a most distinguished black man dressed in a long black coat and wearing a Homburg hat. He was escorting a beautiful blond young lady who had a white Russian wolfhound on a leash. One of his southern friends stopped in his tracks, expressing the view that he had now seen everything. While the man was still making loud derogatory remarks, Gurley grabbed him and pushed him up the sidewalk.

A large number of African French soldiers hung around the outer perimeter of the Vaugirard Rail Yard in a small wooded area. They always had a large quantity of American cigarettes, and Gurley knew their support had to be coming from the American soldiers working there, but could never catch them. He noticed some freight cars were riding high on their springs as they entered the yard. This was an indication they were empty, yet Gurley knew that these cars had left the beach ports of Normandy full of cigarettes.

Late one evening, Gurley was watching a train coming into the yard and noticed someone running beside it. The runner had opened the door, cut open a mail bag, and was pulling out the packages and dropping them on the ground. Gurley stepped out and fired his Luger; at that close range he could not miss, and the runner fell wounded to the ground. Gurley called for the Military Police. As they left with the wounded man in a jeep, the man yelled something to his friends in the woods.

Later, one of the American railroad men stopped by to talk with Lieutenant Gurley. In darkness, the man left the site. He was found later in a ditch barely alive, with multiple knife wounds. Gurley knew immediately that the railroad man had been mistaken for him! The next morning he gave orders to shoot any trespassers. The guards even began shooting over the heads of the African French soldiers in the wooded area to run them off. After a few days, the foreign soldiers disappeared from the area.

The good life in Paris had to end, and after a 40-day stay the men of the 2nd Battalion were told they would be leaving Paris on November 11, 1944.

After a night of hell raising and a few fights, the soldiers loaded up in rough-looking 40-and-8 railroad cars (built for 8 horses or 40 men) and began traveling north to join their parent unit, the 2nd Infantry Division. Lieutenant Gurley and his men never figured out how the lieutenant colonel at the Vaugirard Rail Yard had a large French car and French chauffeur, but someone else would.[3]

16

THE MILLION-DOLLAR BATTALION

Cigarettes and whiskey and wild wild women / they will drive you crazy / they will drive you insane.—Lyrics from a country song of that era that was popular in both English and French

The railway system in France provided some 26,417 miles of single and double tracks. The concentration of lines led from the major ports to the center of France, forming a well-defined railroad transportation system. Prior to the heavy Allied bombing inflicted on the rail yards, the operating and repair facilities were adequate to meet all of the needs of the French population. Every road crossing had a small house for the gatekeeper (generally a man), his wife, and small children who ran out and waved as the train passed.

During their four-year occupation of France, the German military forces requisitioned many of the French lines, especially those in the English Channel section—that is, the northern part of the country directly across from England. The railway lines and equipment had been overworked by the Germans during this time, and maintenance had been neglected. Owing to their strategic value, the French rail centers, yards, junctions and critical points had been the targets for Allied bombings for two years prior to the D-Day invasion. Because of the pattern of German train operations and subsequent destruction by aerial bombing, the rail lines in a great circle around Paris, particularly to the west and at critical points, were badly damaged.

Actual work on the rehabilitation of the railway system of France began after the capture of Cherbourg on June 28, 1944, when the Second Military Railway Service began reconstruction of the waterfront installation using French civilian labor. The first rolling stock arrived in Cherbourg on July 10, consisting of one diesel locomotive and ten flat cars. It was followed by a train ferry carrying the first of 1,521 locomotives and 19,383 freight cars, whose number included box cars, gondolas, flat cars, tank cars, refrigerator cars and cabooses from England.

The first Railway Operating Battalion, the 729th, arrived on July 11. Nine days later, it was operating a short railway line to Carentan and Lison. That day, July 20, the 720 Railway Operating Battalion arrived and took over operation of that rail line. The train initially carried only American soldiers forward and returned with civilian evacuees to the Cherbourg peninsula. However, after the breakthrough at St. Lo on July 26, the rehabilitation and immediate availability of the railway services was a matter of major importance.

During their retreat, the Germans had destroyed rail bridges, tunnels, fuel and water facilities. It was assumed that they would destroy the wooden ties with a "track ripper," a large metal plow connected to the back of a heavy cargo car pulled by a locomotive that ripped and broke every wooden tie. This was not done, however, so no long lengths of track had to be replaced. Thus, while the repair of railroads during the first two months of Allied military operation was given priority, the greatest problem was the repair of destroyed railway bridges.

The first major haul of the Second Military Railway Service took place on August 15, when 31 trains were loaded with high-priority supplies for use of the Third Army, which was approaching Paris from the southwest. At that time General George Patton ordered gasoline, rations, ammunition, and medical supplies to be moved from the beaches to a supply dump at Le Mans, where Third Army trucks would pick them up and deliver the supplies to the fighting troops. The advance of his army during the first two weeks of August had been so rapid that the reconstruction of the railway had been unable to keep pace.

Within the Transportation Corps in Europe was the Second Military Railway Service; reporting to the Second were five Railway Grand Divisions, 706th through 710th. Each Division had four Railway Operating Battalions and one Railway Shop Battalion. The strength of the Second Military Railway Service was 763 officers and 16,763 enlisted men. Within the 709 Railway Grand Division was the 716th Railway Operating Battalion, one of the 20 battalions within the Second Military Railway Service. This unit would prove to be a major embarrassment to the other battalions.[1]

On the day Private Clarence Whitfield was executed in Normandy, the men of the 716th Railway Operating Battalion were crossing the Atlantic Ocean on their way to the Normandy coast. The unit had been activated on December 21, 1943, at Fort Sam Houston, Texas. The cadre for the battalion consisted of former railroad men from the Southern Pacific Railroad. They were a few years older than the average World War II soldier, with their ages spanning the late 30s to the mid-40s.

A railway bridge destroyed by Allied bombing in France.

The battalion consisted of four companies. Headquarters Company handled administrative duties, supply, rations and food, and selection and replacement of personnel. Company A provided the maintenance and structure of the railroad. Repairing railroad bridges, installing switches, bulldozing mud, and excavations were all part of their duties. Company B repaired the locomotives and railcars; it also operated the roundhouses and shops along the rail line. Company C provided the engineers, firemen, conductors, brakemen, yardmasters, switchmen and crew dispatchers—the men who managed the actual functions of the trains. Their mission was to speed supplies and ammunition to Allied troops for the destruction of the enemy.

The men of the 716th got their first look at Omaha Beach on the afternoon of August 26, 1944, when they were offloaded to LST 50 feet below. The ride to the beach seemed long and they grew bored, looking at the hundreds of ships that had been scuttled to create the unnatural harbor that made the D-Day landings possible. Their mountains of duffle bags and equipment were piled onto a steel pier. Every man was fully armed, but not a round of ammunition had been issued to the soldiers. About an hour after their outfit landed,

16. The Million-Dollar Battalion

the men in Company C helped themselves to boned turkey and 10-in-1s at the ration dump because no other provision for their eating had been made.

They remained on the beach in the rain for two days. Then, August 29, they were trucked to the nearest rail point and loaded onto railcars. The train whistled off to Chartres, in the middle of a string of 23 trains going in the same direction. En route, they supplemented their issued K-rations with 10-in-1s and cigarettes taken from trains on the sidings. They passed through St. Lo and other cities that had seen plenty of destruction; traveling only five miles that day, they had plenty of time for sightseeing. The snail's pace continued and they reached Chartres in the late afternoon. The duffle bags were unloaded and the men marched through an underpass headed to a warehouse for a much needed rest. During the march, however, their orders were changed and they were sent back to the train, reloaded, and sent on their way. At dawn the following morning, the battalion arrived in Dreux, ending a five-day trip that in peacetime was a five-hour journey. The old French town of Dreux was to be headquarters for the 716th Railway Operating Battalion.

In a gray dawn that made the battered and windowless ghost-like Dreux station look all the more ghostly, the men stretched as they weaved their way among heaps of duffle bags over to a French engine where the engineer obligingly let them fill their helmets with hot water. Some shaved, some washed, and some just looked at the yard and wondered if they would ever get the mess cleared out.

In charge of this massive cleanup was Captain William P. Olson, 47-year-old Commander of Company C and Trainmaster. Olson had been a corporal in the infantry in World War I. When he entered the army in 1943, he had been employed by Southern Pacific Railroad as superintendent of the San Francisco terminal. In fact, Southern Pacific largely furnished the officers who served in the 716th Railway Battalion. Olson had been informed that there was a vacancy as commanding officer of Company C and, after discussing the matter with his wife, he volunteered for the position. After induction, Olson went to Fort Sam Houston, Texas, where he received training in the army way of operating a railway.

Ninety days later, he was in France answering his men's questions. Where's the roundhouse? Wonder if they have any engines? When do we eat? Where we going to live? While dozens of questions went unanswered, Olson looked the yard over and wondered if this was what he had volunteered for, wartime railroading. Now that he had a job on his hands, what must be done first? The yards looked bad: He needed a couple of mains and a half-dozen auxiliary tracks.

First Lieutenant John W. Springer, a yardmaster for Southern Pacific at

The marshalling yards at Dreux destroyed by Allied bombing.

Sparks, Nevada, and General Yardmaster for the unit, made a hurried survey of the yard. The main tracks looked good, but Company A would have to get on the ball if the junk was to be moved out and the yard made serviceable. Better get a switch engine in there "pretty pronto," he concluded.

Meanwhile, Road Foreman of Engines, Lieutenant Norris E. Loop, an engineer from Rock Island, Kansas, was "casing" the roundhouse, seeing how many engines might be available. It didn't look too good but the men in Company B were reliable.

Fall in! The soldier-railroaders were reluctant and stiff and sore and tired from the five-day trip from the beachhead. They wanted to start railroading, not deal with this army stuff? But fall in they did, with full field packs tugging again at weary shoulders. Up the hill they went, only to wait while the amateur booby-trap "experts" checked the building. A rush for rooms ensued. Everyone finally gravitated into quarters, albeit perhaps not always to their liking. While the group was cleaning up after the Germans, there was also a "chow" call.

Speculation ran high as to when operations would start and who would be on the first crew. "Say, there's a big bridge out here that's got the mainline to Paris tied up. Is that where we run? Here I come, Gay Paree!" "Yeah, and there's another route, a single track line. Looks like we'll use that first. Guess we're stuck here for a while."

But they weren't stuck. Word was sent up the hill that a five-man switching crew would be needed soon to start clearing the yard. There was no reluctance on the men's part to work; rather, they vied with one another to see who would get on the job first.

The test train left Dreux at 10:45 p.m. The whole crew had been over the road before, but only while cramped up in a dark box car, so they didn't know an inch of the road. There was no headlight. Even in peacetime, the French operated without headlights, and those who constructed GI locomotives followed the French custom. In any event, a headlight was a bit too conspicuous in those days. To know where the train was, the crew had to catch the name of the station with a flashlight as they went by. Even that was not much help, though, because the names of French towns meant nothing to them. The important thing was not to go by Chartres and tangle up with something.

Finally the test train reached Chartres at 3:00 a.m.—too much time, but it was only the first trip. The water was low, much too low. "Where's that French pilot? Where's the water spout? Uncouple the engine; we'll have to kill the fire." So ended the first trip: The railroaders were at work.

At Dreux, order of a sort soon emerged from the confusion. While First Sergeant Anderson was having billeting troubles, Tec 4 Constantino J. Lovecchio, the crew dispatcher, began to line up crews for possible movement. A yard office was set up in the Dreux station; Company C was open for business. There was plenty of business backed up along the line, but first the rails had to be opened to Paris.

While waiting for their first calls, the train and engine crews made their quarters as comfortable as possible. They set up stoves and got pieces of furniture here and there. The French people were more than friendly, fresh vegetables were gotten from nearby farms, and women were glad to wash the piles of dirty clothes for a bit of chocolate or a bar of soap. Civilians were in dire want, as the war had been harsh on them and the Germans had taken much from them.

The crew on the test train at Chartres and the one that followed were to be the first members of the 716th to hit Paris. During their time off in Paris, they were called to go to Chartres for a train whose cargo consisted of gasoline and ammunition (later found to be strictly against the rules). At Dreux, Captain Olson told them not to stop, but rather to go on to Paris via Maintenon. While making a switch at Maintenon, Gory flagged a gasoline train that was following and that remained in the block. A few hours later, that train was plowed into by another, with the wreckage tying up the line for some 36 hours. (Neither train was run by a 716th crew.) At about seven in the morning of September 4, the precious load of gas and ammunition arrived in Paris. Later, there was a friendly dispute as to which 716th crew actually got to Paris first.

On September 8, the Dreux bridge was finally completed and eastbound loads started over the main track to Paris. The single track line via Maintenon thereafter was used for the movement of westbound empties. It was also used for other movements when the main line was tied up by wrecks.

The trains successfully hauled bombs, ammunition, gas, pontoons, engineering and signal equipment, and rations. On those first runs the men did not have food issued to them, so they helped themselves to the loads they were carrying. According to later testimony, when one of the men asked the battalion commander what would be done about food, the major replied, in effect, "You're carrying stuff; it's your own fault if you go hungry." Later, organized messes were established and the men were regularly supplied with personal rations before starting trips—but by that time the habit of opening the rations was too strong to break. It eventually developed into a business so successful that some men began referring to their outfit as the "million-dollar battalion."

For the soldiers of Company C, there was no limit on the number of hours they worked. In hundreds of cases, it took four or more days before they returned to their home terminals. Some swore they "met themselves coming back." While the engineer had the toughest job—feeling his way at times, wondering what might be ahead in the pitch black of night, and praying to God that there would be enough braking power to stop—the other jobs were not easy, either. The fireman, often at the point of exhaustion, had to draw on every ounce of reserve strength to keep the steam up: "We can't get hung up on that hill!" The head brakeman was a second pair of eyes for the engineer and aided the fireman on occasions. The conductor, as skipper, completed his inspections, hoping signals would be seen and obeyed, *parleyed avec* by French tower men and agents in an endeavor to move his train forward. The flagman, flashing his lantern occasionally, moved back a sufficient distance to the rear of his train.

The 716th had its share of accidents and wrecks. A few trains were piled up and burned, along with gasoline and supplies that were direly needed. The A and B companies and everyone else quickly cleared the right of way and put the rails down again, and more trains moved up. There was talk about the wrecks and other things, and the men were quick to learn from the experiences of others. Each mission continued to be a separate adventure and a separate story in the mind of every member of the crew.

The members of the 716th worked efficiently as railroad men, but they quickly became experts in the lucrative black market. Rations and cigarettes were easy to carry away from the trains in barracks bags and easy to sell without lining up buyers ahead of time. The crews of Company C obtained their barracks-bag loads in numerous ways. Because of the blackout, the trains ran without lights, relying on manual signals and a safety-block system to prevent collisions. The simplest looting technique was to break into a train when several were held up at the block for a couple of hours, waiting for signals. The conductor of each train carried a waybill describing the contents of the individual cars, so that it was no trick to determine which cars carried the "sensitive items" and which carried heavy stuff that could not be pilfered or sold easily.

More planning went into the siding of cars for looting purposes. Siding means removing a car from the train and putting it on a sidetrack, where it could be pilfered at leisure (generally at night) by the crew of the train and any others in the know.

MPs were detailed to ride trains not long after the lines went into operation. Their customary place was in the caboose at the whip end of the train. The engineers would stop the train on a bend so that the cars at the head of the train could not be watched by the MPs. Then the crews would loot the head-end cars.

At Veilliers, the watering station between Dreux and Paris, where the engine and tender were supposed to uncouple and turn in for servicing, the crews uncoupled not only the engine and tender but many cars containing "sensitive items." They took these cars into the station for looting, leaving the rest of the train and the MPs 5,000 yards or more outside the station. Sometimes six railroad men would generously don helmet liners and carbines and relieve the MPs. When the MPs had gone, their substitutes would join the crew in the looting.

Meat, coffee, cigarettes, canned goods and alphabetical rations (C and K) were the principal items taken, but there was also some minor traffic in army clothing, blankets, and alcohol taken from the westbound hospital trains. The prices varied somewhat, but the standard black market deal was $500 for a case (50 cartons) of cigarettes, $300 for a 20-pound can of coffee, $300 for a box of 50 D-ration chocolate bars, and $100 for a case of 10-in-1 rations. After completing their Dreux-to-Paris run, the looting soldiers completed their transactions with eager awaiting Frenchmen.

Trains carrying slow freight—jeeps, trucks, signal equipment, heavy weapons, ammunition, and so on—were never pilfered because these items could not be carried away in barracks bags or readily disposed of. Also, the railway men themselves thought of these items as essential war products.

Most Frenchmen on the streets and in the cafés around the yards would buy cigarettes or rations. In turn, business was conducted much more casually than in the case of the gas gangs. Early transactions took place in the streets. Later, when town patrols began to crack down, most of the railway men did their business with Frenchmen in cafés, cabarets, restaurants, cheap hotels and houses of prostitution.

Private Robert L. Cosgrove, Company C, joined the army on December, 27, 1943, at 21 years of age. On his first assignment in France in September 1944, he and two other members of his company took a large PX box containing cigarettes, chewing gum, toilet articles and other items from the train at Dreux. Arriving in Paris, they were billeted in a former schoolhouse. One block from where they were staying, Cosgrove sold the box for $450—more money than he cleared in a year. Cosgrove divided the money with several members of Company C, retaining $80 for himself.

After this first deal, Cosgrove began marketing cigarettes and PX items in the cafés of Paris and to Frenchmen directly from the train along the roadside from Dreux to Paris. On several occasions, he sold large boxes of cigarettes to 31-year-old Tec 4 James E. Lemon, who then resold the goods to the interpreters working at the Batignolles railway yard. Frank Crawfield also sold a considerable amount of cigarettes and 10-in-1 rations to the interpreters. From his deal with Lemon, Cosgrove made $800.

Cosgrove worked on the train as a fireman, shoveling coal into the firebox of the locomotive. At Villiers, he helped 44-year-old Lieutenant Ario D. Dal Porto open a refrigerator car and remove a box containing 50 pounds of beef steak. The lieutenant asked Cosgrove to carry the box to his hotel, which he did. Cosgrove's activities are described by him:

> I want to say at this time the manner of operations of the members of my unit. When a train leaves Dreux, the first thing the conductor does is notify the train crew what the contents of the cars are and determine where the best place would be to take some supplies; after that we take off. At nearly all the stations along the line to Paris, if we stop the operators come out and take things off—mostly food but sometimes cases of cigarettes. I don't know the names of these men but could identify them. I was told about a hotel by Fred Smith [34-year-old Tec 4 Floyd M. Smith] of my organization where he, Cranford [John P. Cranford] and Van Volkenburg had a room and where they would take their duffle bags filled with supplies and sell them to the manager. I believe the name of the hotel is Hotel Selter. It is close to our billets in Paris.... I want to tell of the following acts by members of the 716th Railroad Operating Battalion. It was in the beginning of October at Versailles that I saw Sgt. Pete Bazar take a PX box containing supplies and carry it away. Sgt. Blackburn, who used to be in my room, told me he had sold supplies that he had taken from the train. He always had plenty of money. Sgt. Cranford stays at the hotel I mentioned in Paris.
>
> Sgt. Griffin and myself took off PX boxes containing supplies at Versailles, and then again at Chartes, from the train. On one occasion, Sgt. Paul Hart and myself took two boxes of cigarettes and one box of cigars at the Matelot yards. In September, I saw Sgt. Marker with a barracks bag filled with cigarettes. In September,

16. The Million-Dollar Battalion

Sgt. Stephen Roberts divided with myself and six others three cases of PX boxes.... At one time around the 10th of November, I gave T/4 Lemon 23 cartons of cigarettes and 4 boxes of gum for $250.... T/4 Lemon doesn't gamble much. He told me at one time he had $2,000....

I want to add there is a café about 1½ blocks from the schoolhouse where we are billeted in Paris near Bagatelles Yards, and I have heard an unknown American soldier who is always present at night there make deals for the sale of supplies. He buys from soldiers bringing it from the trains. The café is known as the Bucket of Blood.

I also want to add that around 1st October, I was in Dreux station waiting for orders to leave and saw a soldier known to be Stanley Moreschi, Co. A, 716 R.O.B. [Railroad Operating Battalion]. He was standing on a flat car throwing off cases of coffee to another man standing on the platform. He threw off about 6 to 10 cases.[2]

The Matelot Yard was a switching yard. All trains loaded from Cherbourg or the Normandy beaches were sent to the Matelot Yard. Here the cars were rearranged onto one track with Paris as the destination and onto three different tracks for cargo going to Belgium. It was the supreme location for stealing the government property within the railway cars. So lucrative was this business that Cosgrove had been sending his wife $100 money orders about every other day.

On August 2, 1944, an order had been issued by Headquarters, Transportation Corps, Second Military Railway Service, that assigned the 716th Railway Operating Battalion to the mission of operating and maintaining the military railroad of the United States in France from Chartres as far eastward in the direction of advancing military forces as conditions and circumstances would permit. On September 15, 1944, the battalion was ordered to operate and maintain military railways from Dreux to Versailles and from Versailles to Maintenon, with headquarters sited at Dreux. On September 18, it was directed to operate and maintain military railways from Dreux to and including Paris. On October 23, the following territory was added to the battalion's jurisdiction: east switch Dreux to the last connecting switch east of Valeton, and from Matelot Yard to the last connecting track switch east and north of Batignolles Yards. Immediately after the issuance of these orders, the battalion was required to perform these duties. It was charged with furnishing personnel for actual operations of trains and for maintenance of tracks, roadbed and equipment. It was customary to charge one company with the duty of operation of trains, another company with the responsibility of maintenance of tracks and road bed, and another with the task of maintenance of equipment.

Sometime prior to September 12, 1944, a Quartermaster Depot was established in Paris that warehoused and distributed practically all the food and PX supplies sent to troops in Paris and the surrounding area. It also shipped large quantities of subsistence rations and PX supplies to Reims, Liege and other places for distribution to combat troops at the front. During a period in October and November 1944, it furnished rations directly to the Advance Section, Communications Zone, and First and Third U.S. Armies. This merchandise was received from the continental United States at the Cherbourg and Rouen railheads that served the beaches in these areas and was shipped via Dreux, Versailles and Paris to the Quartermaster Depot. The PX supplies included cigarettes, chocolate, smoking tobacco, toiletry accessories and other articles usually sold in Post Exchanges. Such supplies were, at that stage of handling and distribution, property of the United States. Included in the food handled, stored and distributed by the Paris Quartermaster Depot were 10-in-1 rations. Such rations were packed in cases. Each container included food sufficient to feed 10 men for one day as well as cigarettes and soluble coffee. A case (or box) of cigarettes contained 50 cartons—that is 500 packs. Ration Accessory (RAC) Kits were also part of the merchandise handled. Each contained cigarettes, razor blades, a razor, smoking tobacco, chewing tobacco, chewing gum, soap, toothpaste and a toothbrush. There were 20 cartons of cigarettes—200 packs—in each kit.

From September 12 to November 1944, some of the freight cars that arrived at the Quartermaster Depot showed signs of having been opened and rifled. On at least 12 occasions, trains arrived with "badly pilfered" cars. These cars had contained such items as cigarettes, 10-in-1 rations, RAC Kits and PX supplies. Pilferage could be detected by the fact that there were empty spaces near the doors of the cars, which indicated cases or boxes had been removed. In other instances, RAC Kits had been opened and only cigarettes removed. From September to November, badly pilfered trains arrived at the depot at intervals of five or ten days. French civilian laborers were employed at the Quartermaster Depot but they were inspected by military guards on leaving the premises. In addition, guards were posted at each cigarette car.

During the period from September 1 to November 30, 1944, the stock of cigarettes handled and distributed by the Quartermaster, European Theater of Operations, was inadequate to meet the demands of military personnel. There was also a shortage of the 12 basic items contained in the RAC Kits.

As a result of the obvious theft of governed property during the course of its transportation by railroad from French ports of debarkation to Paris, undercover agents were sent to infiltrate the ranks of the 716th Battalion during November 1944. These operatives appeared in the roles of enlisted men of the battalion.

Second Lieutenant Robert P. O'Reilly, Corps of Military Police, Criminal

16. The Million-Dollar Battalion

Officers examining security seals on a box car at the Batignolles Railway Yard, Paris.

Investigation Division, Provost Marshall's Office, became ostensibly a private in the battalion. On or about November 9, he was assigned to Company C as a fireman. He reported for duty at Dreux and served until November 26.

Another undercover CID operative assigned to the 716th Battalion was Bruno James Cozzati, who assumed the role of an enlisted man and was sent to the battalion to act as a locomotive fireman. He performed this duty from November 7 to November 30, 1944.

Within a few days, both O'Reilly and Cozzati managed to get themselves assigned as firemen on the trains carrying supplies to Paris. "We didn't have to lie," O'Reilly said. "No one asked us anything about our previous experience."

During his first night at Matelot Yard on the way to Dreux, Cozzati listened to several crews sitting around a stove and discussing how they had been making plenty of money. Prior to this conversation, one of the men at Headquarters Company told him that he was very fortunate in being assigned to Company C of the 716th, as it was known as the "million-dollar battalion." That same evening, Cozzati and O'Reilly walked across the street and observed an American soldier talking to the owner of a small café—the gist of the conversation was an arrangement to sell government property.

Train guards were on constant patrol at the Batignolles Railway Yard.

During his first day, O'Reilly heard other crew members of his train arranging to open a carload of rations. These men who operated the trains had evolved a fine variety of techniques for making army supplies disappear. It was easy to learn which freight car in a train would be good for looting—the so-called "sensitive" car. If that car was in the middle of the train, crews could cut the train there and take it when the engine sidetracked for water or coal. The car might also "accidentally" develop a hot box and hence be left behind at some siding near a highway. Other members of the looting team would then drive their trucks in, load up from the isolated freight car, and drive away.

On November 11, Cozzati boarded a train at Dreux as a fireman shoveling coal into the large firebox of the locomotive. An American soldier boarded the train and the conductor gave him a car number; he also told Cozzati the number and reminded him not to forget it. The soldier told the conductor not to cut the car off at Dreux. They continued the trip. At about 2:30 on the following morning, about a half mile west of Villiers Station, they disconnected the cars behind the 11th one and proceeded into the station to have the locomotive serviced. As the engine was being filled with water and the rods were being oiled, the rest of the crew went back to the disconnected car. Cozzati watched them unloading cigarettes for about ten minutes. The conductor returned carrying two cases of cigarettes and two boxes of cigars and threw them into the engine area. Cozzati picked them up and placed them back into the tender, the car that contained the coal. Under the pretense of looking for a drink of water, he walked back and watched the crew still unloading the cigarettes. They had been brought to the station, placed into a dark doorway, and then carried into the operator's office.

At the train continued its trip, the cigarettes and cigars were removed and split among the crew. Cozzati was awarded 12 cartons of cigarettes and some cigars. A few days later, an engineer requested Cozzati's help in carrying a heavy duffle bag. When Cozzati inquired about its contents, the engineer told him it was a 50-pound container of lard; he was taking it to Paris, where it was worth $200.

17

THE ARREST OF MEN OF THE MILLION-DOLLAR BATTALION

Beginning on November 8, 1944, additional handpicked criminal investigators working out of the Theater Marshal's Office placed the quarters and personnel of several railroad operating battalions under detailed surveillance. Close watch was kept at Dreux, Villiers, Villeneuve, St. George and St. Cyr; at the Matelot Yard in Versailles; and at the Batignolles Yard in Paris. Some agents stocked locomotives and lived with the men. Others checked the records of army postal units.

The 716th Railway Battalion's transactions in the black market came to an abrupt halt on November 26, 1944, when Colonel James Elder directed a simultaneous raid by CID agents and Military Police on the stations to which the battalion ran the trains. When the gas and cigarette shortages began to grow acute, two husky young CID lieutenants, simply disguised as soldiers, had been sent into an army reinforcement center and then assigned to the 716th Railway Battalion as replacements. They were undercover CID agents Bruno James Cozzati and Robert P. O'Reilly.

Cozzati was on one train as a fireman when it was raided. The conductor, who had left his train as usual and walked into the station for the okay to proceed, was nabbed but released because he had no evidence on his person. He hurried back to his train and warned the rest of his crew, who shoveled their money orders, receipts, 5,000- and 1,000-franc notes, and canned goods into the fire.

O'Reilly was to say, "From the first that I was assigned to the 716th until the day I left the 716th, the most important topic of conversation was the amount of money we could make from the pilfering and sale of the United States supplies aboard the train. While at the station in Dreux, the only topic

17. The Arrest of Men of the Million-Dollar Battalion

of conversation among myself and the other members of the crew was as to what the contents of the train would be that was coming into Dreux."[1]

Most of the men arrested belonged to Company C, the operating company that ran the trains of one railway battalion. The Company C men had greater access to rations and supplies being hauled than anyone in the rest of the battalion. Of all the railway battalions, theirs—which ran from Dreux to Paris—had the greatest access to the Paris black market. This combination made Company C the focus of the army's attention in the concerted effort to stop the theft of government supplies. Members of Company C of this battalion stoutly maintained, however, that "some people may think our outfit is the only one involved, but up and down the line other battalions are doing the same thing."

Some 440 men were seized on the trains and in the yards, billets, and headquarters, together with lots of loot and other evidence—notably, large sums of money, money orders and receipts. At the same time, the French police raided and arrested a number of French café proprietors who had done business with GIs.

The men arrested were taken to the Hotel Montcalm, which had previously been used by the U.S. Army as an officer's billet. Arrangements were made by the CID to obtain exclusive use of the building for housing of the suspects picked up in the initial raid. Because more soldiers were apprehended than had been anticipated, the hotel became overcrowded. More men were placed into each room than was initially contemplated, with insufficient beds and blankets. Some were placed in two small rooms in the basement, which lacked windows, heat, beds, mattresses and blankets.

William R. Smith was taken to the Hotel Montcalm and confined to a room with a large number of soldiers. The men were told they could not sleep until they had signed a confession. He did not recall the exact number of soldiers, but later as they tried to sleep on the floor, they had to lie on top of each other. The men were taken out of the room individually and questioned. The following morning Smith was interrogated by CID agents and asked if he had sold cigarettes; he responded in the negative. The agents told Smith they had a method whereby they could make a person sign a statement. With that, they sent Smith down into the hole—the rooms in the basement.

There were so many soldiers in these rooms that they pulled boards from the wall and laid them across some braces. Some men slept on these boards, while the others slept under them on the floor. More remained standing for lack of room and took catnaps. Smith remained in the hole for two days, then was taken back up for questioning. He was told that if he did not sign a statement of guilt, his family would never hear from him again. If he did sign, the agents promised, he would be back working on the railroad in a week. Smith recalled:

> I wouldn't sign and they sent me back down into the hole. One of the noticeable things [in the hole] was the air. It was very foul. You could put a cigarette in your mouth and strike a match to light it, and the match would go out before you could get it to the cigarette. There was just one door where the MP stood. And also one toilet outside where the MPs were. Then there was the water. They would pass a bottle in for us to drink [a wine bottle filled with water]. Some of the boys had VD and others didn't. We were told that we would all drink out of the same bottle or go dry.[2]

William Smith was taken from the hole and interrogated by three CID agents. They reiterated that with a signed statement he would be back in his company working in less than a week. "I was sitting at the time, so the man in civilian clothes, the CID lieutenant, said, 'Stand up,' and I stood up and he knocked me down. He hit me with his fist, sir. He told me to get up, then he knocked me down again. He knocked me down three times, sir."[3] The accused lieutenant was William C. Yerg.

Smith asked if he could discuss his confession with some of the men in his company and was sent downstairs with the instructions that he had one hour. Smith discussed his dilemma with Sergeant Bert E. Ewing, who later admitted to wrongfully have taken more than 5,000 packs of cigarettes, and Private Charley Isham, who later admitted to wrongfully taking 500 packs of cigarettes and 20 pounds of coffee. Ewing said, "The Lord only knows what Charley has been beat up by the CID lieutenant who is taking the statements. The only thing to do is sign a statement before they kill us here."

Ewing went up stairs with Smith, where they were told to sign the statements and "don't give a damn what was in them." Smith signed a statement that he had pilfered U.S. government property.

Downstairs again, he was given a couple of blankets and shared a bed with Ewing. Smith complained that there was no heat, but in the winter of 1944 the Parisians were suffering the same fate due to the coal shortage throughout Europe. The American soldiers fifty miles away sleeping in foxholes were cold, wet, and under constant threat of death from artillery shelling and automatic weapons fire. Many of the CID agents in Paris had been reassigned from these front-line combat units for the cigarettes investigation and were giving no favors to the American soldiers who were enjoying the "easy life" while stationed in Paris.

From Hotel Montcalm, Smith and Ewing, along with 128 other soldiers from the 716th Railway Battalion, were taken to the Paris Detention Barracks, where they were incarcerated on the fifth floor. The Detention Barracks, an old French military establishment, had been requisitioned by the U.S. Army for the use of the Provost Marshal, Seine Section. It was a cold and dreary place lacking heating and sanitary facilities. Most of the glass in the windows had been broken.

For breakfast, the confined soldiers were marched down to the first floor in Cage B, where they were given a small cup of coffee, a spoon, and a plate and were told to sit at one of the tables. The tables were filthy, littered with prune seeds and stale bread, as the German prisoners of war had eaten first. Smith and Ewing had never seen such a mess and just stood there looking. A lieutenant said, "What are you waiting for? God damn, put down those dishes and start eating."[4] They were doled out a bowl of cereal, three prunes, and a thin slice of bread.

In the cafeteria-style line, the soldiers serving the food did not use spoons or forks. Ernest A. Granelli said, "They just threw the food into the plates with their hands. Just dipped into the meat and break a piece off and throw it on your dish. And after a while you could see a ring around their hands where the dirt was washed off by the grease and that the reason why the guys got the GIs [diarrhea]."[5]

A few of the confined soldiers had worn overcoats, but most had to huddle together in groups of three or four to keep warm. They slept on a cement floor and would lie on one side until it became numb, get up and walk until their circulation was restored, and then lie down on the other side. The fifth floor had a Military Policeman on each end of the floor guarding the stairway and the prisoners could not leave—which was a problem as the floor had only one latrine. It was not unusual to visit the latrine and find 20 to 30 men in line. Unable to wait, the men started defecating in one end of the room; then they would get buckets and wash the waste down the stairways. Not one U.S. Army officer checked on Private William R. Smith or Sergeant Bert E. Ewing while they were confined on the fifth floor. They were incarcerated at the end of November 1944, and it was January 9, 1945, before a stove was installed on the fifth floor and blankets were issued.

During this time, the German prisoners of war had a stove. Smith and the prisoners from the 716th Railway Battalion could look from their floor into Cage C and see the Germans sitting around the stove comfortably in their underwear. They also had wooden bunks, while the American prisoners were sleeping on the cement floor.

At the beginning of January 1945, the commanding officer of the Paris Detention Barracks, his executive officer, and the adjutant officer were relieved and subsequently reclassified to other duties. The 535th Military Police Service Battalion took control of the prison and conditions began to improve immediately.

Smith noted, "After that, the food conditions got much better and the major in charge is now a colonel. I can't think of his name [Colonel Leo Gilbert], but he had a habit of quite often dropping into the mess hall and checking with the boys, always asking if they had enough and if they liked the way it was put out. And he chewed the members working in the mess hall out; he told them they were not feeding pigs, but Americans."[6]

The American prisoners were then housed on the third floor, with the British prisoners on the second floor and the German prisoners of war moved to the fourth floor. Here the American had wooden bunks with straw, good food, and warmth.

Prison life was improving as 200 miles northwest of Paris, the German army launched a bitter winter offensive known as the Battle of the Bulge. Swarms of enemy tanks and men overran the undermanned positions of the Allied defenders and the front lines wavered dangerously. An unrelenting enemy, General Winter sent his legions into the frigid battle. The roads out of towns were jammed with bedraggled American troops and vehicles. The scene was one of weary confusion. American soldiers were swallowed in the red tide that was spread over the map. An unending barrage of artillery and night bombings hammered the American forces. Wounded men were sent back from the front, only to lie helplessly in a village under a continual rain of shell fire. Surrounded, their evacuation was impossible. Doctors and technicians were captured when division aid stations were overrun, which put an added burden on the already overworked and underequipped medical men. One hospital suffered a direct bomb hit—no patient survived.

During this battle, Private First Class Richard Eller Cowan, 23rd Infantry, 2nd Infantry Division, was a heavy machine gunner in the vicinity of Krinkelter Wald, Belgium. On December 17, 1944, his company was attacked by a numerically superior force of German infantry and tanks. The first six waves of hostile infantrymen were repulsed with heavy casualties, but a seventh drive with tanks killed or wounded all but three of his section, leaving Cowan to man his gun while supported by only 15 to 20 riflemen. He maintained his position, holding off the Germans until the rest of the shattered force had set up a new line along a firebreak. Then, unaided, he moved his machine gun and ammunition to the second position. At the approach of a Royal Tiger tank, he held his fire until about 80 enemy infantrymen supporting the tank appeared at a distance of about 150 yards. His first burst killed or wounded about half of these infantrymen. His position was rocked by an 88-mm shell when the tank opened fire, but Cowan continued to man his gun, pouring deadly fire into the Germans when they again advanced. He was barely missed by another shell. Fire from three machine guns and innumerable small arms struck all about him; an enemy rocket shook him badly, but did not drive him from his gun. Infiltration by the enemy had by this time made the position untenable, and the order was given to withdraw. Cowan was the last man to leave, voluntarily covering the withdrawal of his remaining comrades. His heroic actions were entirely responsible for allowing the surviving men to retire successfully from the scene of their last-ditch stand. Pfc. Richard Eller Cowan paid the ultimate sacrifice for his country; for his heroic action he was posthumously awarded the Medal of Honor.[7]

As the Battle of the Bulge continued, trench foot and frozen limbs matched the casualties from artillery and small arms. Men fashioned crude jackets from blankets and tarpaulins and made scarves from supply parachutes. Even cooks and clerks left their pots and typewriters for guns, filling gaps in a depleted line. Tenaciously they clung to frozen slopes and ignored the stiff-limbed piles of German corpses that littered the ground in front of their position. The siege dragged on, but the tide turned as the wreckage of enemy machines cluttered the roads and inundated the slopes. The critical period was over; the enemy encircling the U.S. Army had thrown everything into the assault and failed. It is difficult to come to terms with the comfortable day-to-day situation in Paris while knowing these deadly conditions existed for the Combat Zone soldiers nine months after the liberation of this city.

18

The Cigarette Trials

The largest general court-martial case in all of military history was the railway pilferage case, in which 190 enlisted men and eight officers were tried. Of this number, five officers, including the battalion commander, and 17 enlisted men were acquitted; 176 were convicted. Sentences ranged from 3 to 50 years in prison for dealing in cigarettes and rations on the black market. These trials were conducted by Colonel Carmon Harris of Oklahoma City, Oklahoma, Executive Officer of the Seine Section and Staff Judge Advocate, acting as special prosecutor for railway cases, and his staff.

The first four accused—Alexander A. Fleming, William R. Smith, Arthur Nelson and William Davidson—were brought to trial on January 9, 1945. They were convicted and sentenced to be dishonorably discharged and to serve sentences of confinement at hard labor of 45 to 50 years.

On the morning of his trial, Private Smith had met for the first time with his defense counsel, just ten minutes before the court case began. Smith stated, "He said public opinion was definitely not on our side; that the president of the court was not on our side; and that he had the opportunity to talk with the court and he could state they were not on our side. He said it was in our best interest not to take the stand, but to let him conduct the court in his own way." The counsel further stated, "I want to warn you fellows now, you are going to be convicted and you are going to get a long time."

Based on the advice of his attorney, Smith did not take the stand, nor did he make a statement, hoping for leniency on the part of the court. The damaging statement that Smith had signed while questioned by the CID agents in the Hotel Montcalm was read to the court:

> About 20 October 1944, I was transferred to the Matelot Yards, and for the first three weeks I did not take any supplies from the trains. About 5 November 1944, the wrecking crew was established comprising the following: . . . The repair track is located next to our car, and at the time a box car with cigarettes was placed on

18. The Cigarette Trials

the track for repairs. Sgt. Fleming, Pvt. Davidson, Pvt. Nelson and myself took a case from the car and brought them to our car. These four cases were disposed of to French workers in the yard and some were taken to Paris and sold for 500 francs per carton, making a total of $2,000.00. This money was split 5 ways, but Cpl. Miller never did take part in any of the thefts and the split was forced onto him due to [him being] a member of our car crew. About two days later another car was placed on the repair track, and Pvt. Nelson and myself took two cases of chocolate from this car and took them to our car. The cases contained 144 bars each. The chocolate was sold to French civilians for 40 francs per bar, making a total of $140.00. About two days later Sgt. Fleming learned a ration train was in the yards, and we went to the yards and located a car containing cigarettes. The car was guarded by train guards, but they suddenly disappeared and we received four cases from a soldier who was passing them out of the car. These cigarettes were sold to French workers in the yard for 500 francs per carton, for a total of $2,000.00. A few days later we took several cases of 10-in-1 rations from a car on a train. We sold about 5 cases from our car for 1,500 francs per case, making a total of $150.00.

This edited statement was part of the official trial, but it contained only about a third of Smith's official statement. Missing is the part where he sold $300 worth of coffee and $2,000 of cigarettes to Eugene Pallenger, 15 Rue De Paul, Paris. Also missing is his statement of sharing four cases of cigarettes with a Military Policeman from a company stationed in Versailles. Smith was sentenced to 50 years of hard labor.

The court cases then continued, with four to five soldiers tried jointly. There was no evidence presented—just the preliminary statements made to the CID during the initial arrests. This was enough for a conviction. Following are the confessions made by Sergeant Merel A. Young, age 36; Private Fred C. Jones, age 19; Tec 4 Leonard J. French, age 33; Private Edward N. Wagner, age 22; and Pfc. Thomas G. Harper. All were members of Company C, 716th Railway Operating Battalion.

Young

My first assignment was as "Conductor" at Dreux. The crew of which I was a member comprised T/4 Leonard J. French, Engineer; Pfc. Thomas G. Harper, Brakeman; Pfc. Jones, Brakeman; and a fireman whose name I don't remember. While at Dreux I took a case of PX rations (20 cartons of cigarettes), and about an hour later another member of the crew stole another case of PX rations. These two cases were split among the members of the crew. My one-fifth share was eight cartons of cigarettes. I sold my share of cigarettes for 4,000 francs. I'm not sure if the other crew members sold their shares, but they did receive a share each.

The following day at Paris, I took a PX ration case. I took this case from a freight car, placed it in my barracks bag, and took it back to Dreux. I did not have time to sell it at Dreux, so I waited until my next trip to Paris. On my next trip to Paris, I sold the 20 cartons of cigarettes and 4 boxes of chocolates and received 10,800 francs for these items.

Again while at Dreux, I took one case of PX rations (my next trip) and sold the contents at Paris. I received 10,000 francs for the cigarettes.

I was then transferred to Matelot Yard. My present crew comprised T/4 Leonard French, T/5 Swindell, Pfc. Thomas Harper, and Pvt. Wagner. I had been there about two weeks before the first incident took place. This crew and I during the following six weeks stole approximately ten or twelve PX cartons (20 cartons of cigarettes in each case). Of the 200 cartons of cigarettes that were contained in these boxes, I sold approximately 20 cartons, receiving 500 francs per carton. Pvt. Wagner sold the balance of the cigarettes. The money received from the sales was pooled and split five ways, with each member of the crew receiving an equal share.

While at Matelot Yard I took a PX ration box containing 20 cartons of cigarettes and gave this box to S/Sgt. Possi; he was Yardmaster at Matelot. Possi asked to be taken care of; he stated he knew we were receiving cigarettes. He took the box and proceeded in the direction of the billets.

I sold all the cigarettes to unknown French civilians.

Jones

I wish to state in this supplementary statement the articles I had in my possession at the time I was apprehended: money order receipts #9624 1 Oct. 1944 $50.00 (mother) Mrs. W.E. Jones, #18611 4 Nov. 1944 $100.00 (mother) Mrs. W.E. Jones, #9625 1 Oct. 1944 $100.00 (mother) Mrs. W.E. Jones, #18610 4 Nov. 1944 $100.00 (mother) Mrs. W.E. Jones. I also had in my possession 5,750 French francs and $63.00 in American currency.

I have worked on these train crews from about 1 Sept. 1944 until now, running from Dreux to Paris. When we first started this run, we had no rations and we were taking rations to eat from the train. While doing this, we learned there were PX rations and cigarettes in the cars also. There were always Frenchmen around trying to buy anything they could. I heard there were plenty of rations around and the Frenchmen paid a good price for them. I decided to take a few and sell them. The first box I took, I divided with Sgt. M.A. Young and Pfc. Harper. I received 10 cartons as my share. I sold these to Frenchmen along the run for 500 to 600 francs a carton. The candy, soap, tooth powder, shaving cream and toothbrush, I kept for my own use and to distribute among the men of my company. This was about the middle of September 1944. About the 1st of October 1944 I took another case of rations; I did not divide this

18. The Cigarette Trials

one, [but] sold everything in it except the soap. For this box of rations I received 11,500 francs, or approximately $230.00. About a week later I took another case of rations from a train. This case I divided with Pvt. Culver. My part I sold to various cafés, and 4 or 5 cartons of cigarettes I remember I sold to Frenchmen in the Hotel de Paris, 3 Cité Pusy St., Paris, France. I do not remember the names of the other places I sold cigarettes. I do not know where the other men in my crew who I divided the rations with disposed of their shares. Pvt. Charles McCoy and Pvt. Forrest Scott, both of my organization and company, took a case of rations at the same time I got mine.

I remember on one trip [the crew included] T/4 Neff, Engineer; T/5 or Pvt. Sweatman, Fireman; and Sgt. M.A. Young, Conductor. On this trip, Sgt. Young and I split a case of rations.

When I arrived in France, I had $63 in American currency, I have never changed any of this. I have sent home $150 in money orders. I had in my possession at the time I was picked up (2) two money order receipts, numbers 9624 and 18610, for the money I sent home; (2) two money orders for $100.00 each, #186111 and 9625; 6,250 francs; and the $63 in American currency I brought with me to France. I have received also (3) three months' pay, approximately $90. All except my pay and $63 I brought with me, I received from the sale of cigarettes and rations taken from the trains by me.

French

After spending a week at a receiving area, I was sent to Dreux. I was then assigned as an engineer operating between Lundan, Dreux and Paris.

From the period of the 15th of October 1944 to about the 26th October 1944, I received as my share about eight hundred dollars ($800) from the sale of cigarettes. The other members of my crew were Merel A. Young, Edward W. Wagner, Thomas G. Harper and Paul Swindell. These men received the same amount as I did from the sale of cigarettes. Wagner would usually find the car and then he would take out two or three boxes. Then Wagner, Young, and myself would carry them away and place them in an empty box car somewhere in the Matelot Yards. While we were working, Wagner would take the cigarettes and dispose of them. Where he would go with them, I don't know. When we finished working, the money from the sale of the cigarettes would be divided among us. I have received money about four or five times from the sale of cigarettes taken from the cars at Matelot Yards. Sometimes there would be chocolates in the boxes. The cigarettes that were taken away from the freight cars amounted to about eighty (80) cartons. This money I received from the sale of cigarettes, I used for a good time. The five hundred dollars ($500.00) that

I sent home was money I won in dice games and not one cent of it came from the sale of cigarettes.

When I was taken into custody, I had on my person 11,650 francs. Of this amount, 4,450 francs represents pay I have received since I have been in France.

I at no time broke into or entered any freight cars of the U.S. government or French government.

Wagner

While at Dreux, France, a switchman in the yards, whose name I don't know, took a case of rations containing 20 cartons of cigarettes and various other items. I am pretty sure the switchman took this case of rations off a freight car. We split this case of rations among the crew, consisting of myself and four other men who I don't know their names. I used these rations for my own personal needs.

On or around the early part of September 1944 and in the month of October 1944, I took 10 or 12 cases of 10-in-1 rations consisting of cigarettes and other ration items. Sgt. M. Young, T/4 L.J. French, T/5 Paul Swindell, Pvt. Harper and I split the above mentioned cases of rations. We are all from Co. C, 716 Ry Opn Bn. I sold the above mentioned cases of rations to French civilians, the names of whom I don't know. I only sold the cigarettes from the cases of rations, receiving 500 francs a carton. I split the money five ways among Sgt. Merle Young, T/4 L.J. French, T/5 Paul Swindell, and Pvt. T. Harper.

Harper

I was a brakeman on the train from Paris to Dreux from about the 1st of September until the middle of October. Thereafter I was a watchman at Matelot Yards.

Sometime in September, Meryl Young, Fred C. Jones, Leonard French and I took cases of PX cigarettes and chocolates (20 cartons of cigarettes and 2 boxes chocolates). We split this four ways and I sold my share of cigarettes for 500 francs per carton. We took these cigarettes from a gondola car at Dreux.

About a week after the above incident, Sgt. Paul W. Hart and I took a box of cigarettes out of a box car on the road from Dreux to Paris, which we stopped on the road to clear. This car had already been broken into. I sold my share of 10 cartons for 500 francs per carton in Paris on the street.

About the middle of October I went to Matelot Yards as a switchman. Young, French, Swindell, and Wagner were the other crew members. From the middle of October until I was picked up, Meryl Young, Leonard French and I took from the cars about 10 or 12 cases of PX [goods] containing 20 cartons of cigarettes each; some of them contained boxes of chocolates. We always split evenly on these and I sold my share at 500 francs per carton.

These were typical declarations of guilt for the 176 men convicted. The initial trials for enlisted men were completed on February 13.

As a result of the testimony elicited in these trials, some 60 additional enlisted personnel were implicated and taken into custody about March 1, 1945. These soldiers had been instructed to report to a transient mess in Paris. They were under the impression that they were to be witnesses in the cases concerning the black market activities of their fellow soldiers in the 716th Railroad Battalion. The next thing they knew, a group of armed MPs had assembled and charged the men with conspiracy. After careful screening, it was determined that arrest charges were not warranted in 12 of these cases.

The other 48 soldiers were conveyed to the Paris Detention Barracks. They could not fathom why they were arrested. In jail, they were quite bitter because they felt the members of their battalion had been given unusually stiff sentences, considering that other prisoners had committed more grievous crimes and received lighter sentences. These men sitting in jail felt the previously convicted men of the 716th had not received fair trails, and they were gloomy about getting what they considered a fair deal for themselves.[1]

The results of these trials immediately brought a flock of letters from congressional representatives addressed to the Judge Advocate General, Washington, D.C. For example, the following letter was sent by Senator Chapman Revercomb, Committee on Military Affairs:

> Private Fred C. Jones was a member of Company C, 716th Railway Operating Battalion, in service in the European area. He is nineteen years of age. I do not know the circumstances upon which the sentence is based but it appears to me to be a severe one. Forty years' sentence at hard labor for a boy nineteen years old is virtually a life sentence for theft.... It appears not to be the case of the habitual criminal but, perhaps, that of a country boy who permitted himself to be involved in some thieving in the army.

The Officers' Trials

The court cases of the enlisted men were highly publicized and followed with intense interest by newspapers, magazines and radio commentators. The chief source of this attention was the involvement of practically an entire battalion, with severe punishment that had been extended only to the enlisted men. Were any officers involved? It became clear before the trials concluded that the army had to bring charges against some of the officers of the 716th

Railway Battalion. "Charges against officers were referred to trial upon less evidence than would normally have been the case. This naturally and not unexpectedly resulted in an abnormally large number of acquittals."[2]

Eight officers were tried for their role in the railway pilferage cases. Major Walter H. Marlin was charged with neglect and failure to perform his duties in preventing the known wrongful taking and disposing of rations, cigarettes and other supplies. He was acquitted.

First Lieutenant Ario D. Dal Porto was indicted for conspiracy, converting to his own use two cases rations; receiving and converting to his own use one case rations; receiving and converting 50 pounds of beef; wrongfully converting two shirts and two pairs of pants; and failure and neglect to perform his duties. He was acquitted, but nine members of the court recommended reclassification because he was deemed deficient in knowledge of and ability in military matters.

Captains Samuel B. Gillespie, Harold G. Gould and Neander E. Peterson were all indicted on neglect of duty. The captains were acquitted.

First Lieutenant John W. Springer, 35 years old, 0337667, was questioned by Lieutenant Yerg and signed a sworn confession. He was tried on January 29, 1945, charged with wrongfully disposing of 500 packs of cigarettes, wrongfully removing government property valued at $400, and neglect of duty. Enlisted men of Company C testified that on two separate occasions Springer had received large sums of money from the sale of supplies that had been pillaged from the trains. After a one-day trial he was sentenced to dismissal, total forfeitures, and confinement at hard labor for 35 years.

Later, the reviewing officer recommended that Springer's sentence be mitigated to a forfeiture of pay of $75 per month for 12 months and that the confinement and dismissal be suspended. The Judge Advocate did not concur:

> The accused stands properly convicted of dishonesty and culpable neglect of duty (both admitted by him) meriting punishment—irrespective of lack of fitness as an officer or experience in disciplinary control of subordinates. The conclusion is inescapable that the accused's failure to act as an honest man respecting government property and his failure to perform the duties of an honest man in his position are responsible for some of the like dishonesty on the part of his subordinates who are tried and convicted. He is not deserving of the full measure of clemency extended the 159 enlisted men convicted of similar offenses.[3]

On November 13, 1945, the Theater Commander reduced Springer's sentence to 20 years.

First Lieutenant Norris E. Loop, 45 years old and primarily a railroad technician, was not apprehended with Olson and Springer but transferred north as the 716th moved closer to the advancing front line. He was ordered back to

Paris and arrested on January 24, 1945. He was not questioned and made no statements, but was court-martialed on February 13. He was indicted for conspiracy, wrongfully possessing one box of PX rations, wrongfully possessing one carton of cigarettes, and neglect of duty. He was found guilty and sentenced to dismissal from service, forfeiture of all pay and allowances, and hard labor for 20 years. The sentence was reviewed and confirmed at 20 years.

Captain William P. Olson, as described earlier, was a railroad man in the army charged with performing transportation functions. He was an experienced railway man, but in the point of qualifications not an army officer. On military papers, Olson was a captain and company commander; his real title, however, was trainmaster. The volume of railroad work during this period was at an urgent maximum, and Olson was fully absorbed in the movement of the train's cargo. Because of the pace of work, he visited his company headquarters about once a month. As the duties of trainmaster, which had been his life profession, appeared all-important, this was his military assignment. He knew that government supplies in his custody were being pilfered, but in the confusion of overextended military operations where maximum results were required in a minimum of time, Olson overlooked his Company C administrative responsibilities. In hindsight, he was convinced that he should have devoted more time to being a company commander.[4]

Olson was not taken to the Hotel Montcalm on November 25, 1944, for questioning, but rather went to Lieutenant William Yerg's office, where he signed a sworn statement about what he knew of the activities regarding the theft of government property. Regarding the questioning by Yerg, Olson stated, "I wouldn't say he used any pressure. However, his technique or manner was not what a man my age would expect. He swaggers in and pulls his revolver out and laid it on the table while he was taking it [the statement] down." They then went to the Matelot Yard, just west of Versailles, and inspected Olson's quarters. Two days later, suffering from fatigue and stress, the captain was hospitalized for 11 days. When released from the hospital, he was placed under house arrest. He remained in his billet area until his trial on February 26, 1945.

Olson was accused of wrongfully receiving and converting 80 packages of cigarettes; neglect and failure to perform his duties in preventing wrongful taking and disposing rations, cigarettes and other supplies; and wrongfully receiving and converting one box of razor blades, 20 bars of chocolate, 20 packages of chewing gum, and one pair of paratrooper boots. In a trial that lasted one day, Olson was found guilty and sentenced to ten years of hard labor.

Letters by well-intentioned U.S. citizens were sent to President Franklin D. Roosevelt and to members of the U.S. Senate and House of Representatives attesting to the impeccable character of Captain Olson. They more or less contained the same theme:

> For the past 20 years, I have worked with and under Wm. P. Olson in his capacity of Yardmaster and General Yardmaster in the San Francisco Terminal. During that time, I have never known him to be neglectful of any of his duties. In fact, I have known him to be very diligent in performing all of his duties and always willing to do more than his part. I have never known him to be unfair or unjust to any men under him.
>
> I personally know that he enlisted in the Second World War for the reason he thought that in doing so he would [be] of more service to his country, although he was beyond draft age and would not have to go.
>
> For the above reasons I believe that an error has been made and an unfair injustice done to Wm. P. Olson.[5]

The severity of the sentences doled out to the enlisted men and officers appeared to shock many Parisians, judging by the letters that leading French newspapers received. A group of young girls, for example, wrote: "We would like to find some way of diminishing the rigor of the military laws, though we do not argue against them. We think that we have had, all of us, part of the responsibility for this situation, and that many French persons have been accomplices."

By comparison with the punishment administered to the French fences, the Americans' sentences seemed more severe. Because there was no Parliament to revise the laws, the old French laws still stood, and they did not cover black market operations in time of war. The French were instead punished under statutes forbidding the receipt of stolen property, for which penalties were limited. (On January 13, the military governor of Paris threatened penalties ranging from one to five years' imprisonment for a French national holding or receiving stolen U.S. goods.)

The 716th was by no means the only offender in its light-fringed practice. Rather, its case simply illustrates the opportunities afforded to American soldiers for exploration and the extent to which pilfering and misuse of supplies was carried out. Other railway battalions and innumerable truck companies, including the historical Red Ball Express, were involved in such dealings as well. However, the urgency of the supply problem at that critical time precluded any investigation as extensive at that which brought about the convictions of the officers and enlisted men of the 716th Railway Battalion.

A perplexing fact is that during the trials the declarations taken by the CID were the only evidence presented against the men. These statements were edited, leaving out the involvement of French nationals and crimes committed by the Military Police, which is understandable as the judiciary system would definitely cover for its own law enforcement officers. One piece of testimony especially bothered the author: Tec 4 Charles E. McCoy, 35846720, made a sworn statement regarding Olson's trial that "around 15 October 1944 Private Trimmer under the influence of alcohol attempted to take the carbine from a guard and was shot and killed by him in the Orderly Room of Company C in Dreux, France. Captain Olson was commanding officer. The guard was not arrested and there has been no court-martial." This statement was apparently never investigated.

Reviewing the cases of the enlisted men convicted in the railway battalion cases, General Dwight D. Eisenhower took note of their "effective work under difficulties" and their good previous records, and directed they be given a chance to serve suspended sentences in a special combat company. Eisenhower was correct in his assessment: The men were primarily railroad men and not soldiers. They had been working day and night in moving critical supplies to the front lines. Unfortunately, they began a part-time job of stealing PX supplies that they deemed expendable.

The procedure devised to deal with the situation consisted of a letter addressed to each convicted soldier stressing the cumulated gravity of the offense and the basis of the contemplated clemency as an opportunity to repair some of the damage done. In the petition for clemency, each soldier had to declare under oath the full amount of his profits from illegal trafficking in government property and agree to its full repayment. The convicted man also had to agree to request duty in a combat organization or such capacity as military authorities might determine. The reverse side of the letter contained instructions for the restoration of duty pending final action and directing stoppage of pay of the court-martialed soldier under the terms of the petition. Further, no man would be restored to duty who could not reasonably be expected to be a good soldier— this is, who did not fully repay all profits that he gained through pilfering or authorized through the discontinuance of his pay.

The proposal of clemency was first explained to the entire group of convicted soldiers. Each was given a copy of following letter signed by the Commanding General of Seine Section, Communication Zone:

> You have been convicted, upon your own confessions, of serious crimes against the United States and against our fighting forces at the front lines—namely of the pilfering of trains in your custody and the taking and converting to your own personal profit of the supplies entrusted to your care and handling enroute to the front.
> Some of you have indicated at your trials that you were not properly supplied with food and that you therefore felt obligated to provide yourself with rations in your custody on the trains. If you did this, it was surely irregular; but it was not this for which you were tried and convicted. Your crime was rather the wholesale taking and selling for your own profit of rations and cigarettes brought here from

America at great expense, and urgently needed by your fellow soldiers, some of them working day and night in rear areas, as some of you were doing, and many of them fighting and dying day and night on the battle fronts.

You robbed your comrades of their rations in order to cash proceeds for yourselves. You in effect declared an open season on all rations trains coming through your hands—you who were entrusted as *your* part of the war effort to rush these rations through to the soldiers entitled to them. In trial after trial we have heard hard evidence of entire trains ravaged as though they had been in the hands of bandits, rather than in the care of loyal soldiers of the United States. And though this continued for months, while our armies were at death grips with a most powerful and dangerous enemy, there is unhappily no evidence of even one soldier of the United States in all your group who once raised his hand to stop this wanton plunder, or in any way [protect] the interest of the United States that he had sworn as a soldier to serve.

This is not a pretty picture nor, I am sure, one [on which you] wish to dwell, but it is an aspect of a matter which you may do well to remember when protestations are made that you are unfairly punished, or if it is suggested you are not criminals. Let there be no mistake about it. You *are* criminals, convicted upon your own confessions.[6]

The cigarette conspiracy case had seen 8 officers and 190 enlisted men tried, with 3 officers and 173 enlisted men found guilty. The convicted officers were not offered clemency, but 159 enlisted men were restored to duty under this plan. They left prison immediately and were reassigned to a Ground Forces Reinforcement Center as privates to receive training before being given a chance to redeem themselves at the front. The remaining 14 enlisted men and three officers convicted in the railway cases were to serve out their sentences.

Among the most highly publicized black market operations in France were these railway battalion thefts of cigarettes and rations. These men represented only a part of one railway battalion. The battalion as a whole—like the other railway outfits on the Continent—accomplished an important military mission that was perhaps obscured by this bad publicity. The acute shortage of cigarettes, both on the Western Front and in the United States, at the time made these thefts front-page newspaper stories.

While large numbers of soldiers took part in the railway pilfering, it was never organized on a big-time gang basis like the gasoline racket. Also, the railway men did not go AWOL. Unlike the gasoline racketeers who quit soldiering completely, they stayed on the job of running trains to the front and did their stealing on the side.

At the conclusion of the trials and clemency proceedings, the Judge Advocate Staff made a declaration that $200,000 of government property had been accounted for in these extensive trials. According to their account, however, $28,380,000 in profits was realized from black market cigarette sales during

18. The Cigarette Trials

the three months in which these criminal acts occurred. The CID statements regarding the trucks and half-tracks that backed up to the railway cars and carried off loads of cigarettes were never investigated. A sworn statement on January 23, 1945, by Sergeant Paul M. King, 32212306, is enlightening, as it was never admitted as evidence in any of the trails:

> On another occasion, I was working in Matelot Yard one evening in early November 1944. That evening I received a telephone call from Lt. Col. Neville [710th Railway Grand Division], asking if we had any cigarettes at Matelot Yard. I told him we had some, and he instructed me to save them and he would pick them up the following night.
>
> The next evening I placed three cartons of cigarettes in a paper bag and left them in the office. Later that night I saw Lt. Col. Neville and told him where they were. He stated he would have his driver pick them up.
>
> I do not know this of my own knowledge, but Tec 5 [Robert E.] Nied, H & H Company, who was operator that night, told me Col. Neville picked these cigarettes up himself.[7]

Neither Colonel Neville nor any other high-ranking officer of the Military Railway Service was ever implicated in the pilferage of cigarettes. Without question, though, a U.S. Army soldier, or soldiers, of high rank working with an exceedingly organized bunch of French criminals made a fortune during this three-month time frame of opportunities in war-torn Europe. Moreover, they got away with it, as the "small fish" were incarcerated.

This assessment is reinforced with one statement made by Private James E. Joseph, 38265289, in an unrelated court-martial trial where he was convicted for selling gasoline:

> **Q:** You made a statement that you loaded a truck with rations out in the country. Can you tell us a little more in detail just what extent you participated in this?
> **A:** I didn't know where I was going. I left the hotel that night with two women, myself and another soldier. I took him to be an American GI because he was wearing staff sergeant chevrons. We drove out into the country, out of Paris. When we got there, there were seven GI trucks. It was near a railroad station and tracks. There was one truck out of the seven I was with that made five loads, what kind I do not know. Whether it was food, ammunition, or clothing, I do not know. I didn't help load the truck. In fact, I only picked up three or four pieces to put on any of these trucks. Where they unloaded, I don't know, and where they went, I don't know.[8]

Joseph was living in Paris with Irene, 20 to 21 years old, and Galdys, about 35 or 36, and Joe, an American soldier, 25 or 25, slim with sandy hair. They stayed together for several months, during which time they were involved in money laundering and various nefarious activities. In an episode one night, seven trucks hauled five loads each from a railway station to an undisclosed location in the immediate area of Paris. The 30-year-old Joseph was court-martialed for going AWOL—"although there is some indirect evidence of black market activities." This was the large-scale operation needed to steal millions of packs of cigarettes, not a duffle bag full. The girls were surely part of the French underground of crime. There is no evidence to support that Joseph's sworn statement was ever investigated further.

19

A Review of the Trials

It had taken six weeks, until January 27, 1945, to liquidate the German wedge completely and recover the lost ground on the flanks due to the Battle of the Bulge. Resuming the difficult Allied penetration of the Siegfried Line, the American army broke into the great devastated Rhine city of Cologne on March 6. Small units of the First Army, turning south and bypassing the beautiful university town of Bonn, by a lucky break and quick action seized the Ludendorff railway bridge over the Rhine at Remagen. Rushing tanks and troops across it, a strong bridgehead was established on the east bank before the surprised and demoralized Germans could move many troops to the threatened point. This Remagen bridgehead soon enabled the Allies to secure a dozen other bridgeheads on the east bank by throwing across marvelous prefabricated bridges in place of the bridges destroyed by the retreating Germans. These crossings prepared the way for the spectacular sweep of the Allied armies across Germany to join hands with the advancing Soviet army at Torgau on the Elbe, which occurred on April 27. The Germans, demoralized and uncertain about which way to turn, offered little serious resistance and surrendered on May 8, 1945.

While the war in Europe was over, one of the 14 enlisted men who did not sign the clemency statement, Private William R. Smith, remained in prison. Smith believed signing the clemency could be interpreted as a statement of guilt. When he questioned the document, he was told, "If you don't want to sign it, you will rot in jail. I am just trying to give you guys a break." Smith, still contending he was innocent, would not sign the clemency.

At the war's end, Smith was still serving time in the Paris Detention Barracks along with 11 enlisted men and 2 officers from the 716th. The remainder of the convicted men had been granted clemency and returned to military service. A few months later, Smith was transferred to the Loire Disciplinary Training Center in Le Mans, France, a prison that had been established in the fall of

French women in Paris clothe themselves in dresses representing the flags of four victorious Allies—the United States, Great Britain, France, and Russia—as the French capital celebrates the victory in Europe.

1944 and had room for 4,500 American servicemen prisoners. The prison was rather quickly overpopulated. It was a large area surrounded by a double-apron fence 14 feet high, containing 11 main cages to keep prisoners segregated according to the crimes they had committed. The first big group of prisoners that arrived came from the Paris Detentions Barracks and included Smith and some of the other men from the 716th Railroad Battalion. Prisoners who were considered unquestionably unfit for rehabilitation had already been returned to the United States.

During the confinement of the prisoners in the Paris Detention Barracks, Lieutenant John U. Harris, the chaplain there, became convinced that three of the prisoners from the 716th were innocent. He began writing letters to the Inspector General's office regarding these men. His efforts may have been responsible for another investigation into the cigarette pilfering case because on October 14, 1945, Colonel Lynn H. Stockman was assigned to investigate the cases of the men remaining in jail: "It is desired that you conduct a complete investigation of the circumstances surrounding the trials in connection of the

716th to determine whether or not the confessions obtained were voluntarily given."[1]

Smith was not one of the three men the chaplain had selected as blameless. Because of the small number of men remaining in jail for the cigarettes thefts, Stockman decided to investigate most of the individuals, as it puzzled him why the men remained in jail when they could have "walked free" by signing a clemency statement. During the three-month inquiry conducted by Stockman, Smith was one of the first prisoners whom he interviewed. When questioned about his activity in relation to the cigarette heist, Smith told Stockman he was innocent and that Lieutenant Yerg had beaten a confession out of him. A week later, prisoner Henry A. Murff stated under sworn testimony:

> **Q:** Did you see the CID actually strike anyone during the course of their questioning these men?
> **A:** No, sir. They wouldn't let us watch, but I seen the boys come back with their noses bunged up. There was one boy by the name of Smitty that they pulled some rough stuff on.[2]

With the information from Murff, Stockman met with now Captain William C. Yerg at the Office of the Inspector General, St. Cloud, France, to discuss the case of the 716th Railway Operating Battalion and his involvement in the cigarette heist case. In sworn testimony, Yerg told the colonel that he handled the administrative responsibility for the case for the Criminal Investigation Branch. He further stated he was twice briefly in the Hotel Montcalm. After making this statement, Yerg was read the complete accusation made by William R. Smith.

Yerg was extremely cool and responded that he was sorry to say that he could not help them. He basically avoided the issue by producing file folders that excluded him. Stockman was adamant and told Yerg that the accused men were reasonably intelligent and he questioned their confessions, knowing they could not be compelled to incriminate themselves. Yerg responded, "That is a question that is hard for me to answer."[3]

Following this questioning, Yerg was given a brown suit to wear. He was placed in a line-up with three other individuals dressed in the same attire, without identification or insignias. Smith immediately picked Yerg from the line-up as the officer who had beaten a confession out of him a year earlier. Reminded that he was still under oath, Yerg was confronted with Smith, whom he claimed to have never seen, and denied that any of his claimed beating ever took place. The sworn statement ended:

> **Q:** Do you have anything further?
> **A:** [Yerg] Where did this take place?

Q: At the Hotel Montcalm.
A: [Yerg] I don't know of anything that I can tell you.

Smith remained in prison, even though on August 15, 1945, he signed the original declaration and petition of clemency offered to him on February 22 of the same year. Naturally, it contained the same clause of guilt, and he admitted to stealing government property valued at $1,900.

Captain William P. Olson was released from confinement on December 6, 1945, and returned to duty with the 716th Railway Operating Battalion. The battalion was responsible for a railroad line, 140 miles long, from Heilbronn to Augsburg in the U.S. Zone of Occupied Germany. On November 14, 1945, the 716th had officially ceased as an active railroad operation and had relinquished its territory to the 746th Railway Operating Battalion.

As of December 6, 1945, both First Lieutenants J. W. Springer and Norris E. Loop were confined at the Lorie Disciplinary Training Center in Le Mans, France.

Soldiers at the Rainbow Corner Red Cross club in Paris whoop it up after buying a special edition of the *Paris Post* carrying the banner headline "Japs Quit." The paper quoted unofficial reports stating Japan was willing to accept the terms of the Potsdam Treaty of July 26, 1945.

19. A Review

In 1954, William R. Smith wrote the Judge Advocate Office from his home in Scituate, Rhode Island, requesting a copy of his court-martial. His wife had requested a copy back in 1945.

On August 15, 1945, the war with Japan ended. The celebration of Victory in Japan (VJ) Day in Paris featured a spontaneous parade including WACs, GIs, officers, and nurses that snaked from the Red Cross club at Rainbow Corner down to the Place de l'Opéra and back. Jeeps crawled along in the victory celebration so loaded down with soldiers that the shapes of the vehicles could hardly be recognized. Some GIs showed up with flags to add color and an official note to the procession. By the time the demonstration hit its full stride, trucks and cars were moving five abreast, with pedestrian celebrants marching before and behind and between.

The most unusual note of the day was the spontaneous contribution campaign for the Red Cross, which started out of nothing except good humor when a soldier at Rainbow Corner pinned a couple of franc notes to a tree. That afternoon this gag raised $14,000 for the American Red Cross.

20

THE EXECUTION OF PRIVATE SLOVIK

Most of the soldiers mentioned in the earlier chapters and hundreds more during World War II were charged with violations of the 58th Article of War and given death sentences. After a review by judiciary authorities, the sentence was greatly reduced, except for one soldier in the wrong place at the wrong time—during the Battle of the Bulge.

Eddie D. Slovik, 20 years old, was inducted into the army at Detroit, Michigan, on January 2, 1944. One year later, he would be executed by a U.S. Army firing squad in Germany, in the first execution for desertion since the American Civil War.

During late July 1944, Slovik transferred overseas from Fort George G. Meade, Maryland, as a member of a group of replacements. The group proceeded via England to Omaha Beach, France, thence to the Third Replacement Depot (France), where Slovik was assigned to the 28th Infantry Division. On August 25, the unit traveled to the division headquarters and Slovik, together with the 14 other replacements, was assigned to Company G, 109th Infantry Regiment, 28th Infantry Division.

At division headquarters an officer gave the group, including Slovik, an orientation lecture and ammunition was issued. According to the testimony of one of these soldiers, Private George W. Thompson, it was a matter of common knowledge and general conversation among the members of the group as to which company they were to join, where the company was, and whether it was engaged in combat. Thompson explained that the members of the group didn't know what to expect and didn't come to any definite conclusion about where they were going, but "had a pretty strong suspicion" that the division was engaged with the enemy. They did not know definitely what Company G was doing but just imagined that it was fighting.

20. The Execution of Private Slovik

On the same day, August 25, the group was trucked to division headquarters for Company G, then located at Elbeuf, approximately 80 miles northwest from Paris. En route to Elbeuf, the replacements, including Slovik, saw some damage, including burned-out vehicles and shelled places, but no action. After proceeding for two or three hours, they stopped at what apparently was a rest area, left their duffle bags, and continued on the trucks to the outskirts of Elbeuf, where they unloaded. After moving along the edge of the city, they reached an open lot where they "dug in" at about 11:00 p.m. One of the replacements, Thompson, saw Slovik with the group at this time. A few minutes later the replacements entered the city of Elbeuf to join Company G. There were "a lot of troop movements and shelling, and it took quite a while because there was a lot of confusion. We moved around some but stayed close together so none of us would get lost."

Thompson knew Slovik was at Elbeuf with the group at about 1:00 a.m. August 26, because he knew and recognized Slovik's voice. This was the last time he saw him, however; so far as he knew, Slovik was not present for duty with his company at any time thereafter. The company remained at Elbeuf for two days until Canadian troops took over. Over the next month, the 28th Infantry Division proceeded through Paris, Belgium, and Luxembourg to the Siegfried Line. During this movement, the division was engaged generally with the enemy in fighting and taking part in the invasion.

Captain Ralph O. Grotte, Company Commander of Company G, 109th Infantry, had been in command for a month and a half. When Slovik physically joined the company on October 8, it was reorganizing and not in contact with the enemy. Slovik had been absent without leave and had been returned through the battalion. He was never present with the company for duty except on October 8 for one or two hours. On that day a battalion sergeant major brought him to the company command post, where Grotte assigned Slovik to the 4th Platoon, turned him over to the platoon leader, and forbade him to leave the company area unless Slovik had permission from him. The platoon leader conducted Slovik to his platoon and introduced him to his squad leader. Thereafter Slovik came to Grotte and inquired of him if he could be tried for being absent without leave. Grotte told him he would find out; he then had Slovik placed under arrest and returned to his platoon area, where Grotte directed him to stay. About an hour later Slovik asked, "If I leave now, will it be desertion?" Grotte replied that it would be. Slovik left and thereafter he was not seen in the company area again.

The following morning Slovik went to Military Government Detachment, 112th Infantry, which since the preceding day had been located at Rocherath, Belgium. He handed a cook a green slip of paper containing handwriting and stated that he, Slovik, had made a confession. The cook informed his commanding officer, Lieutenant Thomas F. Griffin, who telephoned the Personnel Section (S-1) of the 109th Infantry and requested that someone call for Slovik. Around noon, a sergeant arrived and drove Slovik to the orderly room of the 109th Infantry, where he handed the green piece of paper to the temporary military police officer, First Lieutenant Wayne L. Hurd read it and directed the sergeant to deliver Slovik to the military police for temporary custody. Hurd then delivered the handwritten slip to Lieutenant Colonel Ross C. Henbest.

Subsequently on the same day, Slovik signed the slip in the presence of Hurd and Henbest, both of whom also signed the note. The paper was a U.S. Army Post Exchange flower order form, with writing in ink on each side, which read, a bit misspelled, as follows:

[Hand-printed in ink]

I Pvt. Eddie D. Slovik #36896415 confess to the Desertion of the United States Army. At the time of my Desertion we were in Albuff [Elbeuf] in France. I come to Albuff as a Replacement. They were shilling the town and we were told to dig in for the night The folowing morning they were shilling us again. I was so scared nerves and trembling that at the time the other Replacements moved out I couldn't move. I stayed their in my fox hole till it was quite and I was able to move. I then walked in town Not seeing any of our Troops so I stayed over night at a French hospital. The next morning I turned myself over to the Canadian Provost Corp. After being with them six weeks I was turned over to American M.P. They turned me lose. I told my commanding officer my story. I said that if I had to go out their again Id run away. He said their was nothing he could do for me· so I ran away again AND ILL RUN AWAY AGAIN IF I HAVE TO GO OUT THEIR.

        Signed Pvt. Eddie D. Slovik
        A.S.N. 3689641511

[Reverse side, on printed form, handwritten in ink:]

Rocherath, Belgium
Oct 11, 1944*

This statement is made in the presence of Lt. Col Ross C. Henbest 0237158 and 1st Lt Wayne Hurd 0-463853.

I have been told that this statement can be held against me and that I made it of my own free will and that I do not have to make it.

        Signed:*
        Eddie D. Slovik

Above statement was signed in the presence of the undersigned:

        /s/ Ross C. Henbest
        Ross C. Henbest *
        Lt Col, Infantry
        /s/ Wayne L. Hurd

20. The Execution of Private Slovik

Wayne L. Hurd *
1st. Lt.Inf *

*Handprinted.

On November 11, 1944, Eddie D. Slovik, 36896415 was tried upon the following charge and specifications:

Violation of the 58th Article of War
Specification 1: In that Private Eddie D. Slovik, Company G, 109th Infantry did, at or near Elbeuf, France, on or about 25 August 1944, desert the service of the United States by absenting himself without proper leave from his organization, with intent to avoid hazardous duty and to shirk important service, to Wit: action against the enemy, and did remain absent in desertion until he was delivered to United States military authorities by Canadian military authorities at or near Brussels, Belgium, on or about 4 October 1944. Sentenced: To be shot to death with musketry.

Upon reviewing the case Brigadier General E.C. McNeil, Assistant Judge Advocate General wrote the following:

This is the first death sentence for desertion which has reached me for examination. It is probably the first of the kind in the American Army for over eighty years—there were none in World War I. In this case, the extreme penalty of death appears warranted. This soldier had performed no front line duty. He did not intend to. He deserted from his group of fifteen when about to join the infantry company to which he had been assigned. His subsequent conduct shows a deliberate plan to secure trial and incarceration in a safe place. The sentence adjudged was more severe than he had anticipated, but the imposition of a less severe sentence would only have accomplished Slovik's purpose of securing his incarceration and consequent freedom from the dangers which so many of our armed forces are required to face daily. His unfavorable civilian record indicates that he is not a worthy subject of clemency.

On January 31, 1945, Eddie D. Slovik was shot at St. Marie aux Mines, France. Here a stack of sandbags, double thick and about 8 feet long and 10 feet tall, had been arranged in the location for the execution. About 18 inches in the center of the sandbags was an 8 by 8-inch post, 8 feet tall. Attached behind the post at a height of approximately 7 feet was a strong peg or hook. Slovik was escorted to the execution area. His legs were tied to the bottom of the post with a leather strap. Then a 1-inch leather strap was run under each armpit and connected securely to the peg or hook behind the post. This had two purposes: (1) if the prisoner was unconscious, he was able to stand erect; and (2) after execution, he was slumping but still in a standing position.

Slovik then had 1.5 minutes to say his last words and had the option of a short prayer. After "amen," a firing squad of 12 riflemen using bolt-action Garand M-1, 30-caliber rifles aimed slightly left of the center of his chest for the heart. The bolt action was used to prevent the accidental firing of two shots or more from a semi-automatic rifle. The five shots were then fired from at least 50 feet, to prevent the shooters from being injured by a ricocheting bullet that could penetrate through the victim's body or a shot that may have missed the intended target. The heart can be mortally injured, but it takes a few minutes to stop beating; thus eight minutes later, the medical doctor examined Slovik and pronounced him dead. More than one victim of the firing squad has died from bleeding to death.

Afterward, the official in charge of the execution, while the body was still suspended, loosened and removed the leg straps, armpit straps, and optional hood and set the body on the ground. They completely opened or removed his shirt and placed the body in a wooden burial box for a photograph and removal. The photographs reveal blood draining down from the bullet holes in Slovik's chest. Considerable blood was smeared on the victim's arms and hands. Apparently his pants were soaked with blood, after remaining upright for eight minutes, and were not removed to prevent the assistant from smearing himself with the victim's blood and possible other discharges from the body.

The so-called standard procedure for a firing squad using a rifle with a blank was, in fact, never used. The recoil from a blank is much less than that of a bullet; thus, it is obvious not only to the individual firing, but also to any witnesses or spectators. Consequently, the blank rule was never followed but was always said to be used.[1]

21

Postwar Paris

World War II had ended, but now all over Europe, the people would face a winter of cold and death. In this gloom American soldiers were left behind to clean up loose ends, to work with the military government, and to route luckier soldiers home. These remaining unhappy soldiers would have to wait endlessly for their own turn to board a liberty ship or a transport and return to the United States.

France had been returned to the French and almost all the U.S. Army offices in Paris had been closed. A lot of official army business still passed through the city, but to the average GI stationed on the Continent, Paris was still the dream place to spend a three-day pass. From every nook and cranny in Europe where Americans were stationed pulling occupation duty, they came on three-day passes, arriving weary and dirty from a two-day combination train and truck trip. These soldiers were mostly loaded with pay that was hard to spend in the small towns of Germany and were busting to get rid of their hard-earned money. After a quick shave, shower, and shine at one of the many Paris billet hotels, they would take off and knock themselves out for 72 glorious hours.

Soon they discovered that, although Paris still retained remnants of the city they heard and read about, it was not all they had thought it would be. On the surface, yes. The soldiers got out in the middle of the Champs-Elysées in front of the Place de la Concorde and gazed down the broad avenue toward the impressive Arc de Triomphe. Paying no heed to the erratic tactics of the French motorists, they took snapshots of each other, legs astride, hands on hips. After half a day of sightseeing at Napoleon's tomb, the Eiffel Tower, and the Louvre—where everything from *Whistler's Mother* to Leonardo's *Mona Lisa* was jam-packed into one gallery—they settled down to the run-of-the-mill GI pastime of drinking bad French cognac at a dollar a snort.

The men who enjoyed "higher-class" entertainment, and who had latched onto a "respectable" date, headed for Paris's most famous nightspot, the Bal Tabarjn, where a bottle of sparkling wine set them back $18. The Bal was the closest thing to New York's Latin Quarter or Copacabana that Paris offered. Its frou-frou revue, with showgirls who wore nothing but a loincloth and a great big smile, would certainly have made a U.S. mayor scream, stomp and call out his vice squad.

The famous sidewalk cafés along the Champs-Elysées were closed for the winter, but street bars, cafés and small night clubs off the street handled the GIs' sidewalk trade. Following the last days of the war, an inkling of what Parisian fashions were like in prewar days hit the Champs promenade. The women dragged out their Sunday-best fineries, which they had stashed away in mothballs during the occupation. They wore these cherished garments because they knew fashion was gradually coming back to Paris and it would not be long before they could replenish their meager wardrobes. Prices were exorbitant: Clothing that could be purchased for $15 or $20 in U.S. department stores sold for ten times those amounts in Paris. But Parisian styling was still tops. Although the materials were inferior, the way the cloth was put together made the GI window shoppers say "Damn, wish I had enough dough to bring one of those home for the wife."

The average soldier limited his Paris-bought gifts to a bottle of perfume, a scarf, and a risqué pastel print of a half-clad femme sprawled on a divan. The shopwise soldier stayed away from the average Parisian main-street stores. Instead, he sweated out a line at the GI gift store PXs or at the Chanel shop where he could purchase a decent-size bottle of the famous stuff for $6.

The black market in watches, binoculars, typewriters, and fountain pens was active in the Rainbow Corner section of town near the Madeleine Church. When a soldier ran out of ready cash, he could always find a buyer for his valuables. Many soldiers wrangled passes to Paris for the specific purpose of buying watches and taking them back to Berlin, Vienna, and other occupation cities, where they peddle them to Russian soldiers for fabulous sums.

The Opéra Comique, French Ballet, and Symphony halls were in full swing again. Except for a few long-hairs and the soldiers studying at the Sorbonne under the Army's Education Program, however, the audience consisted of mostly Parisians.

The WACs had left the Hotel California on the Rue de Berri, so Peeping Toms no longer gathered in the offices across the street to watch the girls get ready for bed. This large army office building on Rue de Berri was now used by the American as the home office for Special Services and Stars & Stripes. The hotel did fantastic business with American and foreign businessmen, but was not as nice as when the tinkle of girlish laughter rang through its halls.

21. Postwar Paris

The only large installations of soldiers left in France were found at the staging areas at the ports of Le Havre and Marseille, where they stepped on the ships returning home. The ports were working two ways, with fresh GIs from the United States unloading for occupation duty. These soldiers knew they had come late to an episode that would last for a long time.[1] One of these soldiers was Manuel Martinez. He had served in Europe during the war, but was now returning to a continent and city that had changed. Could he adapt?

22

Martinez's Early Years

Manuel Martinez's story—a combination of uncontrollable anger, addictions, fabrications, and near-illiteracy—began in the dusty environs of East Texas. The details of his childhood proved difficult to track; his final years, however, are clearly documented by court records and personal testimonies. Unfortunately, his was a life replete with criminal activities that started with theft and fistfights and escalated to murder and tragedy.

Martinez seemed born to lie. Under oath, for example, he swore that he was born in Dallas, Texas, on January 3, 1921; six months later, again under oath, he swore that he first entered this world in Toledo, Ohio. Both his army record and his gravestone inscription record a birth date of January 3, 1926, but even this is doubtful. Given these inconsistencies and lies, logic supports his birthplace as the farming community of Munford, in East Texas. His early years remain a mystery, and his immediate family and mother's family are not recorded in the 1930 census or in any birth records in the Bureau of Vital Statistics in Texas and Ohio.

The family of Martinez's mother lived about six miles down the dirt road from Munford, in a settlement called Mooring, with a given post office address of "Steel's Store." Today the dirt crossing at Mooring shows nothing—no sign that it was ever a community at all. The only evidence of its existence consists of the ruins of Steel's Store, a little roofless structure covered with vines. Munford, therefore, consists mainly of a post office with a past and a modern school situated across the road. Martinez grew up in poverty, but ironically he was surrounded by obvious signs of wealth in this East Texas countryside: vast fields of wheat and oil wells still steadily pumping Texas crude the way they did during Martinez's childhood.

Although no records exist of Martinez's early childhood, it is a fact that his father, Tony, and his mother, Cecilia, were living in Munford in the late 1920s and early 1930s. Logically, their small son also lived there, although

22. Martinez's Early Years

Manuel would swear once that his father was "a tailor in Dallas." He would also add—perhaps significantly, given Martinez's later adult activities—that "the old man was a hard drinker."

Manuel was one of a family of seven children, three brothers and three sisters, of which he was the third eldest. His father Tony was born in Waco and was of pure Spanish descent. This status placed him in the upper class of Latino society. His mother was Mexican, however, so she was looked down upon as low class in the prevailing Texas caste system, as were the children of the Martinez union. This bigotry, combined with a hardscrabble existence, might well have played a part in Martinez's mother contracting pulmonary tuberculosis. She was given some treatment for a year and a half by a doctor in nearby Bryan, Texas, but there was no remedy for her condition. Sadly, on Christmas Day 1931, at 9:30 in the morning, she died at the young age of 26 or 28; on her medical forms, under the field for date of birth, was checked "Don't Know." As a reflection of the social environment of the times, she was buried in the local Mexican cemetery across the cattle path from the black cemetery. The "lower classes" were segregated even in death, a bigotry that persists today.

Little Manuel was five years old when his mother died. A year later, his father remarried and moved to Chicago, taking with him only his oldest son, Tony Jr. Manuel never saw his father again. One of his sisters was sent to the community of Steele's Store to live with her grandmother, Catarina Ramirez. This sister died at the heartbreakingly young age of fourteen (cause unknown). After his mother's death, Manuel's maternal uncle, Mike Ramirez, took him away to live with him in Toledo, Ohio. Martinez claimed that he never went to school, although he did somehow learn to read and write, if only on a very elementary level. At thirteen, he went to work with a cleaning and pressing company for $1.50 a day, working with this single company continuously during that period.

Evidence shows, however, that he eventually left his uncle and lived "on the streets." He was arrested several times in both Toledo and Cleveland for drunkenness; he spent a total of 21 days in jail in these two cities. This drunken behavior, which would be repeated throughout his life, would prove to be his undoing as an adult.

During these days, a judge would often give an offender a choice of punishment: jail or enlistment in the army. This may have been the option given to Manuel, for on March 25, 1944, at the age of eighteen, he was inducted into the U.S. Army at Fort Benjamin Harrison, Indiana. Fort Benjamin Harrison Reception Center was the largest military welcoming center in the United States. (In contrast to Martinez's history, his older brothers, Tony Jr., and Ralph, were also members of the U.S. military during the war. They served in the

Pacific Theater with the ranks of sergeant, were honorably discharged from the service, and returned to their homes in Michigan and California, respectively.)

Manuel took basic training at Camp Blanding, Florida. He then volunteered for paratrooper school and had his initial physical examination on October 17, 1944, at Fort Benning, Georgia, where he received airborne training.

Martinez was ordered overseas. He was processed through Newberry, England, and assigned to the famed 101st Airborne Division—the "Screaming Eagles." In March 1945, he was designated a rifleman with D Company, 501st Regiment, 101st Airborne Division, and continued to serve with that unit in the Ruhr Valley pocket, patrolling and raiding. Three months prior, in December 1944, the 101st had been engaged in the ferocious battle for the village of Bastogne, Belgium. Badly decimated from this month-long struggle, the unit was regrouping. In April 1945, then, the 101st was engaging as an occupying military government unit in northern Germany at Rheydt and München-Gladbach (renamed Mönchengladbach in 1960).

In the last weeks of the war, Martinez's unit moved south 400 miles and then reached Adolf Hitler's hideaway town of Berchtesgaden in the Bavarian Alps, where the war ended. This would seem to have been an excellent opportunity for Martinez to "turn his life around," seeing as how he had become a member of a proud and distinguished military entity, the 101st. But that outcome didn't happen for Martinez: Although his records show that he had endured three months of combat, was wounded in the leg and received a Purple Heart, and was authorized to receive the European Theater Ribbon with two battle stars, he continued to drink to excess. The German government surrendered on May 8, 1945, but "low pointer" Martinez was transferred to the 13th Airborne Division, 515th Parachute Infantry Regiment, Company F.

At this stage in the war, a soldier's future assignment depended on the points value system. Points totals were based on overall time in service and overseas duty. These points were used to determine whether a military man or woman was discharged, reassigned to the United States in a training cadre, remained in Europe as occupational personnel, or (shudder!) redeployed to the Pacific Theater, where the war was still being conducted. The breakdown was as follows: 1 point for each month in service, 1 point for each month overseas, 5 points for combat medals, and 12 points for each of the subject's children under 18 years of age. Eighty-four points was the goal—the "magic number" for discharge. (Each soldier, on a daily basis, could quote his accumulated points and mustering-out pay amount.)

The 13th Airborne Division arrived in France in February 1945 and, as things turned out, was the only division in Europe not to participate in combat

22. Martinez's Early Years

during World War II. Interestingly, the 13th was earmarked to be part of the upcoming Operation Coronet, the March 1946 invasion of Tokyo Bay, but the atomic bombs dropped on Hiroshima and Nagasaki spared these troops from what was sure to be an enormous number of casualties on both the American and Japanese sides. Coronet called for 1 million American troops and their equipment to be immediately transferred from the European Theater to the South Pacific Ocean area to support the invasion of Japan. Thus, lacking the magic 84 points, Private Manuel Martinez returned with the 13th Airborne Division to the United States, arriving at Fort Bragg, North Carolina, on August 26, 1945. Here he was granted a three-month furlough. While on leave during September in his former place of residence, Toledo, he married a Spanish girl, "Mary Rivers." (This is possibly the anglicanization of the Spanish "Maria Rivera.") The couple separated after three months. According to Martinez, "She wouldn't live with me because I was drunk all the time." He had known "Mary" since 1939, and after the separation he is known to have allotted "a dependent" $35 of his pay. This money was most likely set aside for Mary.[1]

23

Martinez Returns to Germany

During Martinez's ninety-day leave, the war with Japan ended. Martinez decided to continue his army career. As a matter of government policy (and more paperwork), he was first honorably discharged and then accepted for reenlistment into the regular army, with an enlistment obligation of three years. From here he was assigned to Camp Pickett, Virginia, a replacement depot for army ground forces. After five months, he was reassigned to a Quartermaster Base Depot in Germany. As was customary with Martinez's self-destructive personality, he decided that he would *not* return to Europe and went AWOL on February 22, 1946. Three weeks later, on March 14, he was arrested and subsequently incarcerated on March 19 at Fort Hayes, near Columbus, Ohio. He was issued inmate clothing and necessary toiletry articles, such as a razor, shaving brush, comb, toothbrush and toothpaste, for which he paid the grand total of $1.02. (It is important to keep in mind that in 1946 an American could buy a hamburger for a dime and see a movie for the same amount.) For this offense, on March 29, Martinez received a summary court-martial and was sentenced to forfeit just $14.00 in pay. The light sentence was in consideration of his combat record during the war. From Fort Hayes, he was transferred to Fort Kilmer, New Jersey, for relocation to Europe. Since his reenlistment Martinez had been promoted to Private First Class and was allowed after his AWOL caper to keep this rank. He wouldn't have it for long.

At Fort Kilmer, Martinez met and befriended Pfc. Manuel E. Castillo. The two were transferred to the 3233rd Quartermaster Service Company in Giessen, Germany. In July 1946, Martinez returned to Germany along with Castillo, and the two were given duties in the mess hall as cooks, despite their lack of any food preparation experience. Martinez and Castillo shared a two-man room in the former German Army (*Wehrmacht*) barracks. Unlike the

23. Martinez Returns to Germany

hastily built barracks in the United States, the German military had built large stone buildings with French glass doors, balconies, and space for two to four men in each room, similar to the setup in an American college dormitory. Castillo kept his watch under his pillow since he had to get up each morning at 3:30 to go to work. Before leaving, he would rouse Martinez at 4:00, so he could wake up the KPs. (As almost every serviceman will recall "fondly," these were the kitchen police—the "sad sacks" who were assigned the unenviable tasks of washing metal trays and eating utensils, scrubbing out huge pots and pans, serving food, and cleaning up the mess hall afterward.) The two men would then report to the mess hall, where Martinez would ensure that the food had been delivered. He had access to an army truck for any necessary short jaunts in the line of duty. This was the duo's daily routine, with one day off each week.

In the meantime, Martinez continued his detrimental pattern of heavy drinking. To this habit he added the use of hashish, which soldiers on furlough to France were able to obtain and smuggle back into Germany. They obtained the "hash" in tablet form for about 33 cents per tablet from Algerians, who called it *gief*. Martinez would take an American cigarette and strip away the paper; he would then grind up the *gief* tablets, mix them with tobacco, and re-roll the combination with brown paper. These hand-rolled cigarettes were called "reefers," and he smoked them very often.

At this new post, the black-haired, dark-complexioned, 5 feet 6 inch-tall, 150-pound Martinez was given the nickname "Pancho." In less than one month, "Pancho" would have his new Private First Class rank reduced to Private because of a misconduct incident on the night of August 23. On that night, Martinez fought with some "Negro" soldiers (as they were referred to at that time) and received the worse end of the bargain; he was beaten up, requiring medical attention on his left eye that resulted in his wearing an eyepatch.

In occupied Germany, drunkenness and fighting were accepted realities when it came to the victorious American soldier. The system made it easy to see why. The officers/NCO/EM clubs opened at 10 a.m. and started selling beer at the astonishing price (compared to today's costs) of a mere five cents a bottle. Drinking all day when not on duty was acceptable, and numerous soldiers were drunk every night. Also, the German *Polizei* (police) had no authority over American soldiers and, when a disorderly event occurred, were required to call an American Military Policeman (MP). These MPs patrolled German cities in jeeps, with two military police in the front seats and a German policeman in the back. The German police did have authority over any Germans involved, which in most cases would turn out to be soldiers' girlfriends. Most often, due to racial tensions involving girlfriends, there were fights between

Caucasian and African American soldiers. In 1946, the U.S. Army was still completely segregated, which meant segregation in churches, parades, mess halls, clubs, troop organizations, and transportation. This inequality existed until July 26, 1948, when President Harry S Truman ordered the desegregation of all military organizations.

In this milieu, Martinez and his roommate/friend Castillo on their day off on Saturday, August 24. At about 2:00 p.m., they went to the downtown Giessen Red Cross club. Most large towns in Europe had a Red Cross club, where a soldier could relax, play cards, read, and get free soft drinks, coffee, and cookies. This was not Martinez's kind of place, so he did not stay long. According to Castillo, however, Martinez remained at the club until he left for the 579th Quartermaster Battalion enlisted men's club about 10:00 that night.

More than any occupying power in history, the U.S. Army brought as much of its homeland culture and customs to Germany as it possibly could. Martinez could listen to American radio stations and read an American newspaper, since his surroundings were carefully contrived to duplicate life back home. Thus, while Martinez did venture into the destruction and gloominess of occupied Germany, he could always hustle back into the brightness of an American environment at the enlisted men's clubs, Red Cross clubs, on-post American movies, bowling alleys, snack bars, stage shows, and most of the other conveniences and entertainments of America. Martinez's and other soldiers' German girlfriends could also gain access to these luxuries; on their own side, the basics of food and warmth were scarce. All of the U.S.-provided comfort was made available at a most affordable price: Beer was a nickel a bottle, a shot of whiskey was ten cents, and a pack of cigarettes cost five cents. The most popular night in most enlisted men's clubs was Friday before payday—free beer night. Cleverly, whiskey was identified as a "Class VI supply," a euphemism to avoid the mentioning of hard liquor. This arrangement caught on, and even today the army refers whimsically to whiskey as a "Class VI supply."

Later that same day, at around 4:00 in the evening, Martinez went to number 19 Weg Alter Krofdorfer, the home of Emmi Reibeling and her cousin, Anneliese Langer. They were the girlfriends of Pfc. Cecil A. Fant and Pvt. Phillip F. Smith. Both soldiers were in the house when Martinez came to the back window and called upstairs asking if he could come up. He was admitted, but once in the room, "Pancho" was told by Anneliese that his girlfriend had not arrived. Martinez then showed the young women a .45-caliber automatic U.S. Army pistol. As Anneliese would later testify, Martinez told the group that he had been "in a house a few doors down" from where they were talking. In that house, according to Martinez, there were six "colored" soldiers, four of whom had jumped him and beat him up. "He had come in to tell us this," said

23. Martinez Returns to Germany

Anneliese. "He had a pistol in his hand at the time and said he was going after them and get even with them." Martinez told them not to mention the pistol to anyone. After about 15 minutes, Martinez said he had to go back into town and left in the direction of "the house a few doors down."

Two hours later, American soldiers Fant and Smith and their young German girlfriends left the house on Alter Krofdorfer to go to the 579th Quartermaster Battalion enlisted men's club. Here, as in most bars, a soldier would take a folded wad of money from his pocket and place it on the right side of the table; then he would place a pack of cigarettes on top and add to the pile by placing his cigarette lighter atop. This "marked" the table and accomplices as his. Most clubs had a band of grubby German musicians whose clothes were always too large, evidence of the wartime shortage of food. They played American songs, and the dance floor was mostly continually full. Soldiers danced with their girlfriends during the slow beat, but with the jitterbug music the German girls danced with each other. It was common in Europe for women to dance with each other, and it took the average GI about fifteen minutes to get accustomed to it. The young German women had a great deal of influence on young American soldiers; there were plenty of them, they were accessible, and there was a free and easy atmosphere about them. These casual contacts often progressed into an enduring relationship, even sometimes leading to marriage.

At the enlisted men's club, Smith downed fifteen to twenty drinks, and Fant and the girls had about "four shots each." They left at about 11:00 p.m. As stated by Pfc. Fant:

> We left the club at 2300 hours and headed for my girlfriend's home. We were stopped on the way home by Pvt. Martinez, who was riding in the front passenger seat of a 2½-ton 6 × 6 U.S. Army truck with a canvas cover. He asked if I wanted a ride and I said "yes." We rode up to my girlfriend's home, and as my girlfriend and I got out of the truck Martinez came up to meet us. On leaving him, as a matter of my usual parting remark to anyone, I said, "Take it easy." As I walked away, I saw he had something in his left hand but I could not make out what it was. It could have been a pistol such as I saw that afternoon. He told me then that he wanted to see the Negro who beat him up.

As he walked around the front of the truck, Pvt. Smith saw a pistol in Martinez's left hand. As they left the truck, Anneliese Langer noticed that Martinez was drunk. He ran around in the street with the pistol in his hand and, using offensive language, said now they "can come who want to kill me."

The area in the vicinity of the German girl's home was a gathering place for young Germans. The vast majority of the German men between the ages of 18 and 50 had been killed during the war or were interned in prisoner of war camps. Any area frequented by American soldiers presented the opportunity to obtain black market items and cigarette butts that were thrown away by American soldiers. The black market thrived, as Martinez and his mess hall buddies had almost unlimited access to sugar, coffee, flour, cooking fat, and butter—items that the Germans did not have and that were in great demand. Trade in such items produced a clear profit without any investment on Martinez's part. A pound of coffee could be sold for $30 and a pound of butter would bring $20. Martinez's military pay was $84 a month. From that was deducted the aforementioned AWOL fine of $14 and the "Mary Rivers" allotment of $35. GI insurance cost him an additional $6.40, thus netting Martinez $37.60 a month. This was pretty good money considering the costs of the time, and with the lucrative black market he lived quite well.

When Martinez stopped in front of Emmi Reibeling and her cousin Anneliese Langer's home, hanging around outside were seventeen-year-old Erich Kraehling and sixteen-year-old Helmut Sack. They recognized Pancho Martinez as soon as he stepped out of the truck; he had been seen there several times before. Erich recognized that the soldiers were all drunk, and then Helmut saw Pancho throw a pistol into the air and catch it. As he placed the pistol back into his pocket, Martinez said (according to young Kraehling), "If he could see black soldiers he would shoot them."

Forty-five minutes later, while at his girlfriend's home, Fant heard a truck drive up to the house next door; it stopped for a minute and then left. Anneliese Langer recognized Pancho's voice as he said something offensive regarding the African American soldiers. The truck left at around 11:15 p.m.

A few minutes later, African American Pfc. Harold Mackel left the enlisted men's club and walked his girlfriend home. Mackel was quite sober, as he was a teetotaler. After saying goodnight, he was walking back to the 3410th Quartermaster Truck Company when he flagged down a truck to get a ride. The truck stopped and a "fellow that was in front with the driver jumped out and came around to the back of the truck about 50 feet from where I was standing. He asked, 'What are you doing over here?" I said, 'Huh.' I then saw a pistol. This fellow told me that 'a bunch of you fellows jumped me the other night.' Then I said, 'Well, craps, fella. It was not me.' He stepped back, pulled his pistol out, and shot me as I turned to run. As I ran, he fired two more rounds at me, one of which went past my head and the other by my feet."

Mackel stumbled, and two young German boys helped him across the street. Here, he flagged down a 1941 Plymouth containing two women and two American officers. They took the wounded Mackel to the 388th Station Hospital in Giessen. He had been shot completely through the chest, three inches from his heart. The following day, Mackel gave the investigating MPs a description of the soldier who assaulted him: "5 feet 8 inches, Mexican or

23. Martinez Returns to Germany

Philippine, stocky with black hair." Later the same day, the MPs brought three "line-up" men to Mackel's hospital room, and Mackel positively identified Manuel Martinez as the soldier that had shot him. Martinez was immediately arrested and locked up in the stockade. Mackel's wounds were serious enough that he remained in the hospital until September 26, 1946.

Pvt. Manuel Martinez's court-martial began at 1:00 p.m. on October 9, 1946. He was charged with assault with the intent to commit murder. Specifically, "Private Manuel Martinez, 3233d Quartermaster Service Company, did, at Giessen, Germany, on or about 24 August 1946, with intent to commit a felony, *viz*, murder, commit an assault upon Pfc. Harold Mackel, by willfully and feloniously shooting him with a pistol."

Mackel testified that he had been shot by Martinez at approximately 23:40 hours on August 24. He was asked the following question by the defense regarding racial tension:

Q: It's not an isolated incident for trouble to develop between white and colored soldiers?
A: No, sir.
Q: It occurs rather frequently?
A: Yes sir, rather.

Pfc. Cecil Fant, Pvt. Phillip Smith, Emmi Reibeling, and Anneliese Langer, under sworn testimony, told basically the same story regarding Martinez's August 26 visit to the German girl's home and the return truck ride. In an attempt to discredit the prosecution witnesses' testimony, the defense attorney questioned them as to how much they had had to drink.

The two German teens, ages sixteen and seventeen, then testified that they knew "Pancho" and that on Saturday night around 11:00 p.m. he was at Alter Krofdorfer, Giessen, the street where the girlfriends of Fant and Smith lived, and that Pancho was throwing a pistol into the air and catching it. They testified that Martinez had proclaimed, "If I see a Negro, I'll kill him." They also testified that he was riding in an army truck.

Next, Martinez's roommate Manuel Castillo stated that he had met Martinez at Fort Kilmer and testified for the defense. Castillo swore that he was in his room at 10:00 p.m. and had gone to bed 45 minutes later. According to Castillo, Martinez came into their room at 11:15 or 11:20. The company cook, Kistler P. Jordan, had looked in and asked if they wanted something to eat. The cook went and prepared some sandwiches, which he brought up to Castillo and Martinez's room. Martinez was in bed, said Castillo, and they sat and talked about their girlfriends. The cook, Jordan, left the room at 11:45. Thus Martinez was in his room when Harold Mackel was shot, or so Castillo and Jordan both swore.

The proceedings ended with a statement from General Prisoner Manuel Martinez. He had the right to do one of three things. First, he could be sworn in and take the stand as a witness. Whatever he said would be considered and weighed as evidence by the court, just like the testimony of the other witnesses, and he could be cross-examined. Second, without being sworn, he could say anything he desired to the court as an unsworn statement, denying, explaining, or excusing any of the acts for which he was charged. This statement could be oral or written. Since such a statement was not given under oath, he could not be cross-examined regarding its content. Third, he could remain silent.

At 4:50 p.m., the members of the court-martial proceeding took a five-minute recess and then resumed their seats. The accused requested counsel to render his unsworn written statement:

> On the 24th of August 1946, I left the club about 10:30 p.m. and picked up a ride in an army two-and-a-half, six-by-six truck. I do not know who the driver of this vehicle was.
>
> About 10:30 p.m. on this night, the driver stopped and picked up Privates Fant and Smith and two German girls who were accompanying them, and drove to the house where one of the girls lived in Giessen and let the four of them out.
>
> I proceeded on in the truck to the main gate at the entrance to the 56th Quartermaster Base Depot Caserne, where the driver let me out. It was about 10:55 p.m. when I got off at the main gate. I walked from the main gate to my quarters in the Caserne, a distance of 500 yards.
>
> When I reached my quarters, it was about 11:00 p.m. and my roommate, Private First Class Castillo, was already in bed, and I started talking to him. A few minutes after 11:00 p.m., Private First Class Jordan came by the room and someone suggested getting something to eat.
>
> The first time I had ever seen the witness, Private First Class Harold Mackel, was when I was taken to the 388th Station Hospital a few days after the 24th of August 1946, and he was then a patient in the hospital.

One hour later at 5:50 p.m., the seventeen-member officers of the court ruled, and the court president made the following announcement:

> Private Martinez, the court finds you Of the Specification of the Charge: NOT GUILTY.

Would this flagrant miscarriage of justice and extremely lucky break teach Martinez a lesson? Unfortunately not. The very next day, October 10, he went AWOL, leaving the barracks at 11:00 p.m. and going into downtown Giessen, where he and Castillo got drunk. He missed his work assignment, and the following day Castillo went to find him. Martinez proceeded to get into a fight with Castillo at the intersection of Wilhelm and Ludwig Streets in downtown Giessen. As Martinez later put it, "Don't know why I go AWOL; I wasn't doing nothing, walked around the company all day long; was drunk all the time; I

23. Martinez Returns to Germany

was put in charge of KP but I never did anything. You see, I have been drinking since I was small, all the time. I have been by myself and all others did it, so I did, too. I have been hit over the head so many times with bottles of beer, I can't count them. My head is full of places [scars]."

For his typical charges of drunk and disorderly and fighting, Martinez was fined $50 on October 24, 1946, and sentenced to four months in the 7720 Rehabilitation Center, Würzburg, Germany. Martinez commented, "They put me in the detention center at Würzburg. The same thing put me there—drunk, drunk, and fighting. I do things when I am drunk I don't remember. Half of them I don't believe because I don't see them. They ain't ever got me in the army for stealing." Remaining in jail throughout the Christmas holiday, Martinez stayed out of trouble and was returned to 3233 Quartermaster Service Company on January 11, 1947.

On January 23, less than two weeks after being released from jail, Private Manuel Martinez slapped a young German woman, Ruth Bender, in the face and tried to choke Pfc. William H. Ray to death with his necktie. When MP Pvt. Glen J. Anderson arrived to stop this altercation, Martinez struck Anderson in the face with his fist. For this offense, on February 19, 1947, he was court-martialed, fined $50, and sentenced to six months in the Giessen military stockade.

While waiting in jail for the conclusion of this court-martial, Martinez was given duty in the mess hall. He disappeared. His escape was recounted by a guard, Private George E. Jacobi:

> On February 15, 1947, at about 1200, I relieved a guard in the mess hall of the 541st Depot Supply Company who was guarding prisoners acting as kitchen police. Another guard with me, his name is Clarence H. Starnard. One of the prisoners for whom I was responsible was named Martinez, nicknamed "Pancho." At about 1230 hours the prisoners ate their noonday meal, after which the dining room was cleaned by three of my men, including Pancho. They finished cleaning the dining room at 1315. I was stationed at one end of the dining room nearest the stairway and Starnard was stationed at the other end. At about 1415 the other guard told me to go to the ration breakdown to get some rations.
>
> I took three prisoners, including Pancho, and we went for the rations. We returned to the mess hall about 1530. After I had unloaded the ration truck, the other guard asked me where Pancho was. I told him he was in the latrine. I looked in the latrines, the soldier's billets and B mess hall but could not find him.
>
> I had to go for more rations so I took three prisoners back through Mess Hall B looking for Pancho, but could not find him. I then took the three prisoners back to the ration breakdown for the other rations. We returned about 1600 when Starnard again asked me where Pancho was. I again made another search but could not find him. I then told Starnard to report Pancho's escape. This was about 1610 when he made the report. I do not know how or when Pancho escaped.

After two weeks of freedom, on March 2, 1947, Martinez was back in the Giessen military stockade. After complaining of being too sick to work ("riding the sick book"), he was placed in solitary confinement for four days. On March 18, he was tried by General Courts-Martial for the offense of escape from confinement. During the deposition of his personal history, Martinez's explanation for his escapes was that he was rather "high" and that he left because he wanted to see a girlfriend in Salzburg.

Upon his fifth court-martial in less than a year, Martinez was sentenced to a dishonorable discharge, total forfeit of all pay, and one year at hard labor. He was to be sent to the maximum-security European Command military prison in Mannheim, Germany, and then transferred to the disciplinary barracks at Greenhaven, New York, for his hard labor. The judge wrote, "The accused does not have any salvage value and should not be retained in service."

Five days later, Martinez escaped again from the Giessen military stockade. This time he was accompanied by Private Junior D. Poindexter.

The escape notification read: "These two men escaped from Giessen Military Post Stockade. Exact time is unknown. Absence discovered after breakfast, 23, March, 1947. Martinez is Spanish, age 21, height 5'6", weight 150 lbs., blue eyes, and black hair (Spanish type). Was general prisoner." Martinez recalled, "I remember I was in the stockade. I go to the mess hall. We get two bottles of schnapps from the Germans [mess hall workers], and the next thing I know I am in Paris."

After his escape, Martinez remained in Germany, living with German civilians in the cities of Frankfurt and Cologne. Wearing a U.S. Army uniform, he had no difficulties eating in the army transient mess halls in the larger German cities. He claimed later, "I stayed in Germany for a while. I would have some boys I met at the replacement depot in Marburg bring me stuff from the PX. They were all AWOL. They are all in prison now."[1]

24

Springtime in Paris

Martinez arrived in Paris in mid–April 1947. Although Paris was not ravaged by the war, the City of Lights, two years later, seemed to be finished in a doomed and listless silence, with few cars on the streets and old women traveling on bicycles. With the shortage of food, fuel and electricity, the theaters, hotels, restaurants and public places were cold, sparsely populated, and forbidding. There was a bright side, though: cheap wine and the young girls, riding their bicycles, short skirts billowing, exposing generously uncovered pink thighs, that helped the Parisians avoid a defeated look.

One of the few places where American soldiers and Parisians seemed to get along was Place Pigalle—or as corrupted by the American soldiers, "Pig Alley." After dark, this small sector of Montmartre devoted itself to the entertainment of the American soldier in its honky-tonks, back alleys, and penny arcades, where black market chocolate and American cigarettes were plentiful. The friendly, free-spending, pleasure-bent soldiers were looking for a good time with the agreeable Parisian girls, and they could certainly find it in Place Pigalle. The area was also known to every American soldier in Europe as the home of the famed cabaret Moulin Rouge and other topless and nude shows, where for a bottle of overpriced champagne one would have an attractive young lady companion for the evening. Unlike in the army, the segregation line for black soldiers hardly existed in Paris and especially in the undecorated nightclubs of Place Pigalle, where the African American soldiers danced with the uninhibited French girls.

Martinez settled here with 9,500 French francs, which he had received from a soldier friend from the sale of two German cameras. He also had about $200 in military scrip money and a PX-purchased watch that cost him $68. He sold the watch for about 7,000 francs ($58), a loss of $10. To further bolster his bankroll, Martinez met a soldier on furlough and gave him the military scrip money to buy PX items. He then sold these goods for francs and shared the proceeds with his partner. A former German soldier asked him if he could get a pistol for him, so he bought an army Colt pistol with some ammunition from an Algerian for 2,000 French francs with the intention of making a profit on it. Life in Paris was expensive, however, and Martinez could not slide back into the inexpensive American environment; instead, he had to pay $20 for a bottle of champagne and $2 for a shot of cognac. It is easy to see why many GIs bitterly complained that "the frogs" were cheating them.

Martinez made contact with several American soldiers in Pigalle, including 27-year-old Private William Stribling and 26-year-old Private William A. Mitchell. Stribling, introduced in a previous chapter, had been arrested in Paris for being AWOL and spent some time incarcerated in the Loire Disciplinary Training Center in LeMans, France. Released back to his unit in Germany, he was now, two years later, on authorized leave in Paris.

Mitchell entered the army on May 6, 1944, at Fort Leavenworth, Kansas. He shipped overseas and was a soldier with the 57th Ordnance Company located in Belgium. He went AWOL and was sentenced to the Military Prison Detention Center at Würzburg, Germany. At the end of his incarceration, he was given orders to report to the staging area in Bremerhaven, Germany, for a return trip to the United States by ship. Mitchell, on his own initiative, decided to travel to Paris.

As his money began to run out, Martinez turned from the black market to an easier way of making money: armed robbery. On the night of April 24, 1947, cab driver Pierre Bourenkoff was sitting in his taxi around midnight when two men, Manuel Martinez and Bill Stribling, approached and asked him in broken French to drive them to the Gare de l'Est, the large eastern train station that served the major cities in Europe and was the starting point of the Orient Express. The pair got into the back seat of the taxi. Upon arriving at the train station, Martinez told the driver to look for a hotel. The taxi driver asked him which hotel they wanted—perhaps they knew of one. Instead of indicating the hotel, they made him drive first to the left and then to the right, and then they ordered him to drive to a small dark street. Martinez clambered over the seat of the car and sat next to Bourenkoff; he had a pistol in his hand and shoved the gun into the taxi driver's side. Martinez then made the driver understand that he must obey them. They proceeded to a small, dark street at Rue Faubourg St. Denis and told the driver to stop. After searching Bourenkoff, they motioned for him to start driving again.

The taxi driver had two billfolds. Out of these wallets, Martinez and Stribling took the sum of 4,000 francs and six ration tickets for ten liters each of fuel. Both men asked the driver if he had more money. Stribling, speaking somewhat better French, repeatedly said, "Money, money, is there no money?"

24. Springtime in Paris

Each time Bourunkoff tried to disobey them and drive to a lighted street, they pushed the pistol in his side and threatened to kill him if he did not drive them where they wanted to go. After he said that he would obey, the two thugs said, "Okay." From that answer he correctly guessed they were Americans. Then they made him drive toward Boulevard Barbes, turn to the left, and go down Rue Clignancourt. Getting out of the car and threatening him with the pistol, they told Bourenkoff not to make any comments to the police. Showing the taxi driver the direction they wanted him to take, they skedaddled in the opposite direction.

Bourenkoff immediately reported the robbery to the police of St. Vincent de Paul at Strasbourg St.-Denise and described the men as "one that looked oriental" and the other "a tall, slender colored man." He reported their approximate sizes and noted that they were dressed in mixed military/civilian uniforms.

The following night, Remy Rouyer was at the Metro station known as Stalingrad, which had been renamed after the World War II Soviet victory at the Battle of Stalingrad. Martinez and Stribling approached his taxi, saying that they wanted to go to the Gare de l'Est. They entered the taxi, and Rouyer turned around. Before the vehicle had covered 400 yards, Martinez had thrust his pistol into the driver's side from the back seat. Stribling was sitting up front and took Rouyer's notebook containing money. They proceeded to help themselves to the driver's wristwatch and then ordered him to turn the taxi around, after which the pair leapt out and scampered away. All of this occurred in about a minute. Like Bourenkoff before him, Rouyer then drove to the police station at St. Vincent de Paul and reported the robbery, describing the suspects just as Bourenkoff had in the same station earlier in the evening.

On April 26, at about 7 p.m., it was still quite light. Near Metro Barbes Rouchechouart, Francis E. Schultz, a civilian employed by the U.S. War Department (later the Department of Defense), was walking across the middle of the street when Manuel Martinez came from behind and asked him in French if he had anything to sell. Schultz told him "no," but Martinez continued to walk alongside Schultz before a taxi came up from behind on their right. Martinez told Schultz to get into the cab. Though reluctant at first, after spying a small revolver in Martinez's hand that was partially hidden by Martinez's jacket, he forced himself into the cab. There, four men plus the driver awaited him. While Schultz was seated on a small folding seat with his back toward the driver, the man with the gun put his hand inside Schultz's jacket and took his wallet. From the wallet he took about $55 in scrip money and four ration cards: two belonging to Janine M. Schultz, Francis's wife, and two belonging to himself. Martinez undoubtedly searched the wallet hastily because he overlooked $20 in folded-up scrip currency. The wallet was returned to Schultz, and the crew released him back onto the street.

Schultz was released just below the Metro Pigalle. He took note of the cab's identification number and wrote a brief description of the vehicle. He noticed as he left that the taxi driver got out of the cab and did not want to go any farther, but the man with the gun rammed it into the driver's stomach and forced him back into the car. Off the group went in the direction of Metro Blanche.

The following day, April 27, Pfc. Victor Zingale of the Army's Special Investigation Section (SIS) received a call that American soldiers had been involved in armed robberies in Place Pigalle, so he drove there to check for suspects. He noticed a "colored person" in mixed GI/civilian attire sporting a suntan shirt, OD pants, no tie, and no cap. The investigator stopped the man and asked him for his papers, to which the man replied in very poor French, "I am French." Zingale understood the language at least well enough to know it was a terrible effort, so he took the "colored man" to the nearest French police station in the Ninth District. The officers there spoke to the man in French, but he did not understand a word they were saying and did not reply to any of their queries. Zingale placed him under arrest, shook him down, and found a PX card and some other identification on him. One of the IDs was marked with the name "Earl Williams" and one of the PX cards belonged to Janine Schultz. Zingale took down the number of the PX card, placed the man—Mitchell—under arrest, and whisked him away to SIS headquarters.

American agents at the SIS headquarters called Francis Schultz down to identify Mitchell, based on the discovery of his wife's PX ration card. He looked a little smaller than Schultz thought, but he was similar to the other black man in the cab. It was rather difficult to identify him. Mitchell told Schultz that he had "found" his wife's PX card.

An hour later at about 3:00 p.m., MP Pfc. Albert S. Kaina received a call at the Paris Detention Barracks and was told to proceed to SIS headquarters and pick up an American soldier. There, Pfc. Zingale turned the black American soldier over to Kaina. The soldier told Kaina that his name was Earl Williams. Kaina took the man into his custody with plans to transfer him to the Paris Detention Barracks, where he was to be confined. Mitchell was riding in the front seat of the open jeep without handcuffs. Kaina had a brassard (armband) on his left arm and was carrying a U.S. Army Colt 45-caliber pistol in a holster on his right hip. Mitchell would say later that he "talked nice to this MP to gain confidence in me." According to Kaina, they even discussed how long each had been in the army. After about ten minutes of conversation, Mitchell pulled the flap from Kaina's holster and jerked the .45 from its holster. Kaina tried to grab

24. Springtime in Paris

it, but the jeep was heading for a telephone pole. The MP had to control the jeep and was unable to take back the weapon. He stopped the jeep and jumped out, with Mitchell holding the pistol. Mitchell pointed the pistol at Kaina, ordered him back in the jeep, and told him to drive to Barbes, a Paris Metro station.

The embarrassed and mortified Kaina told Mitchell to hide the pistol under his shirt so no one would see it. He drove Mitchell somewhere close to Barbes; Mitchell ordered him to proceed around the corner and wait for five minutes. Kaina begged Mitchell not to take the jeep and to please leave the pistol in the seat. Mitchell agreed, but changed his mind and kept the pistol. Ten minutes later, he took a taxi to Pigalle, where he met a girl who took Mitchell home with her.

Nothing is more humiliating or degrading than for a law enforcement officer to have his weapon taken by a prisoner, and that is even more so the case for a young, strapping MP. Would Kaina get revenge? Stay tuned.

Around 8:15 p.m. on April 30, taxi driver Charles Perron picked up three passengers at the railway station, Place de la Bastille. The men—Finis Branham, William Mitchell, and Manuel Martinez—asked the taxi driver to take them to Place de l'Etoile, but to stop first at the Madison Hotel to pick up a girl. They directed the driver to Avenue Daumesnil and then told him to stop under a railway bridge at Rue Tranversiere. All three left the taxi and said they would be back very soon. Martinez, in his broken French, said, "One minute." When they returned, Mitchell was up front while Branham and Martinez sat in the back. They told the taxi driver to continue to Place de l'Etoile. After about 200 meters, while the cab was in motion, Mitchell shoved a large gun into the driver's chest. The driver tried to grab the gun with his right hand and Mitchell then rammed it into his stomach. One of the men in the back seat smashed the back of Perron's head, lacerating his right ear. Perron stopped his cab and started screaming loudly, at several passersby: "Murder! Police!"

The three hoods jumped from the taxi, fired a shot into the air, and began running. Several Paris policemen jumped into the Perron's parked taxi and starting chasing the three men. They spotted Branham and Mitchell running into the Metro station Ledru Rollin. The police and the injured taxi driver jumped out of the cab and soon caught the elusive Mitchell. The police took him back to Perron's taxi, and Perron drove them to the Traversiere Police Station. From there Perron was taken to the hospital and his ear was stitched up; he was prescribed eight days' rest by the treating physician.

The following is Mitchell's story, which borders on science fiction, as he described his arrest:

I had met a girl in Pigalle and she said she lived somewhere in Bastille and I had taken her to the Metro, and we had got out of the Metro and walked up to the top of the steps, and we stood there about fifteen minutes and she said she had to leave and go home. She had some silly little thing to do; whatever her business was, I don't know. I stood there about five minutes after she left, and while I was standing there I seen people passing; and about nine months ago I was on pass, and I knew some girls used to stay in this hotel Grand Central, and I started to go over there and changed my mind at the time when this happened.

I heard people shouting "Police" and everything, and I did hear someone say "American" or something of that sort. I went on to the Metro and I was going down the steps of the Metro and I seen a car from that direction and a French policeman was on it; and I got to the bottom of the Metro steps and this little Frenchman that was here, he is the one that grabbed me, and I don't know what he was saying to the French police.

Well, I seen people over there hollering for police, everything, a crowd of people, and I seen police coming from different direction; and by me being AWOL there was nothing more for me to do than to get out of the way because the French police, I know they would pick me up. So I seen a French policeman on the side of a car coming down in the direction going this way (indicating). Well, the accident seemed to occur on the side of the street where people were on the side of the street like that.

The only time I seen this taxi driver was when he come into the Metro and he grabbed me. I was at the Metro steps and he grabbed me like that. I thought he was drunk. He was speaking to someone and I looked up the steps and I seen the French police, and he had a gun in his hand, and the French police told me to come to the top of the Metro steps; and I come up and he put me in a car and taken me to the French jail. I was there about fifteen minutes, and after they beat me up, beat my face up. They brought another colored fellow I had never seen before [Branham], and they worked him over and took us both out to the Paris Detention Barracks.

No pistol was found on either Mitchell or Branham.

Manuel Martinez had made a clean escape from the Paris police, but had not obtained any money. Later on that same night of April 30, he joined up with Stribling and again hailed a taxi, this time at Place Pigalle. The taxi was driven by Joseph Dejivanni, who was not overly concerned as he recognized Martinez from previous trips. Stribling got in the back seat. Martinez sat beside the driver and, without saying a word, signaled for the taxi driver to drive straight ahead in the direction of Stalingrad Station. Then Martinez pointed to a side street as the taxi driver was wondering to himself where they wanted to go. He took a left and came back again to Stalingrad Station, where they made a stop. Both men got out of the car. Stribling stayed behind and asked whether the taxi driver knew what time it was. Dejivanni had no wristwatch so he took out the watch from his left pocket. Stribling gave him 100 francs for payment. As he took out his billfold to return the change, Stribling noticed

24. Springtime in Paris

that the driver had a big bundle of bills—10, 20, 50, and 100 franc denominations.

Stribling then took back the 100-franc note and said, "Continue to the Gare de l'Est." He was joined in the taxi by Martinez. Upon arriving at the train station, the occupants of the taxi made Dejivanni take several streets, motioned for the driver to go quietly and slowly, and made him stop. Stribling got out through the left door. Martinez, sitting next to the driver, struck a glancing blow off Dejivanni's shoulder, punched him in the side with a pistol, and motioned that he wanted the driver's billfold and watch. Dejivanni gave Martinez his wallet as Martinez pulled the watch from his pocket. Stribling got back in the car, and Martinez motioned with his pistol for the driver to continue on down the street. They stopped on the corner at St. Laurent Church, where Stribling went up to a taxi in front of the Gare de l'Est and climbed in. He motioned for Martinez, who jumped out and ran to the other taxi, and the pair took off. Joseph Dejivanni made a U-turn and took off after the other taxi, hoping to find a policeman. Although he did, the duo lost sight of the taxi racing ahead of them.

After that unsettling experience, Dejivanni would look daily for the two men who robbed him. His vigilance paid off eight to ten days later: Around 7 p.m., he spotted Martinez on foot. There was a passenger in his taxi, but Dejivanni stopped, excused himself, took off his coat, and began following about thirty feet behind Martinez, hoping to find a policeman to make an arrest. It was impossible to find one, and eventually Martinez noticed that he was being followed. He darted into a café and, looking back, saw the taxi driver in the front doorway. Martinez exited a side door and again disappeared.

While identifying his assailants to the police, Dejivanni revealed that they were dressed as Americans, but thought that they were not "real" Americans. "I said to myself, 'It is impossible; they do not look like Americans. They look rather like colonials and they are probably false Americans.'"

After having being apprehended at Ledru Rollin Metro station, Mitchell was taken by the French police to the police station at 58 Rue Galilée, two blocks east of the Arc de Triomphe and also headquarters for the U.S. Special Investigation Section, which occupied the first floor. Here Mitchell was identified as an American soldier and this time successfully transferred to the Paris Detention Barracks. The following morning, May 1, Corporal Milton G. Coppersmith traveled the five miles to the site to bring Mitchell back to SIS headquarters for questioning. Mitchell's old friend Pfc. Albert S. Kaina was assigned to guard the handcuffed Mitchell on this trip. Why was Kaina selected for this duty? Would he extract some vengeance?

Arriving at SIS headquarters, Mitchell was interviewed about the robberies that had taken place on the previous days. He signed a confession for the robberies and the theft of U.S. property—namely, the pistol taken from MP Kaina.

Later, regarding the interview, Mitchell would make the following statement in response to questioning by the SIS:

> **Q:** Did Corporal Coppersmith make any threats or intimations as to what he might do to you?
>
> **A:** Coppersmith told me that if I didn't make a complete statement and sign a statement, that he was going to take me up and work me over, and I told him that I didn't know what he was talking about taking me upstairs and working me over, and he stood me in a corner all day. I was sick and he wouldn't let me go to the dispensary or hospital or nothing, and I wouldn't talk to him at first, so he took me upstairs and took me to the latrine and worked me over, and he said if he had any more trouble out of me he was going to take and get two or three of his bars. I mean two or three of his friends that worked there at the CID, SIS. So he takes me to the latrine and I got my hands handcuffed behind me, and he worked me over with his fist.... Coppersmith worked me over. I was beat by the French police very badly.
>
> He told me, "I'll take you in a jeep by myself," and he can take his forty-five pistol and put on this side of him and I sit right in front seat with you; and he said, "I don't believe you could get the pistol out of the holster." He said, "We will try that sometimes," just like that. "This evening we will try that." And I said I didn't want to take his pistol. I understood that as a threat. [This was in reference to Mitchell forcefully taking MP Kaina's .Colt 45-caliber pistol.]

Mitchell's bruised face did tell a tale of his having been beaten. When questioned, he had to say something about the beating he had taken. It's a good guess that the humiliated MP Kaina settled the score with Mitchell, and that Mitchell had to keep quiet as he was to returning to the prison guarded by Kaina and his buddies. To put it kindly, some of these MPs were tough hombres.

On May 6, 1947, Pierre Dangereux-Dorly, an employee of the Coty Perfume Corporation, and two of his friends arrived at the Le Bridge bar at quarter to midnight for a little relaxation. Around 15 minutes later, two women entered the bar and asked for information from the bartender, then left at once. Pierre and his friends remained, and about a quarter past midnight two men entered. The bar being a rather small one, Pierre sat with his back close to the establishment's entrance. When the door opened, he looked around and quickly glanced at two individuals. At first he didn't pay much attention because he figured they were drunk. The men ordered two cognacs; asked the price, which was 180 francs; and paid with a 200-franc note. They received two 10-franc notes from the cash drawer. Martinez then passed Stribling one of the tens as a signal that he had glimpsed into the cash drawer. It was after this action that Pierre's comrade, who was sitting on his right side, said, "Things are going bad—wrong." Pierre turned around cautiously and saw that the door had been closed by one of the men, who now pulled out a pistol. His partner in crime, meanwhile, was in the process of closing the curtains that covered the front window.

One of the two men—Pierre did not know which one—speaking poor French, ordered them to give up their money. The pair started by robbing the bar man, who took the money out of the cash drawer very quickly. Then Martinez took the bartender's wedding ring and watch. He robbed Pierre's friend, seizing a platinum ring that his friend had on his small finger. He then took all the money in Pierre's billfold and searched his pockets. Pierre had removed his watch from his wrist, but Martinez found it anyway, in Pierre's left pocket. The thieves demanded a bottle of liquor from the barman, which he gave them. Still threatening the patrons and barman with the pistol, the aggressors herded everyone into the men's restroom and then fled. The robbery victims remained in the men's room with the bartender for perhaps another minute. When it was obvious that the coast was clear, they exited and hurried into the street to look for a policeman. There was nobody on the street, so Pierre telephoned the police. The robbers were described to the police as a tall, colored man and a smaller "yellow man," and Americans—especially the "yellow man."

During this reckless spree, Martinez and his cohorts also robbed several other bars, as revealed in later court testimony.[1]

25

Murder in La Place Pigalle

On May 22, 1947, Martinez began his daily routine of waking very late in a hotel room he shared with one Madeleine Simon, smoking a reefer or two, and beginning his drinking day with cognac. About 7:00 in the evening he went with Madeleine, also known as "Zina," to see the movie *The Mark of Zorro*, with Tyrone Power. The theater was next to their hotel; after the movie at about 9:00 they stopped in front of and peered into the L'Escale Bleue, the bar located at 16 Rue Victor Massé.

About this time, a 23-year-old professional dancer named Hughette Carmen CiPierre crossed the street from her hotel and entered L'Escale Bleue. She went to the bar and a bit later sat next to the front door eating. She noticed a young man stopping and looking through the open door and the windows, whose curtains were drawn open. Hughette had lived in Paris for six months. She had left LeHavre, where she had been convicted of a crime involving moral turpitude. The young unmarried mother of two left the bar and returned to her hotel room, where she had an "appointment" with an Italian man. She was to reappear at L'Escale Bleue at midnight.

Martinez and his "Zina" continued on to a restaurant near St. Michel and had supper. They took a taxi to St. Paul, where Simon left Martinez. From St. Paul, he went to Stalingrad Station, where he purchased some more marijuana and smoked one or two cigarettes. Martinez continued toward Pigalle, stopping at one or two cafés on his way to enjoy his beloved cognac.

After this last customer had gone, Henri Géliot, the proprietor of L'Escale Bleue bar, counted his receipts for the day and put them in his right-hand pocket. There were 500 and 1,000 franc notes among the receipts, and they made a packet about three quarters of an inch thick. Géliot had 5,000 franc notes in his possession during the afternoon. Therese Lacheroix, a blonde nick-

25. Murder in La Place Pigalle

The L'Escale Bleue bar, located at 16 Rue Victor Massé, scene of the murder of Henri Géliot.

named "Nini," who had been working at the bar for three days, also counted her tips, which amounted to 1,900 or 2,000 francs.

A few moments later, an Italian entered the bar; he seldom came in at night. He asked Lucien Franck, the cook, for a cup of coffee. Frank told him, "You will drink it tomorrow because we are going to close." Then the Italian said, "I need change; here's a thousand francs." Géliot told him to pay tomorrow, but the man said, "No, I need change." Géliot took some notes out of his right-hand coat pocket to make change, searching for small notes among the larger ones. The man told him to hurry—he had to pay a taxi. When he received the change, he left the bar without drinking his coffee. When asked why he did not drink the coffee, he answered that it was too hot.

After this man left the bar, Géliot stood in the doorway, wearing his hat and smoking a cigarette. He told the cook and barmaid to turn out the lights. As they started to comply with his instructions, Martinez, wearing a brown coat and trousers, entered, pushed Géliot inside, and closed the door behind him. The omnipresent pistol appeared in his right hand. Géliot attempted to turn it away, but Martinez walloped Géliot on the head with the heavy handgun. Géliot said, "Are you mad? You are playing the fool, my boy!" as he continued to struggle with Martinez. Martinez disengaged himself and fired a shot toward Géliot, but in a downward direction that grazed his thigh.

At this point the terrified barmaid cried out, "Lucien, they are killing Mr. Henri! Try and open the kitchen door so that we can get away." The pair remained in the kitchen, with the cook replying, "Don't be foolish; I can't open it." The back door was blocked by a heavy motorcycle that was parked by the kitchen. As the struggle between Géliot and Martinez continued, five or six other shots were fired. Géliot fell to the floor and hollered for Nini to get the police.

Nini returned to the barroom and saw Martinez "working with his pistol pulling, or attempting to pull, the slide or something." Operating on instinct alone and ignoring the danger to herself, she picked up two heavy glass ice buckets filled with ice. At a distance of less than 10 feet, Nini threw them at Martinez, hitting him in the head both times with each one, causing the large one to break entirely and the small one to break in several places. She sprinted around the bar past Martinez, who was facing the rear of the bar and still drunkenly fooling with his pistol; she opened the front door of the bar and ran into the street. As Nini turned, speeding away, she heard a shot fired behind her. Martinez had shot at her, with the bullet passing completely through the brass door handle. Hearing the sound of the broken ice buckets, Franck, the cook, looked out to the barroom, where he saw Martinez lift up the body of Géliot and fire a last shot into his head. Then he turned Géliot's right-hand pocket inside out and took his bundle of money. Covered with blood, Martinez ran from the bar down Rue Victor Massé toward Rue des Martyrs. The cook had remained in the back and hid, naturally fearing that Martinez might kill him, too. When Lucien finally went into the barroom, he felt Géliot and believed him to be dead. He waited until the doorkeeper of the nearby Shanghai Bar arrived and then left to find Géliot's son, who lived close by. The cook returned soon after the policeman arrived—or so the cook said. How did Martinez know the money was in Géliot's right-side pocket? Did the cook steal some of the money from the dead man?

Hughette CiPierre left her hotel and was crossing the street when she saw Martinez running. She looked into the bar's window and saw Géliot lying on the floor with blood coming out of his head. Then she saw Nini returning with a policeman. The door to the bar was closed and no one was inside except Géliot, who was lying on his back, in a pool of blood, with his feet toward the door and his head toward the bar. Hughette was now inside L'Escale Bleue as the policeman checked Géliot's pulse and confirmed that, although his body was still warm, he was dead. The officer took the victim's wallet from an inside coat pocket and located an identity card bearing the name " Géliot"; he also

25. Murder in La Place Pigalle

noticed that the wallet had no money inside. The police officer wisely touched nothing, but telephoned the main police station to report the murder.

Martinez ran the four blocks to his room at Hôtel du Vert-Galant, which was located across the four lanes at Boulevard de Clichy at 75 Rue des Martyrs. He entered the hotel, took a key from the keyboard, and went to his room. Martinez had a cut on his forehead and his jacket was stained with blood. Raquel Gendre, manager of the Vert-Galant hotel, had seen Martinez when he staggered into the hotel and observed that he took the wrong key from the board; she directed her sister, Suzanne, to take the proper key to him. She followed Martinez to his room 24, located on the second floor at the rear end of the corridor. Going up the stairs, she noticed some drops of blood on the stairs between the first and second floors. More drops were on the carpet leading to Martinez's room. Martinez told Suzanne that he had been in a fight with some Americans.

While Martinez was washing his wound, Suzanne saw that he had placed a large pistol on the glass shelf above the lavatory. This pistol also had blood on it. Suzanne moved the pistol to a table in his room. Raquel followed her sister into the room and took the pistol downstairs to the kitchen. Martinez was bleeding from a cut on the forehead. Suzanne and some of the "working girls" living at the hotel assisted Martinez in washing the blood from his face. He then changed clothes and placed a khaki shirt and beige jacket in the bidet filled with water. They floated on top of the water, which was red with blood. Martinez's "girlfriend" Madeleine Simon was initially in the room but had to leave because the sight of the blood was making her sick. Martinez then gave Suzanne 500 francs to clean up the blood spots in his room. Suzanne ran across the street and fetched a doctor, who came over to treat Martinez.

Dr. Jacques Mazel walked across the street to the hotel to attend to Martinez. His cut was about three centimeters long and the glass had severed an artery, causing a great flow of blood. Mazel attempted to stitch the wound but the stitches would not hold. Martinez was conscious but rather dazed. The doctor finally stopped the bleeding. As he left, Martinez paid him 400 francs for his services and received 600 francs change from him for a 1,000-franc note (which he had just stolen). The doctor insisted that Martinez go to a hospital for proper treatment.

The police had been searching the immediate area for a man with a wound on his forehead. A half an hour after the murder, they arrived at the Hôtel du Vert-Galant and asked Raquel Gendre if she had seen a man bleeding. She confirmed that he had, indeed, entered the hotel.

The 23-year-old Micheline Maupied, who had been living in room 24 with Bill Stribling, entered while Dr. Mazel was attending to Martinez's wound.

Stribling had left a day or two earlier for Germany, and now Martinez was occupying the same room. After the doctor left, Maupied attempted to place a bandage over the cut. A taxi had been called and, as Martinez was waiting to be taken to a hospital, he told Micheline, "I have just killed a man three hundred meters away from here." Micheline was called downstairs and told that a taxi had arrived; in reality, the police were waiting for Martinez to leave his room. Upon hearing the word "taxi," Martinez looked out the window and saw there was no taxi. When Micheline returned, he expressed his doubt, and she told him that a small private car had come to take him away. Maupied stated, "He was quite confident in me and we went downstairs calmly. In the corridor he kissed me on both cheeks and thanked me for having aided him."

At the bottom of the steps, Maurice Lecoz, Inspector of Police, pointed a pistol at Martinez and said, "*Lève les mains!*" (Hands up!). Martinez complied as the inspector handcuffed him. Lecoz made a quick search to see if Martinez had a weapon; there was none, but he found some bullets in Martinez's pocket. Raquel Gendre then gave the policeman the bloody pistol she had taken from Martinez's room. The identification papers found in his possession identified Martinez as "Joseph Salazard," born on January 18, 1918, at Guadalajara, Mexico. Salazard was a lieutenant in the Mexican Army who had been arrested by the Gestapo at Argeles-sur-Mer on the French–Spanish border on March 29, 1943. He was arrested for espionage, although Mexico was a neutral country during this war. Upon his release from the Buchenwald concentration camp by the American liberators, Salazard told them he was going to make his way back to Mexico through France. This may explain the papers in Martinez's possession, but not how he obtained them.

The police went to the Hôtel du Vert-Galant, checked their files and found out that room 24 was registered to "Sam Stribling" (William), born on February 27, 1921, in Chicago, residing in Germany, with an American national identification card, P.36.734. He was listed as being registered on May 18 and leaving on May 19—a mistake since he actually left on May 22, 1947. The police removed Martinez's bloody clothes and found no other items in the room.

"Salazard" was taken to a police station and searched. The investigators found 50,110 bloody French francs in his pocket. Martinez insisted that he was Salazard. With a card in his wallet indicating that Salazard had served in Buchenwald concentration camp, however, his story was coming apart. So Martinez lied again and said his name was Tony Ramirez.

Early the next morning, an English-speaking policeman talked to Martinez, who again told the policeman his name was Ramirez. He claimed that he had received the wound on his forehead from two Algerians who had attacked him at the Stalingrad Metro station. He was informed in English that

25. Murder in La Place Pigalle

he was the suspect in a murder at the L'Escale Bleue; Martinez denied any involvement, stating he was not in that area the previous night. At about 8:30 a.m., French Liaison Police had informed the U.S. Army, Special Investigation Section, that the *Brigade Volante*, Central Police Bureau, Paris, had arrested a man they believed to be an American soldier, and were holding him on charges of having murdered a French civilian named Henri Géliot.

Tec 4 Joseph J. Godek and his staff of investigators were assigned to investigate the case. They proceeded to the offices of the *Brigade Volante*, accompanied by an inspector from the French Liaison Police. Upon arrival, they were requested to question the man held by that office to determine if he was, in fact, an American soldier. Godek presented his official credentials to Martinez and asked if he was an American soldier. The prisoner replied that he was an American soldier and identified himself as Private Tony Ramirez, serial number 35248510, of the 58 Q.M. Company stationed in Munich, Germany. "Ramirez" was then warned of his rights under the 24th Article of War. Martinez/Ramirez stated that he wished to remain silent at that time.

Leaving the *Brigade Volante* facilities, Godek returned to his own offices and began trying to locate Ramirez's unit and determine his status. This work continued until the following day, when all sources of information had been checked without results. Neither Ramirez nor the unit he had given as his were known to officials in Germany.

On May 24, Godek returned to the offices of *Brigade Volante* for the purpose of taking Ramirez's fingerprints, which were to be forwarded to Washington, D.C., for positive identification. Upon being told that his fingerprints were to be taken, Ramirez 'fessed up for once: He admitted that he had given a false name, serial number, and unit to the investigators on the previous day, and said that his correct name was Private Manuel Martinez, #35248810, of the 541st Q.M. Company (S), APO 169, stationed at Giessen, Germany. Martinez further stated that he had escaped from confinement at the Giessen military stockade but was not sure of the date. This information was checked by telephone with records on file at these two units. Fingerprints taken of Martinez were forwarded to Washington, D.C., for a positive identification.

In the early afternoon, Martinez was taken to L'Escale Bleue. The English-speaking policeman showed him the blood on the floor and said, "You did a fine job." Martinez's composure was shaken and for a moment the policeman thought that Martinez would make a confession. Instead, the prisoner shrugged his shoulders and said that he had been drunk and could not remember anything. The police reconstructed the crime scene and took photographs of Martinez and the barmaid. Several bullets and .45-caliber cartridge casings were found in the bar.

The inside of the L'Escale Bleue, the location of the murder.

Earlier, a photograph of Martinez had been taken at the police station. He was again questioned by French police authorities and made another statement in which he admitted having given the French police a false name. In this statement Martinez admitted having fired the gun while in the bar L'Escale Bleue, but claimed he did not remember whether he wounded or killed anyone. Martinez told the investigators that he had got the marijuana at a place near Stalingrad in Paris, but did not remember what happened at the L'Escale Bleue. Nor did he know why the money became blood-stained when he took it out of his pocket to pay the doctor.

Among the persons interrogated was the 28-year-old wife of Henri Géliot, Jeanne Géliot. She stated:

> This morning I learned from my stepson about the aggression my husband had been a victim of last night. I married Mr. Géliot on November 15, 1941, at Lille. We had been together until January 1946, at which time we parted because we did not suit each other any more. I did not have any children from my husband, but he had a son from his first marriage, a 28-year-old boy called Henri. After leaving my husband I went to live with a friend of mine.
>
> The bar at 16 Rue Victor Massé is my own property, as I have purchased it myself on June 1, 1946. My husband asked me to let him operate the bar and I agreed to please him. I used to meet my husband but seldom, and when I called

25. Murder in La Place Pigalle

on him it was only with a view of discussing business. I am painfully surprised to learn about his tragic death. I could not imagine that anyone might wish to harm him.

I don't want my husband's body to be the object of an autopsy, and don't allow any postmortem examination. As to the funeral, I will take care of it.

At the request of the Police Judiciary Bureau, the Bureau of Identity sent an inspector to the scene of the shooting for the purpose of obtaining photos to create a diagram, and to obtain any further evidence that might have been overlooked in the previous inspection of the scene. A ballistics test was also ordered by the Police Judiciary Bureau. The results of this test revealed that the pistol in Martinez's possession had fired the fatal bullet that had killed Henry Géliot.

On May 27, most of the victims whom he had robbed came to the police station to identify Martinez as being involved in armed assaults. At this time he was the only American or person dressed in American military clothes in the line-up that was presented for identification. He was identified as the man involved in each armed robbery, and each victim gave the police a sworn statement. On the same day he was taken to a French hospital and the wound on his forehead was treated.

The only known photograph of Manuel Martinez—taken by the police of Paris.

Martinez was held in custody by French police authorities from May 23 until June 3, when he was released to U.S. Army authorities in the late afternoon. He was immediately placed under their command and informed as to the charges against him. A signed statement from Martinez, in which he acknowledged being under arrest and understanding the charges against him, was obtained at that time and witnessed. Martinez claimed he had been beaten by the French police to make him reveal the circumstances of the murder and the various robberies he had committed.

On June 16, 1947, after all statements of the victims of the several holdups committed by "Martinez and his unidentified Negro companion" had been translated into English, Martinez was taken from Paris Detention Barracks and confined to the offices of the Special Investigation Section. There, he was read all the statements made by his robbery victims. When asked if he desired to make any statement in his defense or denial of the complaints filed against him, Martinez made a statement to the effect that he did not know anything about the holdups. A signed sworn statement was taken from Martinez to that effect:

> Martinez states that on May 22, 1947, he had awakened at about 1400 hours, left the hotel and had something to eat. After eating he took in a movie, and after leaving the movie, he went to St. Michel, where he again had something to eat. Martinez then states that he then went to the Stalingrad section of Paris and obtained some marijuana from an unidentified civilian. He then returned to the Pigalle area of Paris, had a few drinks, and also smoked a couple of cigarettes containing marijuana. He then went to his hotel room and took the .45-caliber automatic pistol, and also the clip, which contained some rounds of ammunition, the number unknown to him. He then left the hotel with the pistol on his person, went to a night club, "Cabin Cuba," where he stayed for about ten minutes. Leaving there, he states he was returning to his hotel but that in passing the bar L'Escale Bleue he decided to go in and have another drink. He states that he remembers walking into the bar, and also remembers "having the pistol in his hand" but does not remember firing the gun. He next noticed the gun in his hand when he had reached Boulevard de Clichy. At this time he also noticed that his forehead was bleeding very badly. The lady at the hotel called a doctor, who arrived at the hotel and washed the gash with alcohol and then left. Previous to leaving the room to call a doctor for Martinez, the landlady had removed the pistol from the pocket of Martinez's jacket and had taken it with her. Shortly after the doctor had left the hotel, Martinez decided to leave the hotel and was arrested.

And then another irony occurred: The Colt .45 pistol used in the murder had been taken on April 25 from U.S. Military Policeman Pfc. Albert S. Kaina, stationed at the Paris Detention Barracks, by none other than Private William A. Mitchell. This pistol passed from Mitchell's possession to Martinez, although the latter claimed to have purchased the pistol from an unidentified person in the Pigalle area for the sum of 2,000 francs.

A letter was received from the Adjutant General's Office, War Department, Washington, D.C., which stated that the fingerprints forwarded to this office had been checked and found to be identical with the prints of Manuel Martinez, who had reenlisted at Fort Bragg, North Carolina, on November 30, 1945.

Martinez was incarcerated in the Paris Detention Barracks, but administratively assigned to the American Graves Registration Command, which had been established in 1945 with headquarters in Paris. At the end of the war, there were thirty-seven cemeteries holding American remains scattered throughout Europe, with the bulk being in Germany. Members of Congress

25. Murder in La Place Pigalle

were upset about American soldiers being buried on German soil, so in 1947 they began a program under which all Americans interred in Germany would be returned home, if the families wanted this option, or reburied in ten permanent cemeteries in Belgium, Holland, or France. Surprisingly, fewer than 30 percent of the families elected to have their next-of-kin returned. The American Graves Registration Command was quite busy with all these arrangements when it took on the added duty of holding court-martial proceedings for Martinez.

When Martinez was jailed, he quickly integrated himself into the prisoner population. Upon the advice of a fellow prisoner, he requested the services of Lieutenant Colonel Westray N. Wilson as his defense council. Wilson received two inquiries from the Commanding General of the American Graves Registration Command regarding Martinez's request and ignored both. Then Wilson received a telegram from the U.S. Constabulary, strongly emphasizing that he should communicate with the Commanding General. A few days later the Commanding General received a short, curt telegram: "Availability of Lt. Col. Westray B. Wilson as individual counsel for Pvt. Manuel Martinez. Subject is not repeat not available." Martinez had already slowed the wheels of justice.

Captain William J. Long was assigned as Martinez's defense counsel instead, and in doing his job to the best of his ability began to protest the proceedings immediately. On August 27, 1947, Long wrote that the robberies should not be tried simultaneously with the murder charge as the offenses were in a different class. Long also emphasized that military courts did not have jurisdiction to try a person charged with murder in peacetime in the United States. His request for severance was quickly denied, as the alleged offenses were not considered minor.[1]

26

The Trials

There are no records to indicate that Private First Class William Stribling was ever charged with a criminal act by the U.S. Army regarding his participation in the robberies in Paris, which may have made him one of the luckiest criminals in Europe. Private William A. Mitchell, in contrast, was tried in Paris on July 10, 1947, and found guilty of "stealing a pistol from and also intent to do body harm to Private First Class Albert S. Kaina. Also guilty of force and violence by putting in fear, feloniously take, steal and carry away from the person of Francis E. Schultz $55. Guilty with intent to do him body harm, commit an assault upon Charles J. Perron with a dangerous weapon." For these crimes, Mitchell was to be confined to hard labor for fifteen years. He was assigned to confinement in the U.S. penitentiary in Terre Haute, Indiana.

Martinez's trial began at 10:00 a.m. on September 3, with a trial judge, the defense counsel, and six officers making up the jury, and a court reporter also being present. One of the officers serving on the jury stated he had formed an opinion as to the guilt of Martinez and was excused. The members of the court were asked if they had scruples that would prevent them from voting for a death sentence; apparently there were none. The defense, led by Captain William Long, challenged the entire court proceeding. After a lengthy exchange with the prosecution, he settled the matter by the court's being closed and reopened immediately. These verbal challenges between defense and prosecution continued for several hours. Then the first witness, Pierre Bourenkoff, testified. The following is a paraphrase of the prosecuting witness's testimony:

The Taxi Robberies

PIERRE BOURENKOFF: I am a taxi driver and on 24 April 1947, at 0030 hours, I was robbed of 4,000 French francs and some gas coupons by two men. I perfectly recognize the man you name, Martinez, as the man who threatened me with the gun and took my wallet.

REMY ROUYER: I am a taxi driver. On April 25, 1947, at about 2345 hours, I was robbed of about 2,200 French francs and a wristwatch by two men. I positively recognize the man you name, Martinez, as the man who put a revolver to my stomach and took my money and watch.

JOSEPH DJIVIANNI: I am a taxi driver. On April 30, 1947, at about 2100 hours, I was robbed of about 3,500 French francs and a chronometer and chain by two men. I recognize the man you name, Martinez, as the man who threatened me with the pistol and took my watch and chain, while the other man took my wallet containing the money.

The Bar Robberies

RENE LABARTHE: I am the manager of a bar. On the night of May 6 or 7 at about 0001 hours, two men robbed me in the bar of about 6,500 French francs from the cash box and also 4,000 French francs I had on me, my gold ring, and a bottle of liqueur. I positively recognize the man you name, Martinez, as the man who held us up with a pistol and took the money and my ring.

BERTHE BAZIER: I am a waitress. I was in the restaurant at 36 Rue Condorcet on May 6, 1947, at about 2245 hours when I was robbed of about 1,000 French francs and a pair of sunglasses by two men. I recognize the man you name as Martinez as the man who covered us with a pistol and stole my money and glasses.

OLIVE DEBIASE: I am a waitress. I was in the restaurant at 36 Rue ConcIorcet when I was robbed of about 750 French francs by two men. I recognize the man you name as Martinez as the man who covered me with a pistol while his accomplice robbed me.

CORNELIE WEYNANT: I positively recognize, among the people you showed me a moment ago and among the American soldiers wearing the same uniform as him, the Asiatic-looking man who, together with a Negro, committed armed robberies, at about 2330 hours on May 7, at the Bar de l'Isly, of which I am the directress.

This man, clad in an American soldier uniform and wearing no cap, accompanied by a Negro dressed in a brown suit, drank at the bar and paid for his first drink. The two men ordered a second drink. Then the Negro took out a 10-franc note, which he handed to his companion. At this moment, the latter took out of the inside left-hand pocket of his blouse a pistol, big caliber, and pointed it at us. The Negro then said the following words, looking at us and at the customers: "Everybody in the bar!" He repeated this sentence several times. The Negro had his hand in his pocket. We obeyed, but still he threatened, with the Asiatic-looking man at us with the American pistol. We were robbed of the money we had. The Negro took my husband's wristwatch. The American searched my handbag, out of which he took about 10,000 francs and then took the contents of the cash box, about 20,000 francs.

The Negro took, from the persons present in the establishment, the money they had then. When everything was over, the Negro and the American I have just recognized walked away. At least I believe so, because we did not hear any motor noise.

Testifying About the Murder

THERESE LACHEROY: I am the barmaid at L'Escale Bleue. On 23 May 1947, at 0005 hours, I was behind the bar when a man entered and assaulted my boss by hitting him on the head with a pistol. When my boss tried to free himself, he was shot dead by this assailant. I threw two ice glasses at the murderer, hitting him on the head, and then ran for my life. As I ran out of the bar, another shot was fired and I think it was for me, as the bullet went through the handle on the door. The cook, Mr. Franck, also witnessed the murder.

LUCIEN FRANCK: I can perfectly identify the man who murdered Mr. Géliot and tried to shoot the barmaid. I was at the bar when the shooting started and then ran to the kitchen to escape by the rear door, but it was locked. Then the barmaid returned to the barroom and hit the man you name as Martinez on the head with two glasses. The barmaid then ran out and as she did so, he fired at her. I remained in the kitchen and saw him fire a shot into the boss's head. I perfectly recognize the man you name as Martinez as the man who murdered my boss.

HUGUETTE CARMEN CIPIERRE: Mr. Henri, whom I have known for three years, was a very good friend of mine. I was in the bar L'Escale Bleue on May 22, at about 2100 hours, when I saw a man looking through the window. He had curly black hair, oval eyes, a bad look. Then he went away. I came back to the bar again this night at about ten minutes before midnight. As I came up to the door, someone opened the door, and the same man who had been looking through the window came out running. He was bloody all over his face and had a gun. He ran toward his left. I did not follow.

INSPECTOR SCOCKER, BRIGADE VOLANTE: Inspector LeRoy and I apprehended the man you name as Martinez in a hotel at 75 Rue des Martyrs. His pistol was picked up at the hotel also. His face was bandaged where he had recently been cut, and had entered the hotel shortly after the murder.

RAQUEL GENDRE: At about 0035 hours, May 23, Martinez entered the hotel and went straight to room 24. His face was covered with blood, and I called a doctor at his request. I took a gun which I saw in the bathroom and hid it.

MADELEINE SIMON, ALSO KNOWN AS "ZINA": I know the accused as "Tony." I went to the movies on the 22nd of May. When I entered the hotel, the proprietors told me Martinez had been wounded in a fight. I entered the room of Martinez. Raquel was there; Michele was there. I did not see a large blonde. The doctor was not there yet. I left before the doctor and did not return. I went to Michele's room. She was there in her room. I can't say that she was always with me. She left and came back. I always stayed in Michele's room and did not go back to Martinez's room.

I never saw Martinez smoke reefers. I didn't know Martinez very well. I was in room no. 26. I wasn't afraid of Martinez or of others. I left Paris because I wanted to return to my parents. Martinez tried to date me. Martinez did not leave drug tablets in my room. I saw him smoking cigarettes but not reefers. Martinez did not always have the same room. Martinez was kindly toward all of us.

Martinez liked me very much and wanted me as his girlfriend. I had known him 8 to 12 days before that night. I met him there at the hotel. I didn't know him

26. The Trials

long. Martinez asked me to get a taxi. I got 100 francs from Nellie for a taxi. I gave it back to her. Tony asked me for 100 francs and I borrowed it from Nellie. I gave the 100 francs to Martinez. I think he asked for the taxi before the doctor arrived, because I didn't go to Martinez's room after the doctor arrived.

SUZANNE GENDRE: I am a chambermaid at the Hôtel du Vert-Galant, located on Rue des Martyrs. On the night of May 22–23, 1947, Martinez entered the hotel about midnight. Blood was running from his head. He was in a hurry and took the wrong key from the key rack. My sister told me to take the right key up to him. I did this. I entered the room and saw Martinez at the lavatory. He put a large pistol on the shelf above the lavatory. I took up this pistol, which was covered with blood, and laid it on the table. Later, I saw sister walk in and take it downstairs. As Martinez was bleeding, I ran across the street and called Dr. Masel, who came after and treated Martinez. I was in and out of the room while Martinez was there. As the doctor was leaving, Martinez handled him a 1,000-franc note and the doctor gave him some change. Martinez then gave me 500 francs, pointing to the various spots of blood on the bed, the lavatory, and various other places, as he did so indicating that the 500 francs was for cleaning the room.

I don't recall who was in the room with Martinez all the time, but I did not see Madeleine Simon in the room with Martinez at any time, although I know she was in the hotel that night. I don't know who called the taxi for Martinez. I did not see a police car parked in front of the hotel. There was a car parked there, but I don't know whose it was. I don't recall that at any time when I left Martinez's that he was left alone with any one person. People, however, were standing in the corner outside of the room.

INSPECTOR LA PIERRE: I first met Martinez at the Police *Judiciaire* at about 07:30 hours on May 23, 1947. Since there was no regular interpreter and since I understand and speak English to some extent, I talked to Martinez. He told me his name was Ramirez. I asked him where he received the wound on his forehead, and he said he had been attacked by two Algerians at Metro Stalingrad the night before. I told him we suspected him of murdering the proprietor of the L'Escale Bleue the night before. Martinez denied this, stating that he wasn't in that area the night before; that, in any event, he could not have committed the murder because he had no weapon and was not around the night before.

The defense, Captain William Long, did little to rebut the testimony related to the taxi and earlier bar robberies. For the murder he tried, unsuccessfully, to establish that Martinez was under the influence of drugs and could not differentiate between right and wrong. The defense also tried to discredit the female witnesses, who were unemployed dancers—professional "mannequins"—and could not otherwise produce evidence of receiving pay for employment in the past year. The defense also implied that Hughette CiPierre and the Italian who purchased the coffee were working with Martinez and that the Italian had indicated to Martinez where Henri Géliot had the money:

DEFENSE: The defense feels this witness has a particular personal interest in seeing this accused convicted, and that interest extended to her association with an individual that was in the café, at five minutes to 12 that night, met her after he was in the café and got the change for 1,000 francs. Now I should think the court would want to know the entire background of the witness that was picked up in Pigalle neighborhood, without profession other than dancing. Certainly you are not going take that testimony the same as someone engaged in business and with a good reputation.

CiPierre's testimony for the prosecution and the major part of her involvement were targeted by Martinez's defense lawyer, who sought to discredit her by admitting evidence that she was a prostitute. Long also cast doubt on whether the man purchasing the coffee was really a customer. Six months previously, CiPierre had been convicted in LeHavre of a crime involving moral turpitude. The defense lawyer asked her about her occupation when she was living in Leave. The prosecution objected to the question and Hughette answered in English, "I object, too." It was not exactly equivalent to Hermann Göring distracting Justice Robert Jackson during his interrogation at Nuremberg, but the results were the same.

Franck, the cook, had quickly been convicted of a crime and was placed in confinement and charged with stealing money. He may well have taken some of the money from Géliot's body. He, CiPierre, and the coffee-buying customer were French citizens, and the U.S. Army was not about to become involved with their possible roles in this crime. It left these matters up to the efficient French police.

Martinez's defense counsel guided him in preparing and presenting an unsworn three-page statement in defense of the charges against him. The statement was a rehash of the entire case that ended as follows:

> I make this unsworn statement because of my lack of education and inability to understand and answer questions that might be asked on cross-examination. I have no recollection of what might have happened on the night of May 22 after 10 o'clock, and I have heard so much told to me that is supposed to have happened, so I fear that I might not be able to answer all questions truthfully as I would like to. However, the statements herein made are the same as I would make if I were sworn to tell the truth.

The most serious charge against Martinez was Violation of the 92nd Article of War—specifically, "That General Prisoner Manuel Martinez, did, at Paris, France, on or about May 22, 1947, with malice aforethought, willfully, deliberately, feloniously, unlawfully, and with premeditation kill one Henri Géliot, a human being, by shooting him with a pistol." After four days the court was recessed and the jury members had three options to consider—life imprisonment, "musketry," or hanging. On September 10, 1947, upon secret written ballot, "all of the members present at the time the vote was taken concurring, sentenced the accused to be hanged by the neck until dead."[1]

27

Mannheim Prison: Maximum Security

Martinez was immediately transferred to the European Command Military Prison in Mannheim, Germany, to await execution. In typical Martinez fashion, he again created a problem by the "willful misuse of Government Property" and began "Seven days solitary confinement on a diet of bread and water, beginning 1500 hrs. 16 Sept. 47 and ending 1500 hrs. 23 Sept. 47." For these seven days, Captain Walter F. Saunders certified that he issued Martinez five gallons of drinking water and eighteen ounces of bread every day. Martinez was released from solitary on September 23.

Knowing that he was in serious trouble, on September 25, 1947, Martinez sent a letter to his Uncle Mike Ramirez in Steel's Store, Texas (the aforementioned rural community with a population of about 300 people, a church, a school, four businesses, and a number of scattered dwellings). The misspelled semiliterate letter was written by a left-hander and was neat and legible. It was signed in a different hand, "Manuel Martinez."

Sept. 25, 47

Hello Mike!

While sitting here in deep meditation I have decited to drop you these few lines to let you hear from me.

I am fine and sincirely hope you are the same. I am sorrie I haven wrote you before now but you see it is like this I have been locked up in Paris jail for quite a lot and now the oppertunty has just become minds to write you. I was tryed the 10 of Sept for killing a man and robbing some people so they say but you know I wouldnt do nothing like that but they found me guilty and sentance me to be hunge. I am waiting for it to be aproved of or cut.

If you wish to do me a favor you can write the President and ask him to cut it because he is the only one whom it can be aprove by you tell brother and Louis to get togther and do something for me because they know some people in the

States who can write and ask for mercy for me because now is the time a need help my life is at stake.

That is all you can do for me in that case. I am in germany now waiting for my time to be cut. I will have to stay over here untill it is aproved or disaproved

Give my regards to all the folks and the friends I new.

Tell mother don't worrie about me because if it turns out for better or worse than you know everyone has to go some times and it might just be my time to go.

Write and let me know if Raff is still in the Army or is he out.

Tell all my little brothers to be careful because to be behind bars is no where.

You know I'll be here quite a while and I would like for you to send me a box with any thing but cigertes

I want a good pipe and some candy nuts and a good fruit cake.

Well this is all I have to say today so I'll say good-by for now looking for a quick reply from you.

Sincerely Yours
Manuel Martinez

Martinez's letter must have be sent by airmail, which was unusual at that time, because ten days later on October 4, a typed one-page letter from Martinez's 93-year-old grandmother, enclosed along with Martinez's handwritten letter of September 25, was on the way to the president of the United States. The letter stated: "He is in trouble and has asked me to help him out.... This boy, one of three brothers who served in World War II, is supporting one small sister and brother.... I am trusting that you will have Mercy on my boy. /s/ Mrs. Catarina Ramirez."

On October 29, Mrs. Ramirez received a letter from the Adjutant General's Office, Washington, D.C. It stated the matters contained in her letter "would be given careful consideration before final action is taken." Martinez's court-martial was under review by the Office of the Judge Advocate General in Washington, D.C. That office concluded that the trial was legally constituted, but a month later wrote, "In order that the issue of mental responsibility may be free from doubt it is suggested that the accused be transported to a general hospital for observation and report by a Board of Medical Officers with respect to his mental responsibility. At least one member of the board should be a psychiatrist."

Each day in jail was basically the same for Martinez, with an officer checking on him and entering a good conduct entry, and later the same day another officer entering a good condition entry in an Inspection Record of Prisoners in Safe-Keeping. This lasted until October 15, 1947, when Martinez was again placed in solitary confinement for four days, charged with "defacing walls in cell with his name." Again he was placed on a bread-and-water diet under the certification of Captain Walter F. Saunders.

27. Mannheim Prison

On October 19, 1947, Martinez was placed back into safe-keeping and remained there until January 5, 1948. He was transferred to Mannheim prison and forwarded to the 327th Station Hospital in Wiesbaden, Germany, to determine "whether or not he was now and at the time of his offenses free from mental defect, disease or derangement and [able] to distinguish right from wrong and to adhere to the right." The hospital staff was also to evaluate whether he possessed sufficient mental capacity to understand the nature of the proceedings and was intelligent enough to conduct and cooperate in his own defense.

Captain Joseph S. Jacobs was assigned the case and gave instructions that the patient was to be watched closely, as he was in for observation before a final decision on a death sentence would be made. In the first week Martinez was under constant observation of the guards and due to being very tense was unable to sleep.

On January 21, he was given a Wechsler-Bellevue Intelligence Test and a Rorschach Personality Diagnosis. The intelligence test revealed he had an IQ of 65 and the mental age of a nine-year-old. This immaturity was clearly displayed in the Rorschach test with his frequent reference to the "ink blocs" resembling female genitalia. Martinez's five responses to the first ten Rorschach cards: "Woman's cunt there. That reminds me of like a cunt, too, sir. That looks like a cunt, too, sir. Sir, that's a cunt, too. Could be a cunt in there, too." His responses to the remaining 10 cards were even more sexually graphic.

While in the mental hospital, Martinez did considerable reading in his confined area. He requested reading material and was furnished with Ernie Pyle's 1944 book, *Brave Men*. He did not read it. Indeed, when questioned how he liked the book, Martinez responded that he was reading a magazine, remarking, "I like to read murder stories."

By the end of January, Martinez was complaining of a persistent headache and prescribed a dosage of all-purpose capsules (APC pills). Due to the headaches, on January 26 Martinez had his eyes checked; they were found to be normal. He continued his daily routine until February 9, when he broke down the door of his cell and pulled his mattress into the latrine. He refused to return to his cell, yelling that there were snakes and bugs in his cell. The guards forced Martinez back into his cell. The report states: "Patient rest of night slept fairly well after 0200."

On February 11, the last night in the clinic, the entry reads: "Patient asks for sleeping pill—a little restless and moves about a good deal, but he is quiet and well mannered." The following day, February 12, 1948, Martinez was discharged to the prison guards at 1 p.m. and returned to safe-keeping in the European Command Military Prison in Mannheim.

On January 12, Captain Jacobs wrote that his patient, Martinez, "had practiced most of the sexual perversions—"bung-holing," being "sucked off," enjoys "sucking off a woman"—but "will have intercourse in the normal fashion. Enjoys one about as much as the other." Jacobs further wrote: "The patient has been well-behaved and cooperative. The patient has complained frequently of frontal headaches and he shows some difficulty in sleeping. He gives the impression of having an organic brain syndrome but there has been no objective basis for such a diagnosis. It is possible that his low mentality, the schizophrenic tendencies and the after effects of drug addiction have combined to create this impression. The patient was presented to a 35c Board 4 February 1948, at which time no mental disease was found in an individual of borderline intelligence."

After his month at the neuropsychiatry clinic, the board of medical officers ruled that Manuel Martinez was at the time of the alleged offenses free from mental defect, disease, or derangement and able, concerning the particular acts charged, to distinguish right from wrong. They also ruled that he possessed sufficient mental capacity to understand the nature of the proceedings and was intelligent enough to conduct and cooperate in his own defense. These findings were sent to the Office of the Judge Advocate General in Washington, D.C.

A week after returning to Mannheim, on February 17, Martinez had the nerve to register a complaint with the Office of the Inspector General as to the whereabouts of the 50,000 francs ($405) taken from him at the time of his arrest!

On March 19, 1948, the Secretary of the Army sent President Harry Truman a three-page letter outlining the case against Martinez. The last paragraph read, "I concur in the recommendations of the Judge Advocate General and enclose a form of action designated to carry it into effect should it meet with your approval." The president's response was as follows:

> In the foregoing case of Prisoner Manuel Martinez, the sentence is confirmed and will be carried into execution under the direction of and at a time and place to be designated by the Commander-in-chief, European Command.
>
> The White House
> s/ Harry Truman
> March 23, 1948

On April 13, Martinez was informed that the 50,000 French francs he had inquired about earlier were taken by the finance officer in Paris, where duplicate receipts had been issued. Further, if the francs were the property of the persons robbed, and if his sentence was approved and executed, neither he nor his estate would be entitled to the money. Surprisingly, no claims were made from heirs

27. Mannheim Prison

or next of kin regarding the murder of Henri Géliot. Further, no claims for restitution of property were received from the victims in the series of robberies committed by Martinez. Two days later, his death sentence was reconfirmed for execution at "1000 hours 23 April 1948 at War Criminal Prison No. 1, Landsberg, Germany. No band, escort or troops will be present for the execution."

Manuel's brother, Ralph Martinez, living in Houston, Texas, had officially requested information regarding his brother's execution. The Army informed Ralph of the designated place and time. In addition, the Special Delivery letter contained this paragraph:

> The Army will prepare the remains for burial and your brother's body will be transported to the United States at Government expenses. However, if you desire to claim his body, the expenses of transportation from port of entry to the place designated by you for burial must be borne by you. If you do not desire to claim your brother's remains, they will be buried by the Government in a cemetery near the port of entry. Please be assured of my sympathy.

On April 16, Martinez was transferred from Mannheim to Headquarters, Heidelberg Military Post, a distance of about 10 miles. Here he was placed under a suicide watch. It is not known when Martinez, under heavy guard, was driven the 187 miles to Landsberg, Germany, home of War Criminal Prison No. 1 and the abode of hundreds of Nazi war criminals. The prison had an experienced hangman and two scaffolds that recently had seen considerable use. Martinez would be the 183rd prisoner executed there in the three years since the end of the war.[1]

28

THE INEVITABLE END

Landsberg, 40 miles west of Munich, derived its Nazi fame from its prison. That facility contains Cell #7, where Adolf Hitler wrote *Mein Kampf* after he was jailed following his famously unsuccessful Munich "Beerhall Putsch"—an attempt by the Nazis to overthrow the Weimar Republic in 1923. This town had not changed outwardly in 500 years. Nestled in the valley of the Lech River, it was hemmed in on both sides by steep wooded hills. An ancient wall pierced by watchtowers surrounded it. To get to the prison, one crossed the Lech, which was scarcely more than a gushing stream. On the hill ahead appeared the prison and fortress, a complex of grayish-white buildings encircled by a high stone wall. The prison was divided into two sections: one for ordinary prisoners and the other for political inmates.

Hanging has been employed as a mode of execution for as long as humans can remember. There have been more executions by this method than by any other means. The procedure is simple, yet there have also been more botched executions with this method than by any other. The most famous botched hanging at War Criminal Prison No. 1 had been on May 28, 1947, with the execution of August Eigruber. His hanging was the most brutal of the 306 executions at Landsberg. Maybe his fate was sealed by his arrogant attitude and last words:

> Lord take care of Germany.
> Lord take care of my family.
> Lord take care of my children.
> I regard it as an honor to be hung by the most brutal of victors.
> Long live Germany.

From under the hood that covered his face, Eigruber said to Father Morgenschweiss, "Farewell, Father."[1] The hangman pulled the lever and Eigruber fell through the trap door. Eigruber should have been unconscious, but then a strange thing happened. Morgenschweiss heard Eigruber say in a dialect, "Pfiat di, Pfarrer" (in proper German, "Behüt Dich Gott, Pfarrer") or "God bless you priest."[2]

August Eigruber was conscious. Did the hangman botch the execution on purpose? Priest Morgenschweiss thinks he did, but we will never know. After ten minutes, the curtain on the side of the gallows was opened and Eigruber was still alive. His body was placed on a gurney and according to the priest, the doctor was requested to smother Eigruber to death. The medical team refused, and the Polish guards carried out the gruesome request by stuffing cotton and wool swabs into Eigruber's mouth and nose until he suffocated.[3]

Now came another strange twist. During his incarceration, Eigruber's ex-wife had remarried and chose not to receive Eigruber's body after execution. In January 1948, the Landsberg Prison Director received a letter from her, requesting that Eigruber's body be exhumed and cremated. She explained that her present husband had died the previous December. Now she wanted her former husband, August Eigruber, cremated by the same Munich mortuary and his ashes placed with her current husband's. The U.S. Army approved of the request and apparently Eigruber's final resting place was with his wife's most recent husband. Was this spitefulness by Eigruber's former wife? If so, directed toward which man—Eigruber, the last husband, or both? Is she today interred with them and spending eternity with both husbands?

At this site on April 22, just before noon the officer charged with the execution and a chaplain entered Martinez's jail cell and read him the order directing his execution at 10 a.m. the following morning. Martinez was then told that any reasonable request, including special food, would be allowed and that it would be arranged for him to have in his possession a Bible, rosary, or other religious articles during the execution. He would be supplied with sufficient writing paper and envelopes, with no limit placed on the number of letters that could be written, although the letters would be subject to censorship and might or might not be forwarded.

In the early-morning hours, Martinez attempted suicide by cutting the veins in his left wrist with his fingernails but was discovered by guards of the death watch. He spent the remainder of the night in handcuffs, dressed in regulation uniform from which all decorations, insignia, and other evidence of attachment to the U.S. Army had been removed.

The hangman had selected a manila hemp rope approximately 30 feet long. The rope had been boiled and stretched during the drying process to eliminate any spring, stiffness, or tendency to coil. The hangman then made a loop approximately eighteen inches long and proceeded to wrap the rope six times around the loop. The knot was then tightened by pulling the longer end.

It had to be done with almost no extra rope remaining at the top of the knot. The executioner then took the portion of the rope that slid through the noose and greased it to ensure a smooth sliding action. Next, he determined the proper "drop" for Martinez through the trap door; at Martinez's weight of 145 pounds, it was to be a 6 foot 9 inch drop. Last, he procured a sandbag, the weight of which matched Martinez's weight, and rehearsed the execution to ensure that the gallows, trap door, and noose functioned properly.

On April 23 at 10:00, the sergeant of the prisoner guard and a sergeant from the main guard walked Martinez to the platform of the gallows; the officer charged with the execution and the chaplain were a few steps in front of Martinez as he walked up the steps. The officer charged with the execution faced Martinez and read aloud to him the charges, findings, sentencing, and orders. He then told the chaplain and Martinez that a brief time would be allowed for any last statement. Martinez had one: "Everything is all right. I am sorry for what I did and my whole past life."

The hangman placed the black hood over Martinez's head, bound his ankles, and adjusted the noose around the prisoner's neck, directly behind the left ear. He stood beside him. The sergeant of the prisoner guard, who was charged with successfully carrying out the execution, then placed himself in position at the trigger and, upon a signal from the execution officer, sprung the trap door. The violent stop broke the bones in Martinez's neck and severed his spinal cord, causing him to go into shock and lose consciousness. This was accompanied by slow strangulation. The medical officer examined the body for time of death nineteen minutes later and made a pronouncement of death.

Martinez's body was transferred to the 539th General Dispensary in Augsburg, Germany. His personal articles consisted of a brown leather wallet, seven pictures, and a black broken rosary; these were taken and sent to the Quartermaster Depot, Kansas City, Missouri. This was the standard procedure for the personal effects of any soldier killed in combat during World War II.

Three days later, the Adjutant General's Office, Washington, D.C., received from HQ EUCOM Frankfurt, the following telegram:

> 26 April 1948
>
> The sentence of execution of death by hanging general prisoner Manuel Martinez RA-35 248 810 was carried out at 1019 hours 23 April 1948 at the War Criminal Prison No. 1 Landsberg, Germany, which is the place designated for the execution of death sentences of all personnel subject to military law. No unusual circumstances incidents to the death by hanging.

Now the army needed instructions as to the disposition of the remains. Martinez's Uncle Mike Ramirez was listed as the next of kin. A letter sent to him at Steel's Store, Texas, did not receive a response, nor did a letter to his

28. The Inevitable End

wife, Mary, at a different post office box in Steel's Store. This letter included a telegram to her stating that it was "difficult in ascertaining your address." The army exhausted every channel, including through various postmasters, but it appeared that not one relative could be located to claim Martinez's remains.

On June 1, 1948, the body of Manuel Martinez was shipped aboard the United States Army Transport *General Patrick* and arrived in the New York City Port of Embarkation on June 10, 1948. By now, family members had been located and the family paid the cost for Manuel's

Above and below: Manuel Martinez's birth and early life are an enigma, but his body rests in this cemetery at the end of this dusty dirt road in East Texas. His last name is spelled incorrectly on his tombstone. He is buried between his mother, Cecilia R. Martinez, and his caring grandmother, Catarina Ramirez.

remains to be sent to Mumford, Texas. His funeral procession followed a dusty southeast Texas dirt road to a wagon trail and then into a meadow. Manuel Martinez was buried next to his mother. His tombstone is marked with his dates of birth and death and the inscription "Remembered by Bros & Grandmother." Five years later, his 98-year-old grandmother, Catarina Ramirez, would join him in eternal rest.

As might be expected, his father, Tony, who had abandoned the family when Martinez was just a lad, now showed up and made an application to the Kansas City Quartermaster Depot on December 23, 1948, for Manuel Martinez's personal effects. The army ruled that "Tony Martinez, c/o F.M. Guy, RFD #1, Lilbourn, Missouri, [is the father] of the decedent and appears to be entitled to receive his or her effects."[4]

Manuel Martinez's remains now lay at the end of a dusty trail in Texas—but what about Milbert Bailey, James L. Jones, Benjamin Pygate, Clarence Whitfield and John Williams? They are interred in the Oise-Aisne American Cemetery and Memorial in France with the remains of 6,012 American war dead who lost their lives while fighting in this vicinity during World War I. These soldiers' headstones, aligned in long rows on the 36.5-acre site, rise in a gentle slope from the entrance to the memorial at the far end. The burial area is divided into four plots by wide paths lined by trees and beds of roses; at the intersection are a circular plaza and the flagpole. Interred across the highway and deliberately hidden from view with their headstones numbered on flat stone markers are Bailey, number 90; Jones, number 84; Pygate, number 85; Whitfield number 37; and Williams, number 94. They are bured with 94 other executed American military prisoners, known as the dishonorable dead.

Chapter Notes

The gruesome execution procedures are based on examination of archival photographs and notes from the Commonwealth of Virginia, Office of Chief Medical Examiner Dr. Marcella Fierro. Much of the information was obtained by e-mail correspondence with Fred Leuchter, an expert on execution technology and the inventor of the lethal injection machine.

The Web address for court-martial reviews follows and is referenced in the notes as www.loc.gov (the Library of Congress). The full address is http://www.loc.gov/rr/frd/Military_Law/ETO-Board-of-Review-Decisions.html. These pdf files are books cited as follows: The United States Army. Branch Office of Judge Advocate General. European Theater of Operations (ETO). Board of Review. Volumes 1 through 34 are located in the University of Virginia Law Library.

Chapter 1

1. Helmuth Greiner, MS# C-0654, Foreign Military Studies Branch, NARA. This source can also be accessed at www.fold3.com; click and follow the path "World War II/WWII Foreign Military Studies, 1945–54/Chapter 4—C Series Manuscripts."

Chapter 2

1. Pete Martin, "We Shot D-Day on Omaha Beach," *American Legion Magazine*, June 1964.
2. Junius J. Stout, National Personnel Records Center, St. Louis, MO.
3. Excerpt from newspaper clipping, no date or headline.
4. Obituary, "John Black Reybold, No. 6782, Class of 1920, Died July 5, 1987, in Leesburg, Virginia."
5. "The Lion Rampant: A Brief History of Combat Operations in the European Theater during 1944–1945 of the 15th Cavalry Group, Mechanized, RG 407," National Archives.
6. Edward Clark, *Escape from Jersey Island* [Self-published booklet?], Jersey Archives CCLC732.
7. MS # B-833, 47. This source can also be accessed at www.fold3.com; click and follow the path "World War II/WWII Foreign Military Studies, 1945–54/Chapter 3—B Series Manuscripts.
8. Clark, *Escape from Jersey Island*.
9. Ibid.

Chapter 3

1. Record Group 498, Diary—Machine Records Unit (Mobile), NARA. This source can also be accessed at www.fold3.com; click and follow the path "World War II/WWII European Theater Army Records /4—Staff Section Report/571h—Ground Forces Replacement Command—annexes III & IV; 88."

Chapter 4

1. Colonel William H. S. Wight, provost marshal, "Proceedings, At a Point near Canisy, France, 1635 hours, 14 August 1944," St. Louis, MO: NARA.
2. "Morale and Discipline in the European Command," *Occupation Forces in Europe Series*, 6.
3. Privates John Williams, 32794118; Milbert Bailey, 34151488; and James L. Jones,

34221342; Branch Office of the Judge Advocate General, Board of Review.

4. Privates John Williams, 32794118; Milbert Bailey, 34151488; and James L. Jones, 34221342; Personnel folders, National Archives, St. Louis, MO.

5. "Morale and Discipline in the European Command," *Occupation Forces in Europe Series*, 15. www.loc.gov: Vol. 8, Whitfield ETO 3141 CM 293083; Bailey, Jones and Williams, Vol. 28, ETO 7518 CM 286135.

Chapter 5

1. Record Group 498, Diary—Machine Records Unit (Mobile), NARA. This source can also be accessed at www.fold3.com; click and follow the path "World War II/WWII European Theater Army Records/4—Staff Section Report/571h—Ground Forces Replacement Command—annexes III & IV; 88."

Chapter 6

1. *Geography*, Seine Section, Special Service, 7.
2. Arthur Moore, musician and veteran of World War II.
3. RG 498, *Geography*, Seine Section, Special Service.
4. RG 498, *Geography*, Seine Section, American Red Cross.
5. RG 498, *Geography*, Seine Section, Special Service.
6. RG 498, Lt. Colonel Kenneth P. Gilson, I.G. General Inspectorate Report #50, Report of Visit to Paris Leave Center, March 12–30, 1945.
7. RG 498, Lt. Colonel K.P. Gilson, I.G. General Inspectorate Report # 50, Report of Visit to Paris Leave Center, March 12–30, 1945, 6. This source can also be accessed at www.fold3.com. For footnotes 1–5, click and follow the path "World War II/WWII European Theater Army Records /5—Geographical Commands Reports/599—Seine Sections a–k: Vols. For footnotes 6–7, click and follow the path "World War II/WWII European Theater Army Records /4—Staff Section/555B—General Inspectorate Section, Inspection and Survey Reports, 336–356." Page 344 is used for footnotes 6–7.

Chapter 7

1. Roland G. Ruppart, *Logical Support of the Armies* (Washington, DC: U.S. Government Printing Office, 1959). This source can also be accessed at www.fold3.com; click and follow the path "World War II/WWII European Theater Army Records/5—Geographical Command Reports/599e—Seine Section, Vols. XIV and XV, Histories, 32."

Chapter 8

1. Kenneth D. Alford, *Allied Looting in World War II: Thefts of Art, Manuscripts, Stamps and Jewelry in Europe* (Jefferson, NC: McFarland, 2012).
2. Rene C. Pollard, Board of Review No. 4, November 10, 1945, 4, 5.
3. www.loc.gov: CM ETO 16835, General Court-Martial, St. Louis, MO.

Chapter 9

1. Sgt. Allan B. Ecker, *Yank—A Weekly Magazine*, May 4, 1945.

Chapter 10

1. RG 498, Colonel Eugene N. Slappey, I.G. General Inspectorate Report #34, Report of Visit to Paris Detention Barracks, March 1–2, 1945. This source can also be accessed at www.fold3.com; click and follow the path "World War II/WWII European Theater Army Records/4—Staff Section/555B—General Inspectorate Section, Inspection and Survey Reports, 36–56, 51."

Chapter 11

1. Court-martials of James C. Blackburn, 15082471, and James E. Dugger, 39083211, NARA, St. Louis, MO. This source can also be accessed at www.loc.gov, Vol. 25 (Johnnie Porter) and Vol. 28.
2. Court-martials, James Mills and Haywood Madison, Branch Office of the Judge Advocate. www.loc.gov, Vol. 20.

Chapter 12

1. Missing Air Crew Report, AFPPA-11 file #12266. This source can also be accessed at www.fold3.com; click and follow the path "World War II/Missing Air Crew Reports, WWII (search name)."
2. L. P. Sinel, *The German Occupation of Jersey* (London: Corgi, 1969).
3. Junius J. Stout, National Personnel Records Center, St. Louis, MO.

Chapter 13

1. www.fold3.com: "World War II/WWII European Theater Army Records/4—Staff Section/559a—Digest of Facts—Death Sentences in the ETO, 600."
2. General Court-Martial of Ervine Furman, 32601803, Alvin Davis, 34139863, and Herman Francis, 32684769, NARA, St. Louis, MO; www.loc.gov, Vol. 26.

Chapter 14

1. General Court-Martial of Jerome M. Ciullo, 36570676, NARA, St. Louis, MO; www.loc.gov, Vol. 25.

Chapter 15

1. *The Stars and Stripes*, December 14, 1944.
2. Interview with Lt. Colonel Carmon C. Harris, Judge Advocate General Division, May 4, 1945, signed by Harris.
3. Charles D. Gurley, *How a Ninety Day Wonder Survived the War* (Petersburg, VA: Dietz, 1991).

Chapter 16

This chapter is adapted from a public domain book, *The Soldier-Railroaders' Story of the 716th Railway Operating Battalion*, composed by members of that unit in 1945–1946, Stuttgart, Germany.

1. www.fold3.com: "World War II/WWII European Theater Army Records/4—Staff Section/582g."
2. Robert L. Cosgrove, statement on November 16, 1944.

Chapter 17

1. Branch Office of the Judge Advocate General, Board Review No. 1, May 3, 1945.
2. Investigation of General Prisoner William R. Smith, 31446204, taken by Lt. Col L. H. Stockman, IGD, October 18, 1945.
3. Ibid.
4. Ibid.
5. General Prisoner Ernest A. Granelli, sworn statement taken by Lt. Colonel L. H. Stockman, IGD, October 18, 1945.
6. Investigation of General Prisoner William R. Smith, 31446204, taken by Lt. Colonel L. H. Stockman, IGD, October 18, 1945.
7. "Medal of Honor," U.S. Army, Center of Military History.

Chapter 18

1. RG 498, Colonel Eugene N. Slappey, Report of Visit to Paris Detention Barracks, March 1–2, 1945. This source can also be accessed at www.fold3.com; click and follow the path "World War II/WWII European Theater Army Records/4—Staff Section/555B—General Inspectorate Section, Inspection and Survey Reports, 36–56, 51."
2. Report of Investigation, IG, December 15, 1945, Exhibit D-1.
3. Report of Investigation, IG, December 15, 1945, 15.
4. C. E. Brand, "Official Opinion of the Staff Judge Advocate," June 29, 1945.
5. William P. Morehouse to Bertrand W. Gearhart, House of Representatives, March 3, 1945.
6. Pleas B. Rogers, brigadier general, Headquarters Seine Section, February 22, 1945.
7. Criminal Investigation Division, "Statement of S/Sgt. Paul M. King," January 23, 1945.
8. James E. Joseph, 33553268, Court-Martial, St. Louis National Archives, 9. www.loc.gov, Vols. 19, 25, and 26.

Chapter 19

1. Ira K. Evans, TSFET (Rear), October 14, 1945.
2. Investigation of General Prisoner Henry A. Murff, taken by Lt. Colonel L. H. Stockman, IGD, October 24, 1945.
3. Sworn statement of Captain William C. Yerg, 0886325, taken by Lt. Colonel L. H. Stockman, IGD, October 26, 1945.

Chapter 20

1. www.loc.gov, Vol. 15, 151; www.fold3.com: "World War II/WWII European Theater Army Records /4—Staff S, 559A, 601."

Chapter 21

1. European staff, *Yank*, n.d.

Chapter 22

1. Elizabeth C. Franks, "Special Examination or Additional Data," January 7, 1948; Mary E. Farley, "Memo Routing Slip," September 2, 1947; "Physical Examination (Jump Training)," October 17, 1944; "Final Payment Work Sheet," November 29, 1945.

Chapter 23

1. "Toilet Articles Issued," March 19, 1946; "Special Orders Number 156," July 3, 1946; "Misconduct," August 3, 1946. "Record of Trial of Manuel Martinez," Bad Nauheim, Germany, October 9, 1946—testimony and sworn statements of Pfc. Harold Mackel, Pfc. Cecil A. Fant, Pvt. Phillip F. Smith, Emmi Reibeling, Anneliese Langer, Helmut Sack, Erich Kraehling. "Record of Trial of Manuel Martinez," CM# 321457, Bad Nauheim, Germany, March 18, 1947—testimony of Sgt. Arthur R. Koch, sworn statement of Private George E. Jacobi, "Special Court-Martial Order 128, October 30, 1946. "7720 Rehabilitation Center," January 11, 1947; "Special Court-Martial Order 33," February, 19, 1947; Elizabeth C. Franks, "Special Examination or Additional Data," January 7, 1948; personal experiences of the author.

Chapter 24

1. "Record of Trial of Manuel Martinez," Paris, France, September 1947; "Record of Trial of William A. Mitchell," July 1947—testimony of Francis E. Schulz, Cpl. Victor Zingale, Pfc. Albert S. Kaina, and S/Sgt. Victor Husband." "Record of Trial of William Stribling," November 1945; William Stribling, "Affidavit," September 13, 1945; Sgt. Philip R. Randolph, "Affidavit," September 24, 1945. "GIs in Paris Flock to Pig Alley," *Life*, November 26, 1945.

Chapter 25

1. "Record of Trial of Manuel Martinez," Paris, France, September 1947. Salazard, Buchenwald Concentration Camp: Fragenbogen filed out by Salazard upon release by U.S. forces.

Chapter 26

1. "Record of Trial of Manuel Martinez," Paris, France, September 1947.

Chapter 27

1. Elizabeth C. Frank, "Special Examination of Additional Data," January 1948; "Final Summary," February 5, 1948; Mary E. Farley, "Memo Routing Slip," September 2, 1947; "Rorschach Method of Personality Diagnoses," January 8, 1948.

Chapter 28

1. National Archives, August Eigruber's 201 File.
2. Heinrich Pflanz, "August Eigruber Profile," letter to the author, July 19, 2002.
3. Ibid.
4. Department of the Army, "Procedure for Military Executions," December 1947; Lloyd A. Wilson, "Execution of General Prisoner Manuel Martinez," April 23, 1948; "Clinical Record Brief," April 23, 1948; "Inventory of Effects," April 23, 1948; "Telegram to Mary R. Martinez," May 10, 1948; Army Effects Bureau, December 28, 1948.

Bibliography

Alford, Kenneth D. *Allied Looting in World War II: Thefts of Art, Manuscripts, Stamps and Jewelry in Europe*. Jefferson, NC: McFarland, 2012.
_____. *Great Treasure Stories of World War II*. Mason City, IA: Savas, 2000.
_____. *Hermann Göring and the Nazi Art Collection: The Looting of Europe's Art Treasures and Their Dispersal After World War II*. Jefferson, NC: McFarland, 2012.
_____. *Nazi Millionaires*. Haverty, PA: Casemate, 2002.
_____. *Sacking Aladdin's Cave*. Atglen, PA: Schiffer, 2013.
_____. *The Spoils of World War II*. New York: Birch Lane, 1994.
Beevor, Antony. *Paris after Liberation*. New York: Penguin, 1994.
The Best of Yank. New York: Arno, 1980.
Botting, Douglas. *The Aftermath: Europe*. Fairfax, VA: Time-Life, 1982.
Bradley, Omar N. *A Soldier's Story*. New York: Holt, 1951.
Butcher, Harry C. *My Three Years with Eisenhower: The Personal Diary of Captain Harry C. Butcher, USNR, Naval Aide to General Eisenhower, 1942–1945*. New York: Simon and Schuster, 1946.
Collins, Larry. *Is Paris Burning?* New York: Simon and Schuster, 1965.
D'Este, Carlo. *Eisenhower: A Soldier's Life*. New York: Henry Holt, 2002.
_____. *Patton: A Genius for War*. New York: HarperCollins, 1995.
Eisenhower, Dwight D. *Crusade in Europe*. New York: Doubleday, 1948.
Gurley, Charles D. *How a Ninety Day Wonder Survived the War*. Richmond, VA: Ashcroft, 1991.
Harrison, C. A. *Cross Channel Attack*. Washington, DC: U.S. Government Printing Office, 1951.
Joseph, Jeremy. *Swastika Over Paris*. New York: Arcade, 1989.
Kluger, Steve. *Yank*. London: Arms and Armour, 1991.
Price-Jones, David. *Paris in the Third Reich*. New York: Holt, Rinehart and Winston, 1981.
Ruppart, Roland G. *Logical Support of the Armies*. Washington, DC: U.S. Government Printing Office, 1959.
Shirer, William L. *The Rise and Fall of the Third Reich: A History of Nazi Germany*. Norwalk, CT: Easton, 1991.
The Stars and Stripes. New York: Hugh Lauter Levin, 1985.
World War II. New York: American Heritage, 1966.
Ziemke, Earl F. *The U.S. Army in the Occupation of Germany*. Washington, DC: U.S. Government Printing Office, 1975.

Index

Adams, Ansel 69
Albertone, Giuseppe 70
Albertone, Marie 70, 71
Alexander, James E. 106, 107
American Red Cross, Paris 51, 56, 58, 59, 61, 62, 65, 84, 85, 87, 166, 167
Anderson, Glen J. 177
Anderson, Woodrow W. 104
Arroya, Raphael 68
Astaire, Fred 55

Bailey, Milbert 36, 222
Barnett, George M. 31
Baurche, Jean 72
Bazar, Pete 138
Bazier, Berthe 209
Bell, Harold 116–125
Bell, John D. 101
Bell, William L. 37
Bender, Ruth 187
Berry, Sergeant 112, 113
Blackburn, James Clyde 89–98
Blackburn, Sergeant 138
Blackler, Robert B. 103, 105
Blein, Mildred 70
Bobesco, Lola 68
Bourenkoff, Pierre 190, 191, 208
Bouvier, Louise 91–93
Boyken, Booze 90, 91, 93, 94
Bradley, Omar N. 11, 14, 23, 40
Branham, Finis 193
Butts, Walter *see* Orville

Camelia *see* Slagmudler, Herminne
Carroll, Sergeant 105
Carter, John D. 91–94
Cartier, Jacques 23
Cartier, Lola Alfreda 118–120, 122
Castillo, Manuel E. 118, 119, 120, 122

Cercle Militaire (officer's mess) 63, 64, 67, 68
Chaplin, Charley 55
Chilengrerian, Charles 111–113
Choltitz, Dietrich von 10, 17
Christiane 106, 109
Churchill, Winston 10, 17
Cinema Marignan 52, 55
CiPierre, Hughette Carmen 198, 200, 210–212
Ciullo, Jerome 85, 116–125
Clark, Edward R. 19, 20, 22, 24, 25, 104, 105, 126
Clavier, Jean 122
Cleyet, Georgette 118–120, 122
Coppersmith, Milton G. 195, 196
Coreno, Armand J. 96, 97
Cosgrove, Robert L. 138
Cowan, Richard Eller 148, 149
Cozzati, Bruno James 141, 143, 144
Cranford, John P. 138
Crawfield, Frank 138
Crockett, Woodrow W. 93
Cuegnez, Jacqueline 117, 120, 123–125

Dal Porto, Ario D. 138, 156
Dangereux-Dorly, Pierre 196, 197
David 106, 108–110, 115
Davidson, William 150, 151
Davis, Alvin 106–112, 115
Davis, Frank E. 75
Deason, Walter B. 91–95, 98
Debesse, Louis 108, 109, 112, 114
Debesse, Marie 108, 112, 114
Debiase, Olive 209
de Gaulle, Charles 40, 52
de Haven, Gloria 55
Dejivanni, Joseph 194, 195, 209
Dempsey, Miles C. 11

Dicks, R.A. 95
Dietrich, Marlene 57
Dominique, Di Rosa 73
Dookie, Austin C. *see* Boyken, Booze
Dugger, James E. 90–94
Durant, Suzzane F. 91, 92

Earnest, Herbert L. 15
Eickenburg, M.W. 62
Eigruber, August 218, 219
Eisemann, C.P. 62
Eisenhower, Dwight D. 10, 23, 40, 68, 69, 159
Elder, James 144
Empire Theater 52, 56, 68
Ewing, Bert, E. 146, 147

Fain, Sidney 102
Fant, Cecil A. 182–186
Fiset, Joseph 103, 105
Fleming, Alexander A. 150, 151
Ford, John 11, 14
Francis, Herman M. 108–112, 115
Franck, Lucien 199, 210, 212
Franklin, Henry E. 86
French, Leonard J. 151, 153, 154
Furman, Ervine 108, 109, 113–115

Gahagnon, Louie 97
Garrison, Harold S. 18
Géliot, Henri 198–200, 204, 205, 212
Géliot, Jeanne 204
Gendre, Raquel 201, 202, 210
Gendre, Suzanne 201, 211
Gilbert, Leo 148
Gillespie, Samuel B. 156
Giraud, Henri 7
Godek, Joseph J. 203
Göring, Hermann 4, 212
Gould, Harold G. 156
Granelli, Ernest A. 147
Griffin, Sergeant 138
Griffin, Thomas F. 170
Grotte, Ralph O. 169
Guilbert, Reine-Marie 174
Gurley, Charles D. 14, 15, 126–128

Haas, George 19, 24, 25, 104, 105
Hal *see* Bell, Harold
Hanson, James R. 18, 23, 24
Harper, Thomas G. 151–154
Harris, Carmon 150
Harris, John U. 164
Hart, Paul 138
Hebert, Adrien 115
Henbest, Ross C. 170
Hileash, Adrian 111

Hitler, Adolf 1–3, 8, 20, 40, 178, 218
Holt, Jennifer 55
Horkott, George 22–24
Hotel Astra 69–75
Hotel Lotti 65, 67
Hubert, Lucienne Juielette 106, 107
Hurd, Wayne L. 170, 171
Ickler, Rittmeister 25

Isham, Charley 146

Jacobs, Joseph S. 215, 216
Jacquier, Pierre 107
Jamison, Jewel L. 99
Javelle, Maria 73
Jean, Monsieur *see* Oudart, Stephane
Jocobi, George E. 187
Jones, Forrest L 99, 100
Jones, Fred C. 151–153, 155
Jones, James L. 36, 222
Jordan, Kistler P. 185, 186
Joseph, James E. 161

Kaina, Albert S. 192, 193, 195, 196, 206, 208
Kearns, William H. 104
Kenny, Vincent 111
King, Paul M. 161
Kisley, Pfc. 113
Kraehling, Erich 185

Labarthe, Rene 209
Lacheroix, Therese 198–200, 210
Lange, Arthur H. 73
Langer, Anneliese 182–185
La Pierre, Inspector 211
Lassetter, James P. 101
Lecoz, Maurice 202
Lefebvre, August 35, 36
Lefebvre, Eugene 35, 37
Lefebvre, Madam 35–37
Lefebvre, Marguerite 35, 36
Le Marinel, M. 104
Lemon, James E. 138, 139
Lidya *see* Hubert, Lucienne Juielette
Long, William J. 207, 208, 211
Loop, Norris E. 134, 156, 166
Lovecchio, Constantino J. 135

Maciejczak, John 107–115
Mackel, Harold 184–186
Madeleine Theater 56, 68
Madison, Haywood 102
Mama Russky *see* Vissokinsky, Madam
Marker, Sergeant 138
Marly, Pauli 106, 109, 111
Marquard, Carl F. 14

Index

Martin, Walter H. 156
Martinez, Cecila 176
Martinez, Manuel 85, 176–222
Martinez, Mary *see* Rivers, Mary
Martinez, Ralph 217
Martinez, Tony 176, 177, 222
Maupied, Micheline 201, 202
Mazel, Jacques 201
McCoy, Charles E. 159
McNair, Leslie 29
McNeil, E.C. 171
Medici, Catherine de 45
Medley, Walter 106–115
Middleton Troy H. 15
Miller, Glenn 56
Mills, James R. 100, 102
Mitchell, William A. 190, 192, 193, 196, 206, 208
Montgomery, Bernard Law 10
Moreschi, Stanley 139
Morgenschweiss, Father 218, 219
Moses, Gilbert 98, 100
Moulin Rouge 189
Murff, Henry A. 165
Murphey, Randall W. 111, 112, 115

Nauche, Henri 74, 75
Nazaret, Roger 71
Nelson, Arthur 150, 151
Neville, Lt. Col. 161
Nicoud, Rene Alberte 109
Nini *see* Lacheroix, Therese
Nordling, Raoul 40

Odett 117
Olson, William P. 133, 135, 157, 158, 166
Olympic Theater 55, 56
O'Reilly, Robert P. 140–142, 144
Orville 95–97
Oudart, Stephane (Jean) 97, 107, 110

Pallenger, Eugene 151
Pallentine, Ermine E.G. 104
Patton, George 15, 40, 68, 131
Peck, Henry L. 37
Perron, Charles 193, 208
Peterson, Benjamin J. 111–113
Peterson, Neander E. 156
Pierrepoint, Thomas William 33–35
Pig Alley *see* Pigalle
Pigalle 57, 189–194, 198, 206, 212
Poindexter, Junior D. 188
Pollard, Rene C. 69–73
Porter, Johnnie L. 98, 100
Pycz, Edward J. 104
Pygate, Benjamin 106, 107, 222
Pyle, Ernie 215

Queulvée, Henri François 101, 102

Rainbow Corner, Paris 58, 166, 167, 174
Ramirez, Catarina 177, 214, 222
Ramirez, Mike 177, 213, 220
Ramirez, Tony *see* Martinez, Manuel
Ray, William H. 187
Raymond, Frenchman 123
Reed, Ronnie 30
Reibeling, Emmi 182, 184, 185
Reilly, Vincent S. 113
Rene, Mouton 101
Revercomb, Chapman 155
Reybold, John B. 15–19, 23–25, 104, 126
Rivers, Mary 179, 184
Roberts, Stephen 139
Rogers, Pleas B. 65, 66
Romanauskas, Stanley J. 112, 113
Roosevelt, Eleanor 16
Roosevelt, Franklin D. 6, 16, 21, 157
Rouyer, Remy 191, 208
Royer, Camille 101

Sack, Helmut 185
Salazard, Joseph 202
Saunders, Walter F. 213, 214
Schultz, Francis E. 191, 192, 208
Schultz, Janine M. 191, 192
Scocker, Inspector 210
Searle, Helen 71
Sence, French Captain 92, 93
Shore, Willie 55
Siciah, Walter S. 34
Simon, Madeleine 198, 201, 210
Sinatra, Frank 55
Skipton, Gerald 95
Skrzyinarz, Aniela 33, 34
Slagmudler, Herminne 107, 114
Slovik, Eddy D. 168–171
Smith, Bedell 68
Smith, Floyd M. 138
Smith, John D. 102
Smith, Phillip F. 182, 183, 185, 186
Smith, William R. 145–148, 150, 163, 165–167
Smith, Willie 92–95, 98
Snyder, Walter, D. 73–75
Sondej, Zofia 33, 34
Springer, John W. 133, 156, 166
Stage Door Canteen, Paris 56, 58
Starnard, Clarence H. 187
Stelly, Lee R. 99, 100
Stockman, Lynn H. 164
Stout, Archibald J. 12, 105
Stout, Junius J. 11, 12, 14, 103, 104
Stribling, William 125, 190, 191, 194, 195, 197, 201, 202, 208

Index

Suggs, James I. 117, 118, 124
Summersby, Kay 68
Suzanne *see* Marly, Pauli

Tanguy, Raymond 74, 75
Tanguy, Yvonne 74, 75
Tauscher, Roland L. 34
Tavernir, Joseph 120
Taylor, Cephas 111
Taylor, Hoyle S. 98–100
Thompson, George W. 168, 169
Thompson, James R. 94
Thunderoz, Andre 107
Truman, Harry 182, 216

Urich, M. 96

Villars, Michel 119, 122
Vincennes Gang 88–99
Vissokinsky, Madam 118
Vissokinsky, Martin 119, 124

Voltaire *see* Medley, Walter
Voltaire Gang 106–115

Wagner, Edward N. 151, 154
Wagner, German Master Sergeant 25
Walsh, David E. 27, 41, 42
Warren, Sidney 19–22
Webster, James P. 34
Westemeier, William H. 105
Weynant, Cornelie 209
Whitfield, Clarence 33–35, 131, 222
Williams, Earl *see* Mitchell, William A.
Williams, George 98, 100
Williams, John 36, 222
Wilson, Westray N. 207
Witting, Aileen, M. 61

Yerg, William C. 146, 156, 157, 165, 166
Young, Merel A. 151, 152

Zina *see* Simon, Madeline
Zingale, Victor 193

www.ingramcontent.com/pod-product-compliance
Ingram Content Group UK Ltd.
Pitfield, Milton Keynes, MK11 3LW, UK
UKHW041943140426
5217IPUK00014B/635